AF575738

YOU WILL BE ABLE TO

DRAW ANIMALS

BY THE END OF THIS BOOK.

An Hachette UK Company
www.hachette.co.uk

First published in Great Britain
in 2024 by Ilex, a division of
Octopus Publishing Group Ltd
Carmelite House
50 Victoria Embankment
London EC4Y 0DZ
www.octopusbooks.co.uk
www.octopusbooksusa.com

Additional picture credits:
ilimi/iStockphoto.com; mcbadshoes/Deviant Art;
Courtesy photos-public-domain.com

Distributed in the US by
Hachette Book Group
1290 Avenue of the Americas
4th and 5th Floors
New York, NY 10105

Distributed in Canada by Canadian Manda Group
664 Annette St, Toronto, Ontario, Canada M6S 2C8

Publisher: Alison Starling
Commissioning Editor: Ellie Corbett
Managing Editor: Rachel Silverlight
Editorial Assistant: Ellen Sleath
Art Director: Ben Gardiner
Designer: Sarah Strandoo
Production Controller: Lisa Pinnell

ISBN 978-1-78157-867-4

A CIP catalogue record for this book is available from the British Library.

Printed and bound in China

10 9 8 7 6 5 4 3 2 1

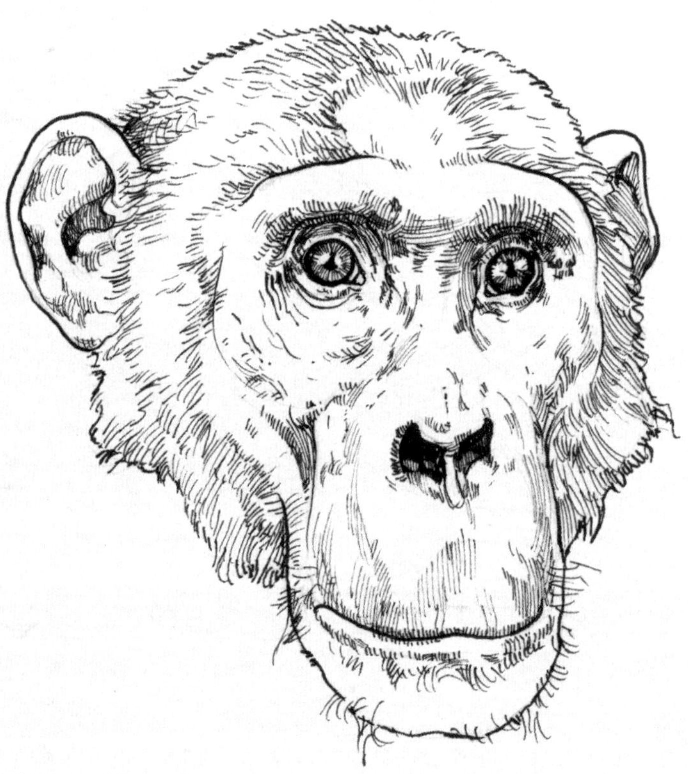

YOU WILL BE ABLE TO DRAW ANIMALS BY THE END OF THIS BOOK.

JAKE SPICER & LANCELOT RICHARDSON

ilex

IN THIS SKETCHBOOK

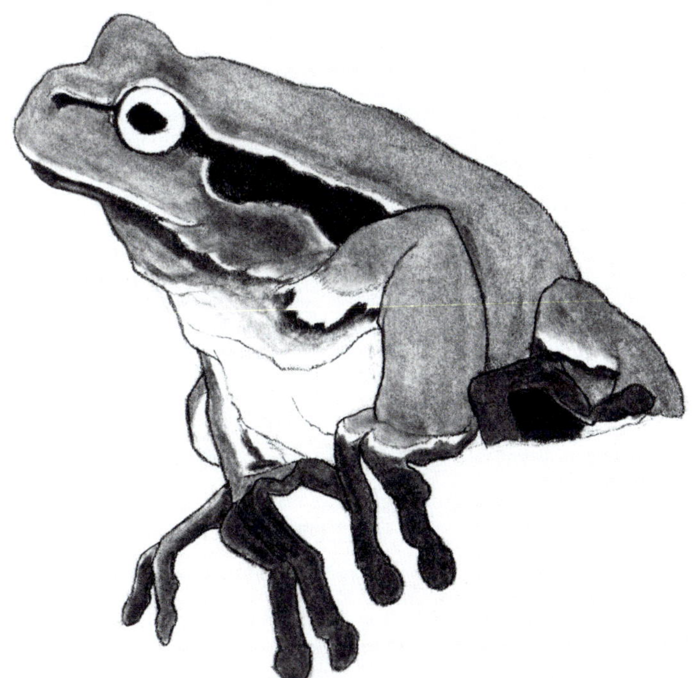

WHAT DO YOU WANT TO DRAW TODAY?

WARM-UPS & QUICK SKETCHES

LONG STUDIES

- Part 01: Observational drawing
- Part 02: Structures
- Part 03: Surfaces
- Part 04: Application

BY ANIMAL

DOGS

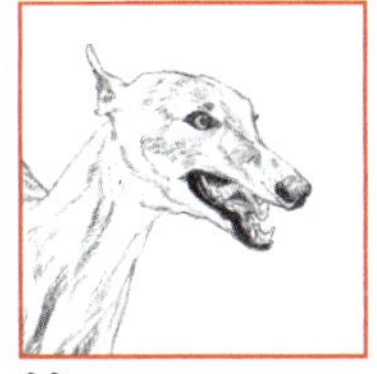
66

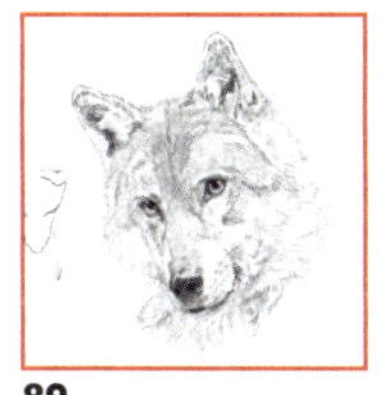
89

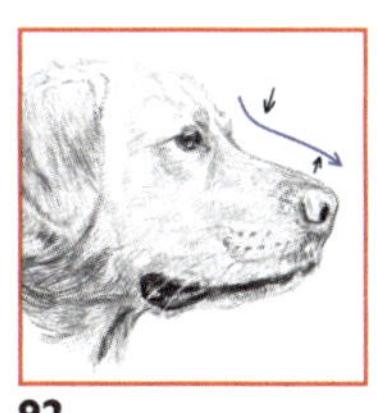
92

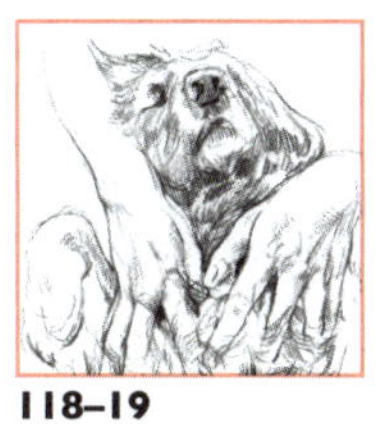
118–19

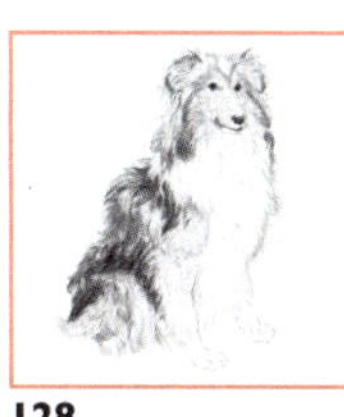
128

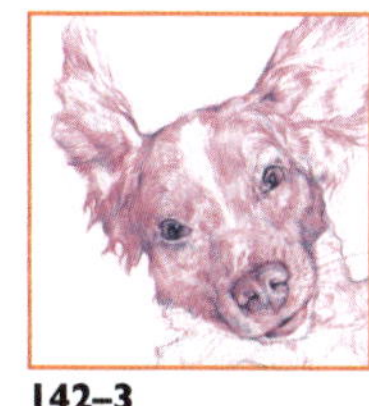
142–3

DOMESTIC & WILD CATS

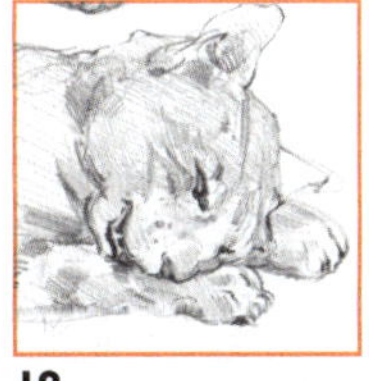
19

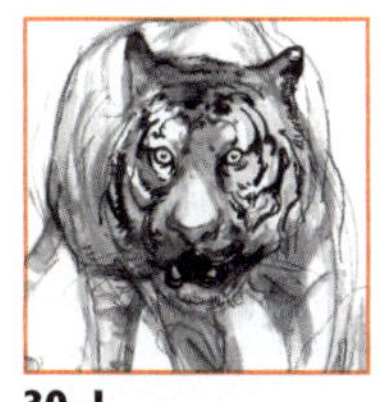
30–1

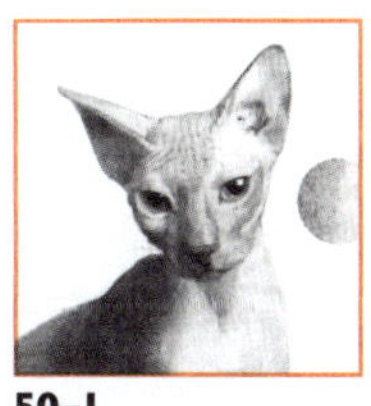
50–1

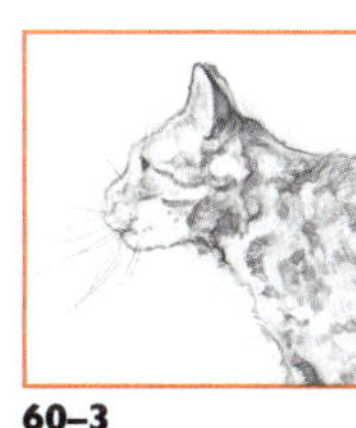
60–3

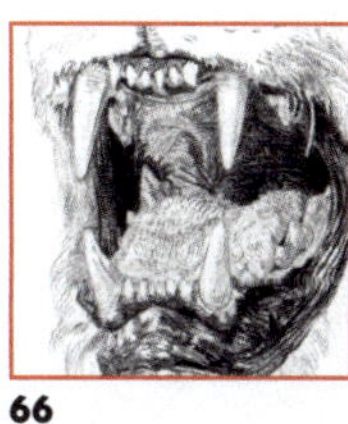
66

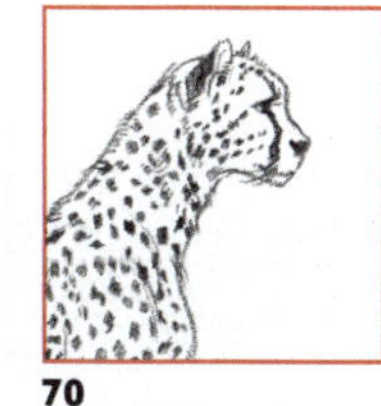
70

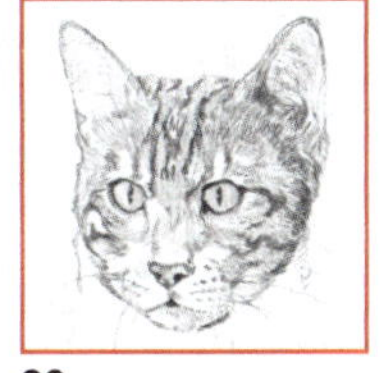
90

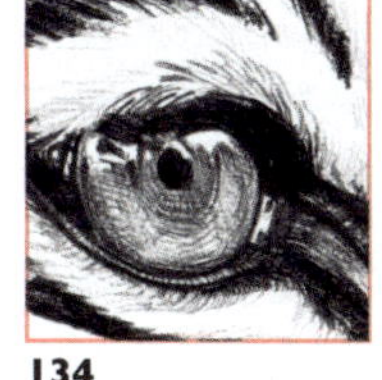
134

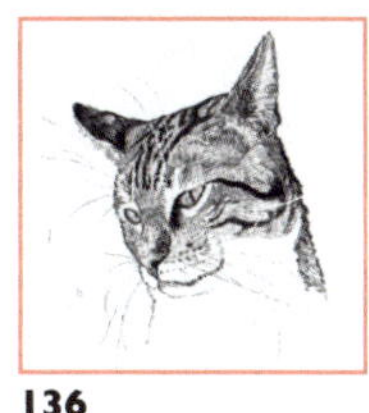
136

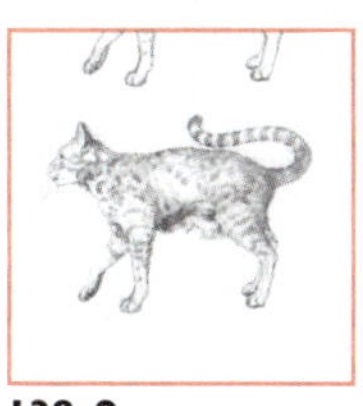
138–9

HOOFED MAMMALS

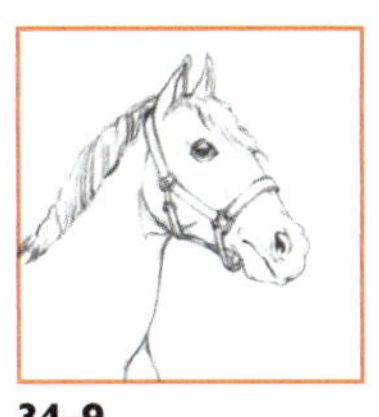
34–9

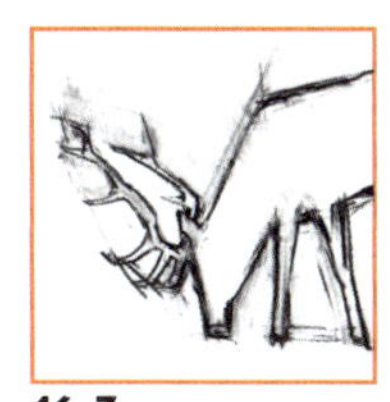
46–7

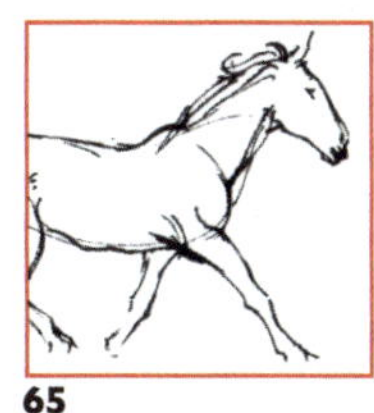
65

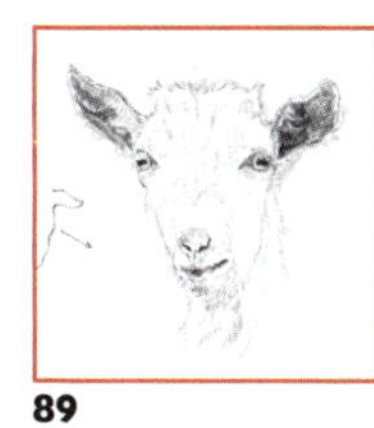
89

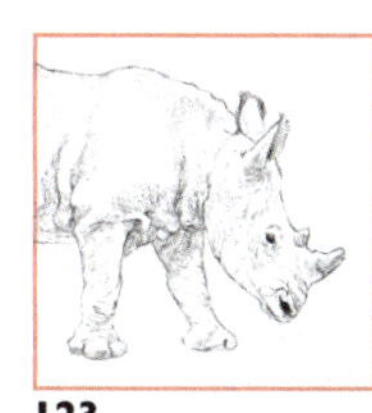
123

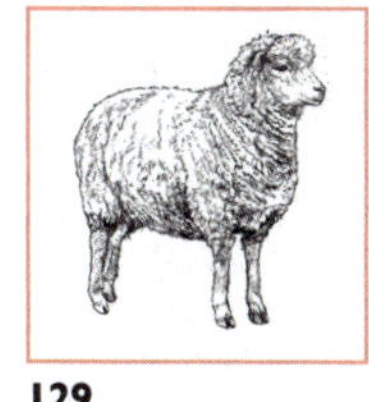
129

129

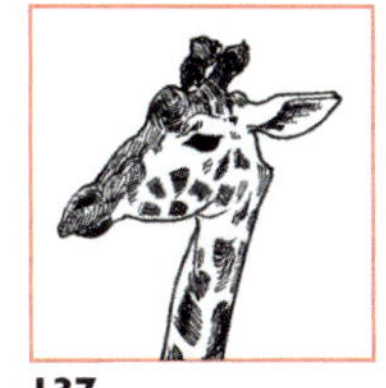
137

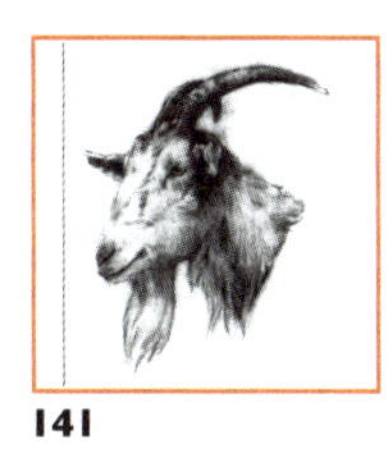
141

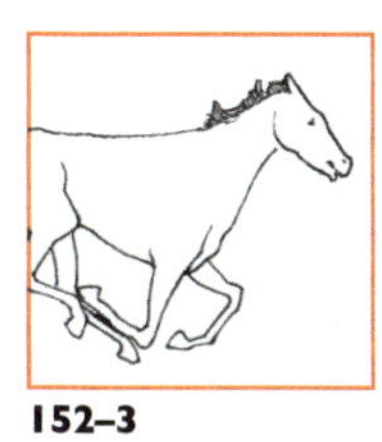
152–3

OTHER MAMMALS

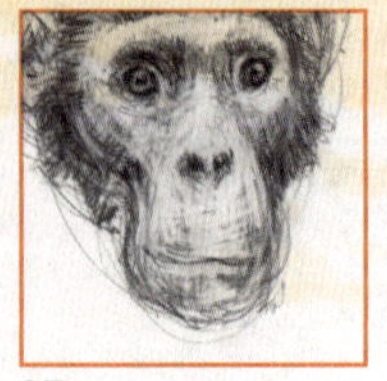
27

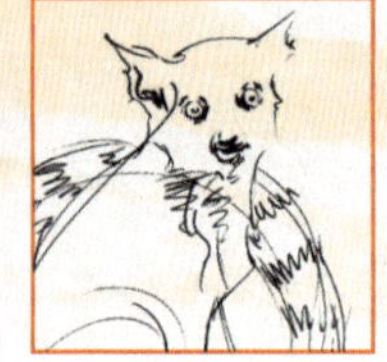
32

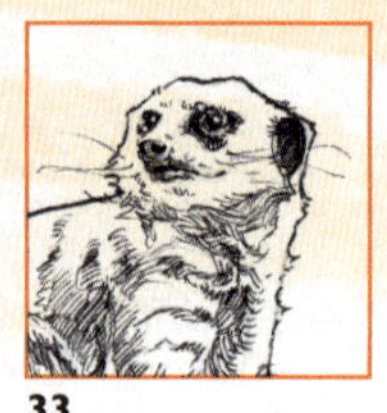
33

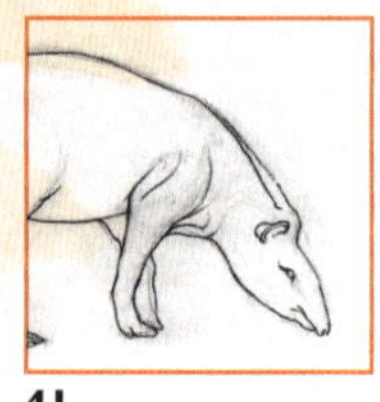
41

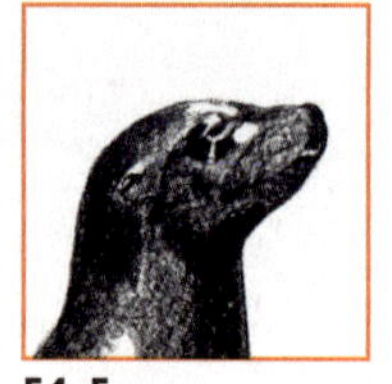
54–5

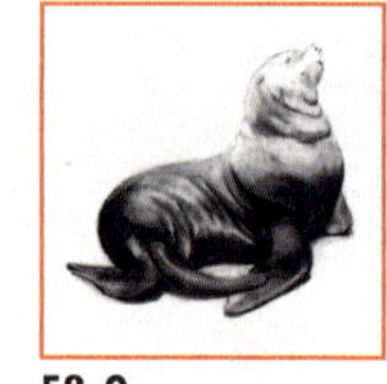
58–9

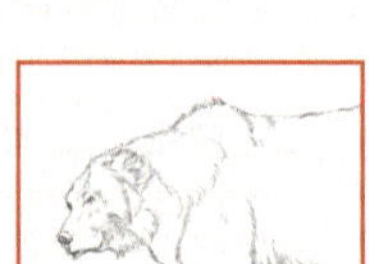
72

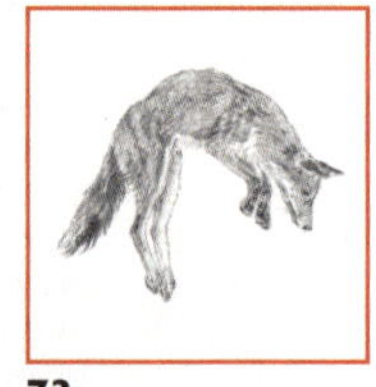
73

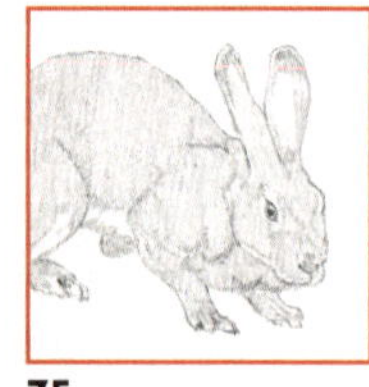
75

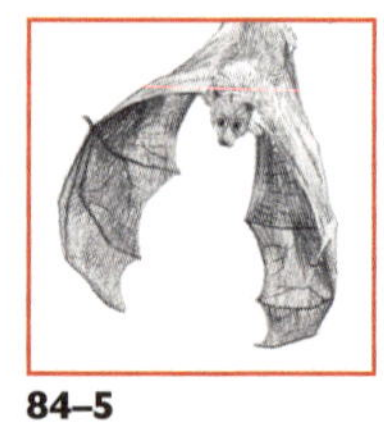
84–5

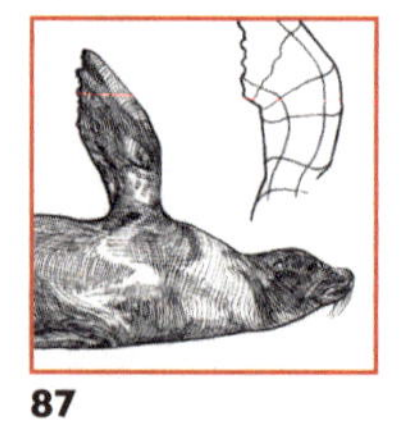
87

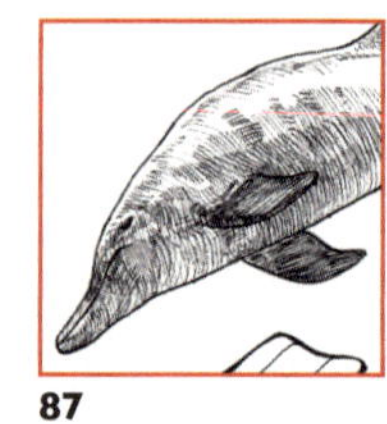
87

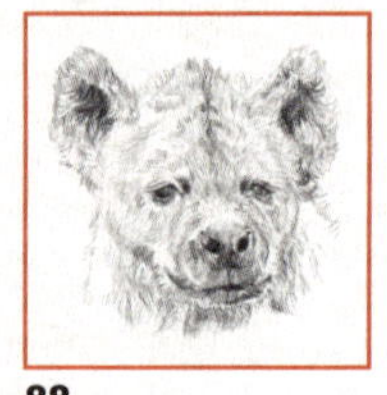
88

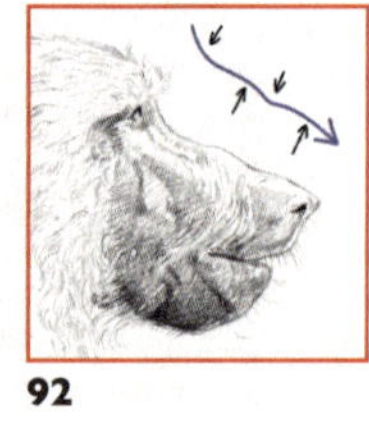
92

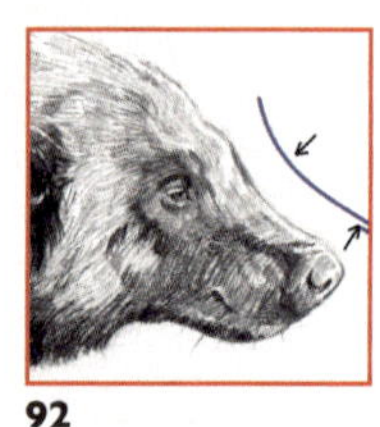
92

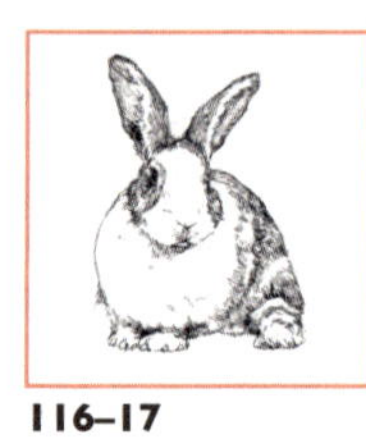
116–17

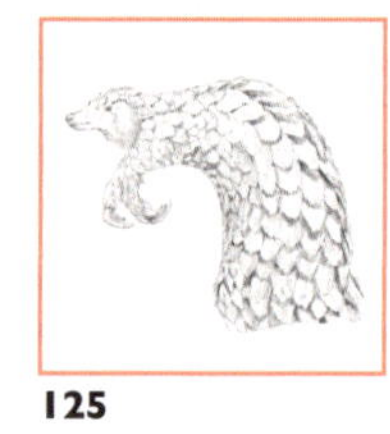
125

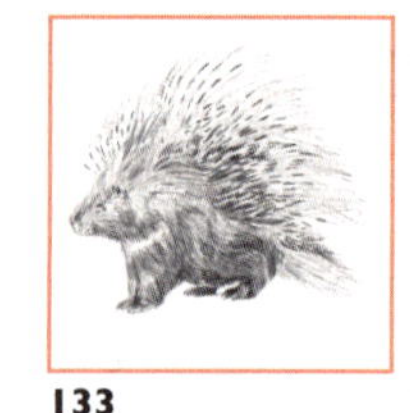
133

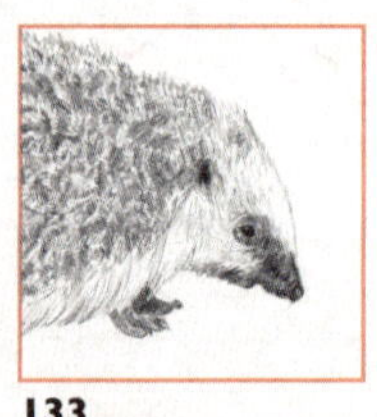
133

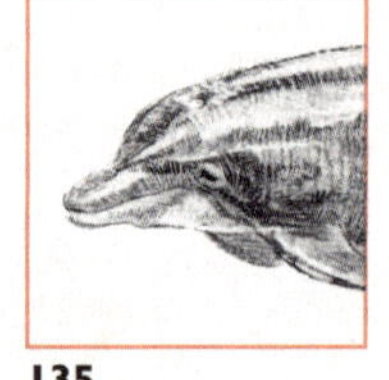
135

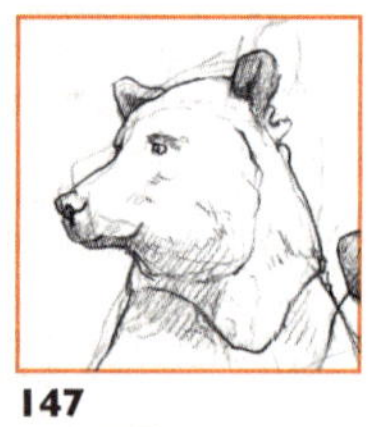
147

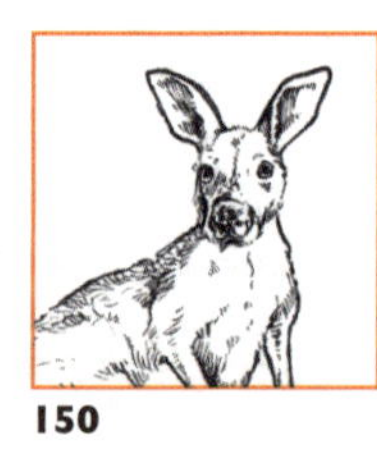
150

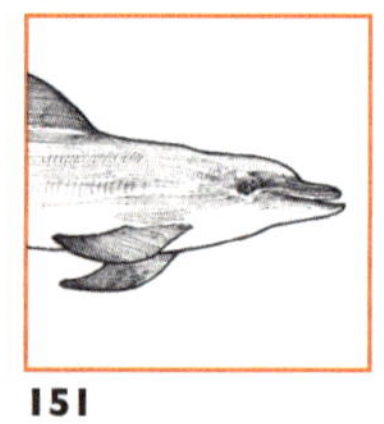
151

REPTILES & AMPHIBIANS

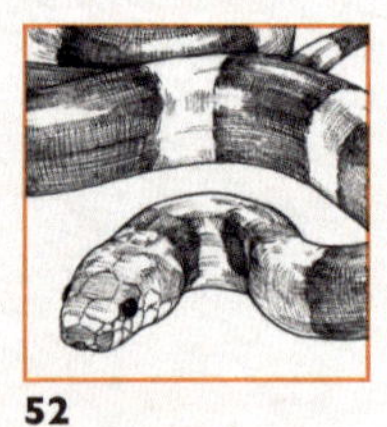
52

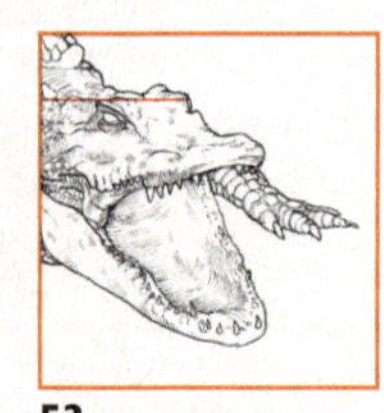
53

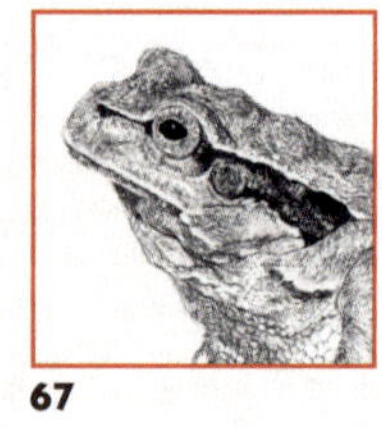
67

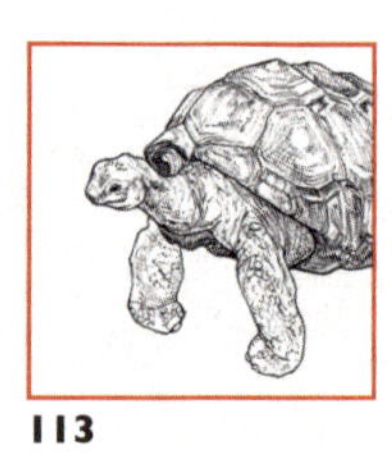
113

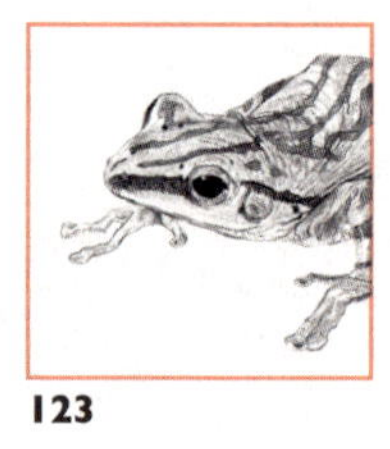
123

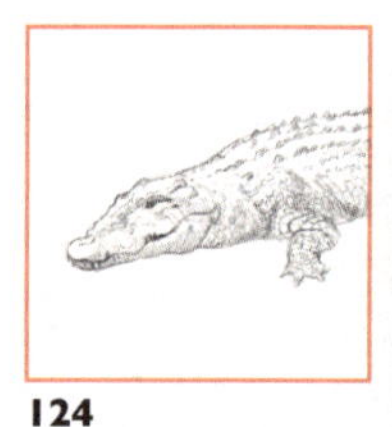
124

CEPHALOPODS & CRUSTACEANS

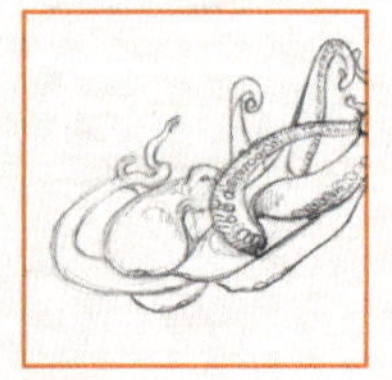
44–5

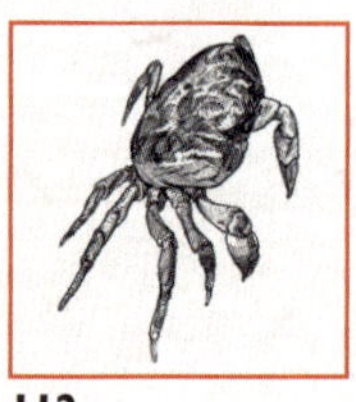
112

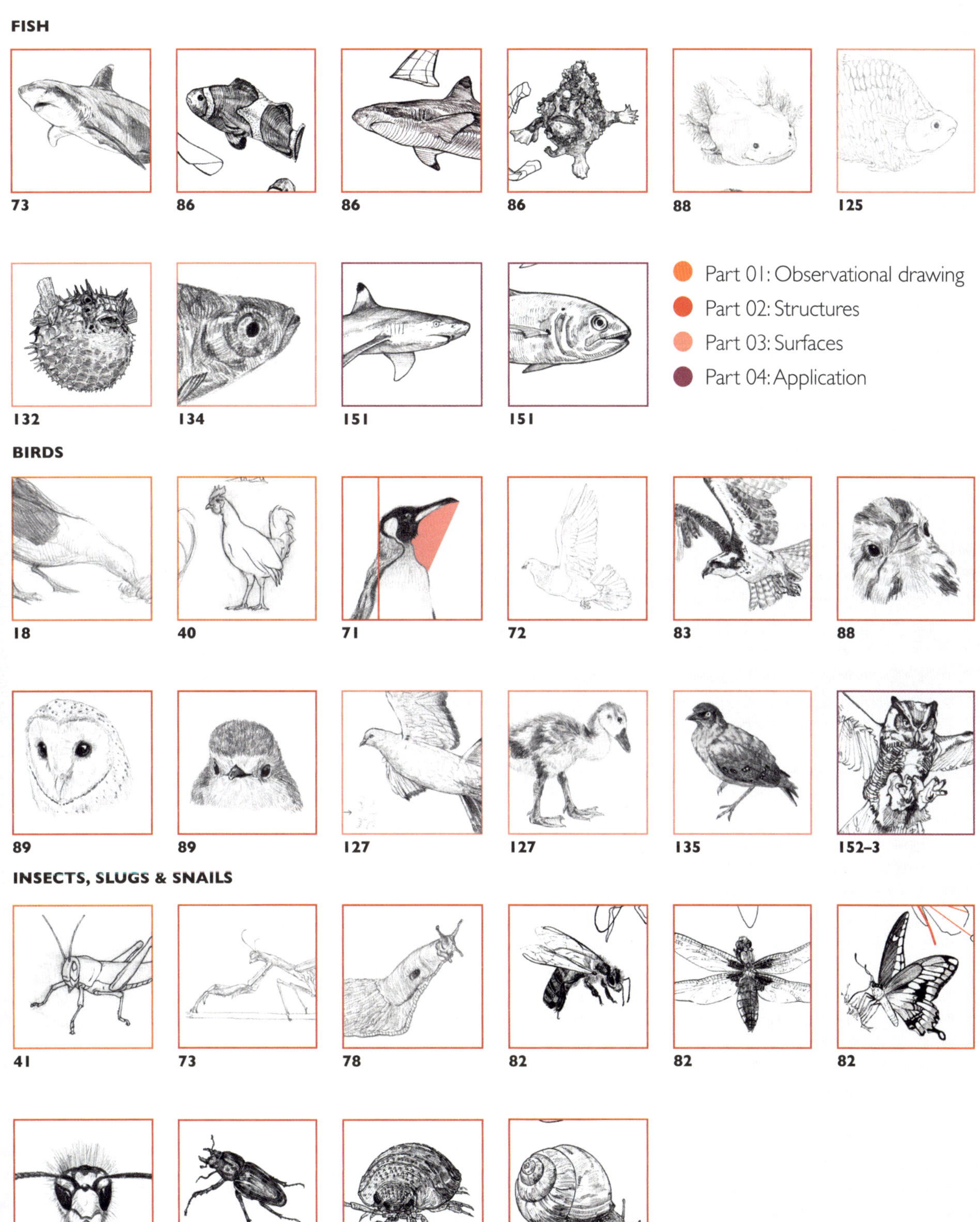
FISH
73
86
86
86
88
125
132
134
151
151
Part 01: Observational drawing
Part 02: Structures
Part 03: Surfaces
Part 04: Application
BIRDS
18
40
71
72
83
88
89
89
127
127
135
152–3
INSECTS, SLUGS & SNAILS
41
73
78
82
82
82
88
112
112
113

INTRODUCTION

This book will help you to draw animals more confidently and competently. From the prehistoric paintings of bison, birds, cattle and horses that cover the walls of the Lascaux caves to kitten memes, animals have always had a central role in our visual culture. We have drawn animals to deify them, to study them, to tell stories about them or to simply appreciate looking at them.

As little children we draw animals as readily as people, from the pets that define our earliest relationships with animals, to the mythical beasts that spring from our vivid imaginations. As we get older and lose confidence with our drawing, we can also forget the wonder that inspired our love of the natural world – drawing can be a powerful way to rediscover that connection. Whether you are 11 years old and want to make better drawings of animals, 31 years old and trying to find a new connection with nature, or 81 years old and sketching animals with your grandchildren or for your own pleasure, this book is for you.

LEARNING TO DRAW WITH THIS BOOK

Drawing is a skill that can be learned, like riding a bicycle or playing the guitar – even if you feel like you have no initial talent, you'll be able to improve with practice and time. The book that you'll learn the most from is a blank sketchbook, so this book is a sketchbook with training wheels, full of blank spaces for you to practise, and room in the margins for notes and exercises to get you drawing.

Your first sketches will be awkward things, and you'll be starting from where you left off; so if you haven't drawn since you were ten, then you'll make your first drawings like a ten-year-old. Don't rush to finish the book but allow yourself time to linger on processes that you enjoy, to repeat favourite exercises, and to go off on exploratory tangents. Learning to draw is not a race to a finish line, but an ongoing adventure through an unfamiliar landscape that rewards curiosity and patience.

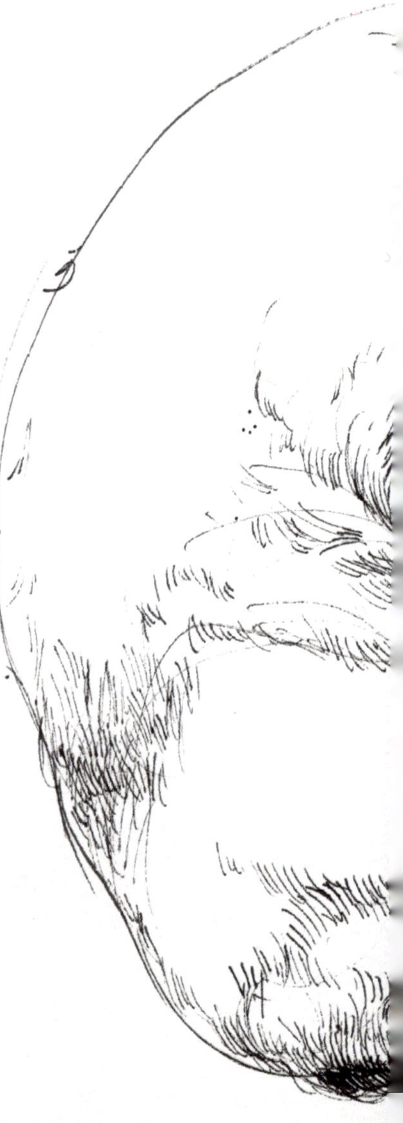

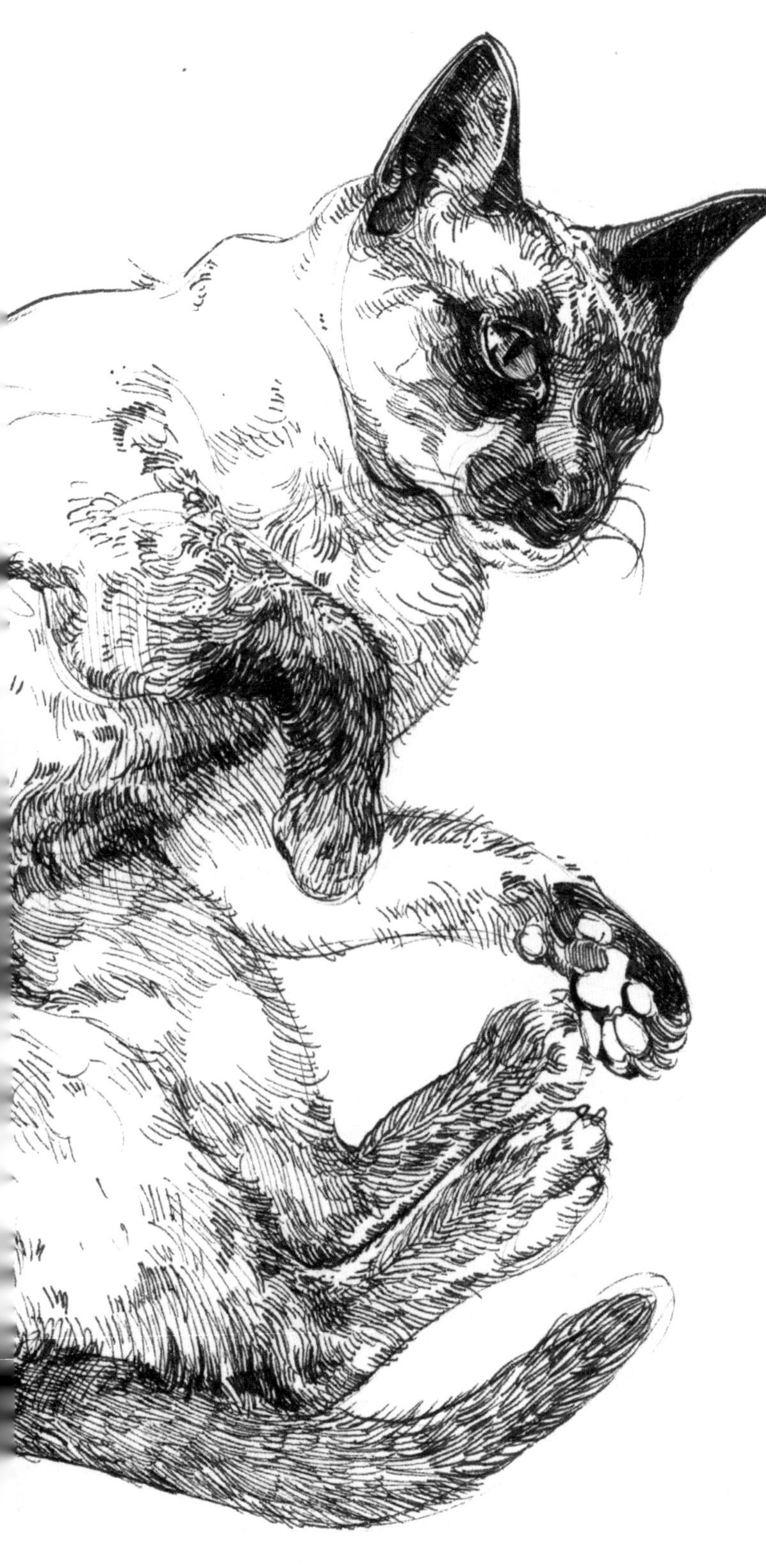

DRAWING WITH INTENTION

Drawing is more than just picture-making, it is a way of practising your ability to look, a tool for translating your curiosity into tactile marks to help you foster a deeper connection with the world around you. Don't judge the success of a drawing by how it looks, but by how well it meets your intentions – if you know why you are making a drawing, then you'll know when it has succeeded.

If you are drawing to learn, then even a messy and amateurish drawing might be a success if you learned a useful lesson while making it. If you are drawing to get to know an animal better, the drawing will be successful if it helped you notice something about that animal that you hadn't seen before. If you are drawing to foster a deeper appreciation of the natural world, then, regardless of outcome, the drawing can be successful if it has simply created the opportunity for you to get out in search of animals to draw.

OBSERVATION VERSUS IMAGINATION

If you've ever tried to draw a horse from imagination and struggled to work out which way its legs should bend, that isn't an indicator that you lack talent but a sign that you haven't spent enough time looking at horses. We are not born with an innate knowledge of how other animals look; we build up our internal bank of animal reference through looking and drawing. Learning to look is the cornerstone of all observational drawing – that is why this book focuses on drawing animals from observation.

All artists who draw animals from their heads also make repeated studies of those creatures from life and/or from images such as photographs or other artworks in order to build up a memory bank of poses to draw upon. If you intend to draw animals from your imagination, then this book will help you to lay strong foundations. If your aim is to learn to draw animals from life or from photographs, the coming parts will introduce all the skills you need to draw well.

GETTING STARTED

If you feel like the greatest barrier to making good drawings is a lack of skill, don't worry – that is a barrier that can be overcome with practice. First, you'll need to address everything that holds you back from practising, then you'll need to make a habit of drawing.

TIME

Find time every week to draw. You'll learn more from making several short sketches than from making a single, sustained drawing, and if you only make one six-hour study a month, you'll feel dispirited if it goes badly. Drawing in short bursts every week will help you to get used to the rhythm of better and worse drawing days that is inevitable at all levels of study. As well as carving out dedicated hours in the week to draw, fill moments of slack time with drawing – replace 15 minutes on social media with a quick 15-minute drawing from your phone or make short sketches of passing dogs while you're waiting at a bus stop. Every moment spent looking and making marks from what you see is valuable.

SPACE

You don't need a dedicated art studio to learn to how to draw, but you will need to make sure that you have a favourite drawing space to return to each time you want to put in some practice. Whether you are drawing at the kitchen table, on the sofa or out at the zoo, it is important to make sure that your drawing area is well lit, that your paper is supported on a flat, rigid surface, and that the surface is tilted towards the plane of your face.

AVOID THIS

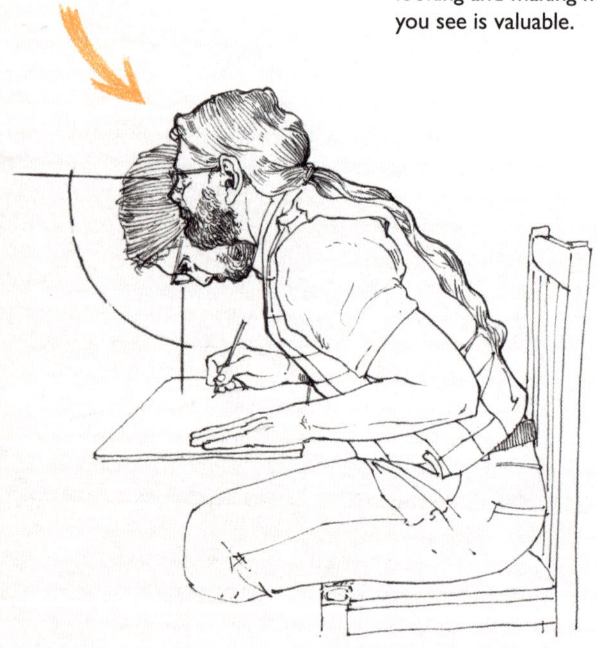

THIS IS GOOD

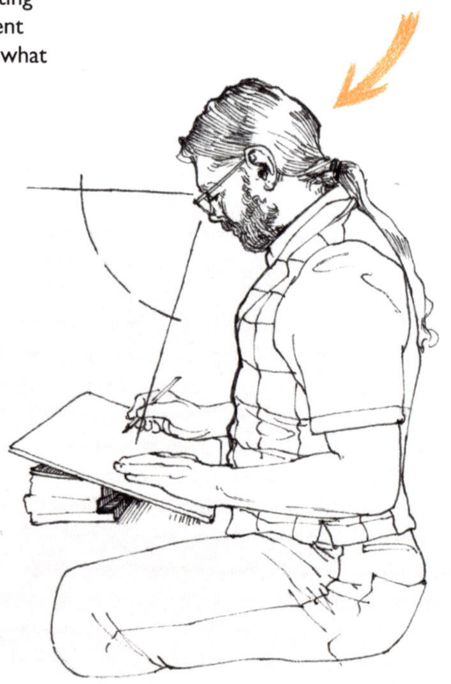

MATERIALS

Make sure you always have something to draw with and something to draw on. Think in terms of three kits:

1. ***An improvised kit***

Be resourceful – in an emergency you can make a drawing with a ball-point pen and a piece of scrap paper.

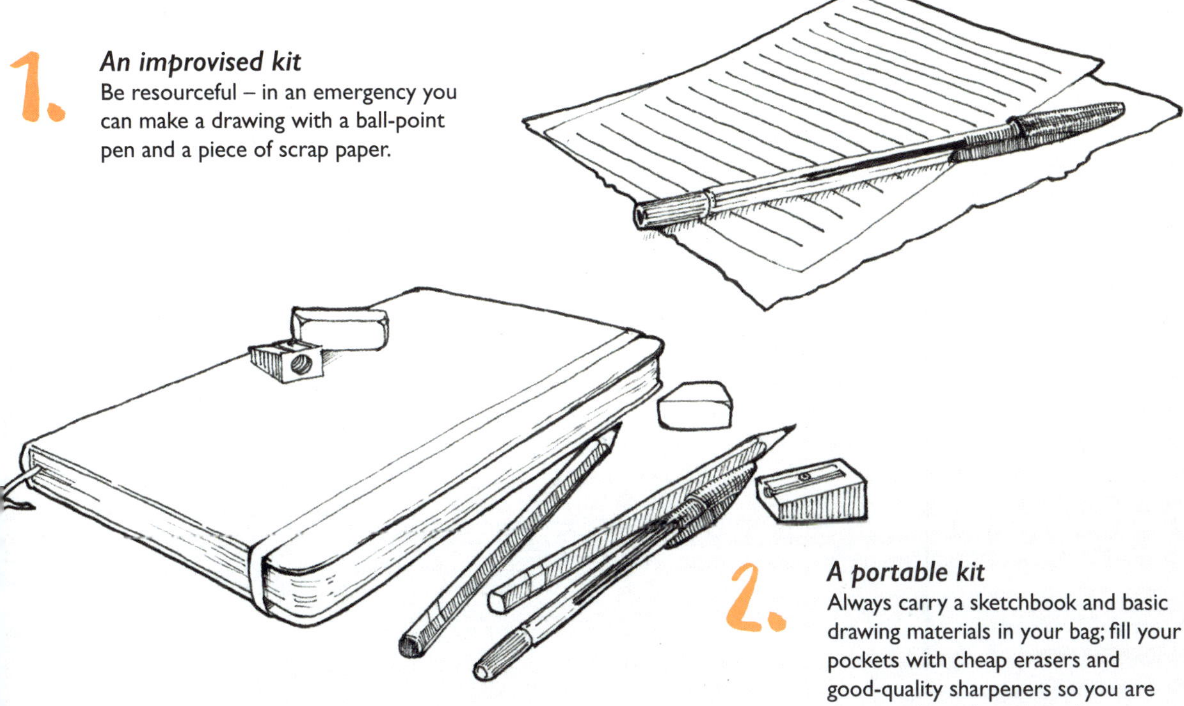

2. ***A portable kit***

Always carry a sketchbook and basic drawing materials in your bag; fill your pockets with cheap erasers and good-quality sharpeners so you are never without drawing tools.

3. ***An expanded kit***

Pack a folder or toolbox with your favourite drawing materials so that it is easy to get them out at home or to take away to draw with on location. Keep it somewhere accessible so you are always ready to set up to draw.

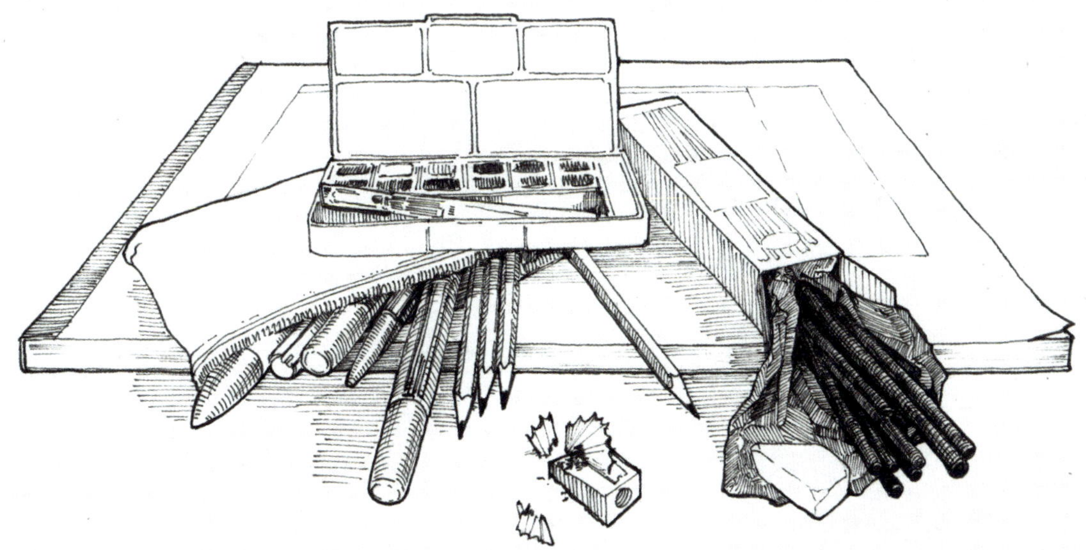

DRAWING FROM ANIMALS

One of the greatest pleasures of drawing animals is the search for a subject. At our unique moment in history, we are able to access images of any animal we like at the click of a button. However, until recently, artists incorporating animals into their work had no choice but to make studies of animals from life. While it is tempting to resort to a quick image search of the animal that you're keen to draw, it can be even more rewarding to seek out subjects away from a screen.

Select the source of imagery that best suits the drawings you want to make. Drawing from the work of other artists can help you to understand the language of marks they apply to their subjects, while drawing from photographs will allow you to make detailed studies, and paused videos will help you to sketch animals in motion. Alternatively, drawing animals from life can allow you to have the encounters that deepen your connection with those animals – there is an urgency to working from a live subject that is difficult to recreate when you're working from a photograph. Even posthumous drawings of an animal will allow you to make sustained, reflective studies that honour its life, whether it is recently deceased or preserved as taxidermy in a museum. Over the next few pages, you'll find suggestions of drawing opportunities that might present themselves in different spaces.

DOMESTIC DRAWING

From sleeping cats to pond-bound goldfish, the home can yield a wealth of opportunities to draw animals from life or to record your own reference material. Gardens and windowsills might offer opportunities to draw semi-tame birds and squirrels, while nearby parks allow you to draw dogs being walked.

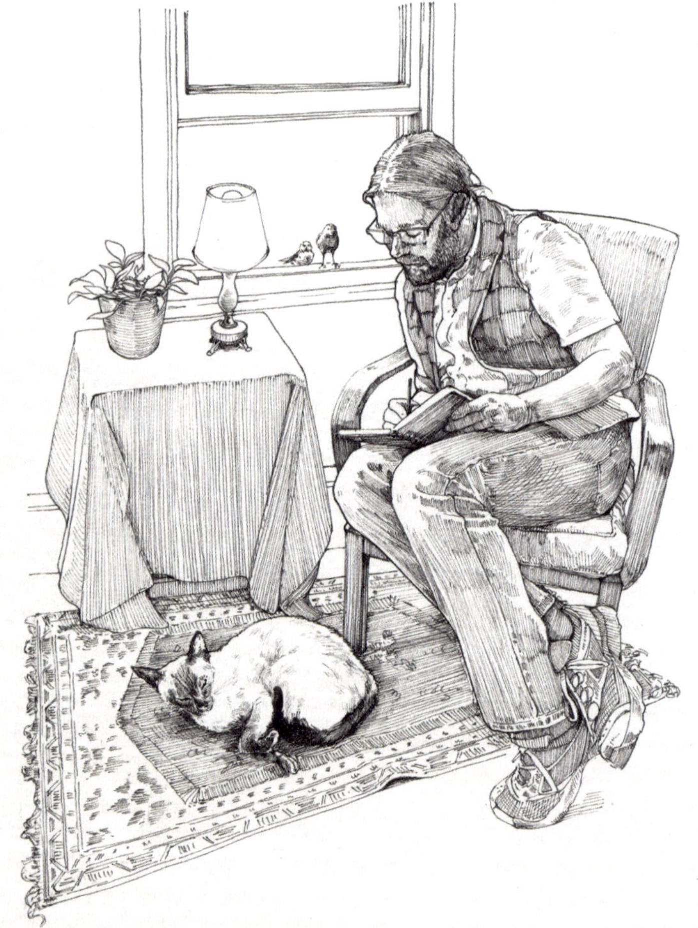

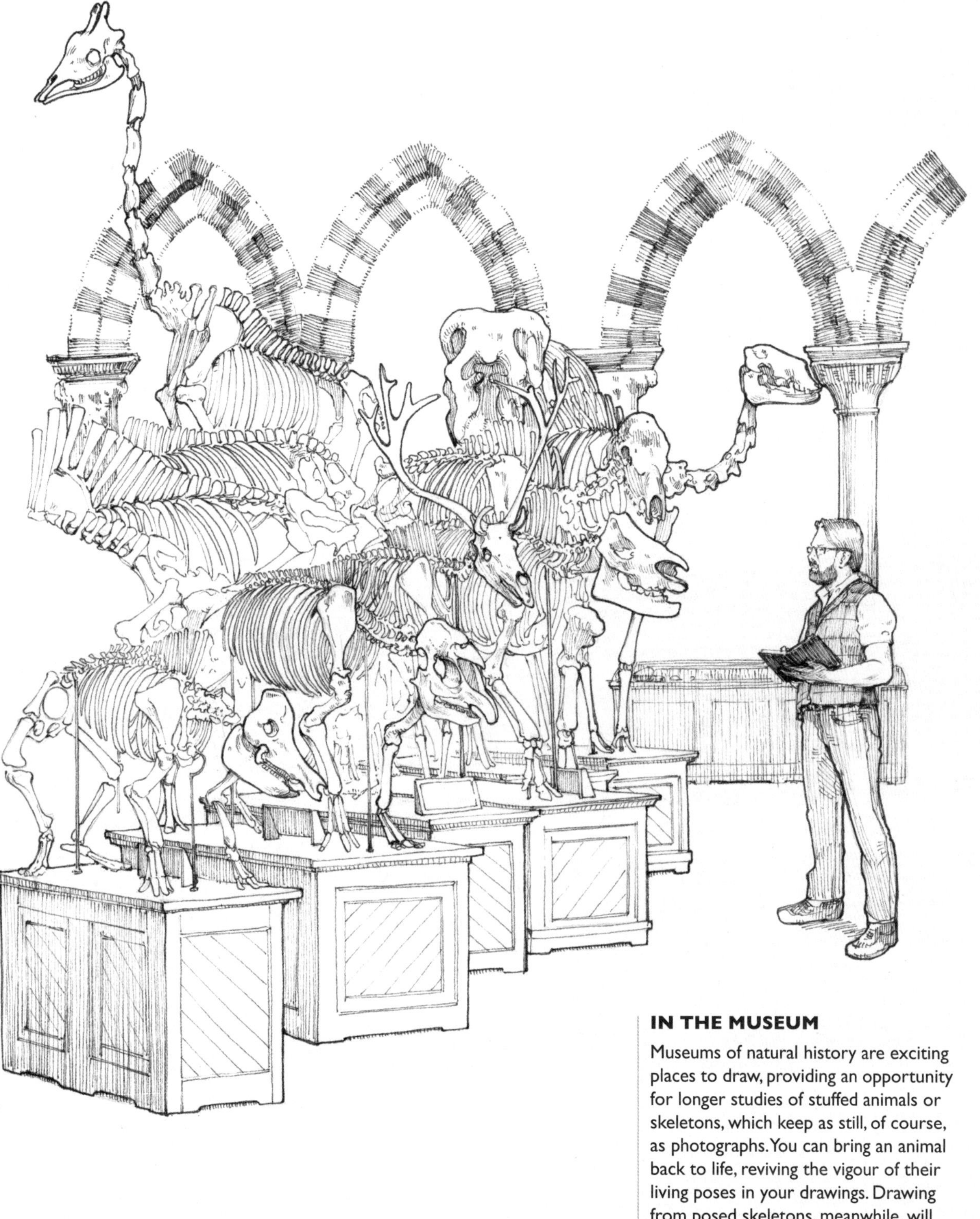

IN THE MUSEUM

Museums of natural history are exciting places to draw, providing an opportunity for longer studies of stuffed animals or skeletons, which keep as still, of course, as photographs. You can bring an animal back to life, reviving the vigour of their living poses in your drawings. Drawing from posed skeletons, meanwhile, will help you to gain a deeper understanding of animal anatomies.

ZOOS, FARMS AND AQUARIUMS

It can be challenging to draw animals in the wild, and zoos can provide the opportunity to draw not only exotic species but native ones, too. Domesticated cows, goats, horses and sheep can be sketched from the paths that border farmland. An aquarium will provide unusual views of aquatic animals: often, fish will swim in repeated cycles of movement allowing you to draw them from recurring snatched glimpses.

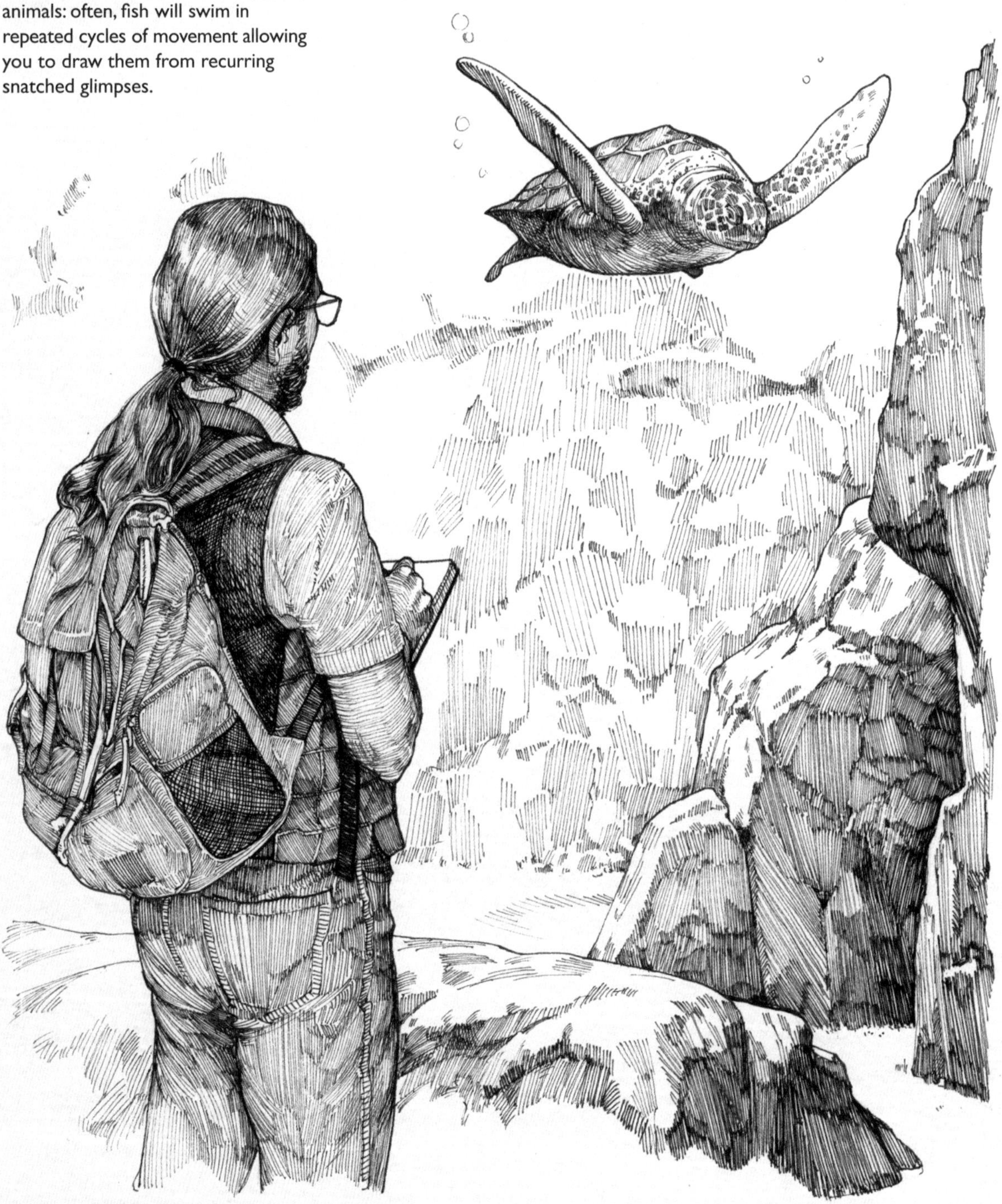

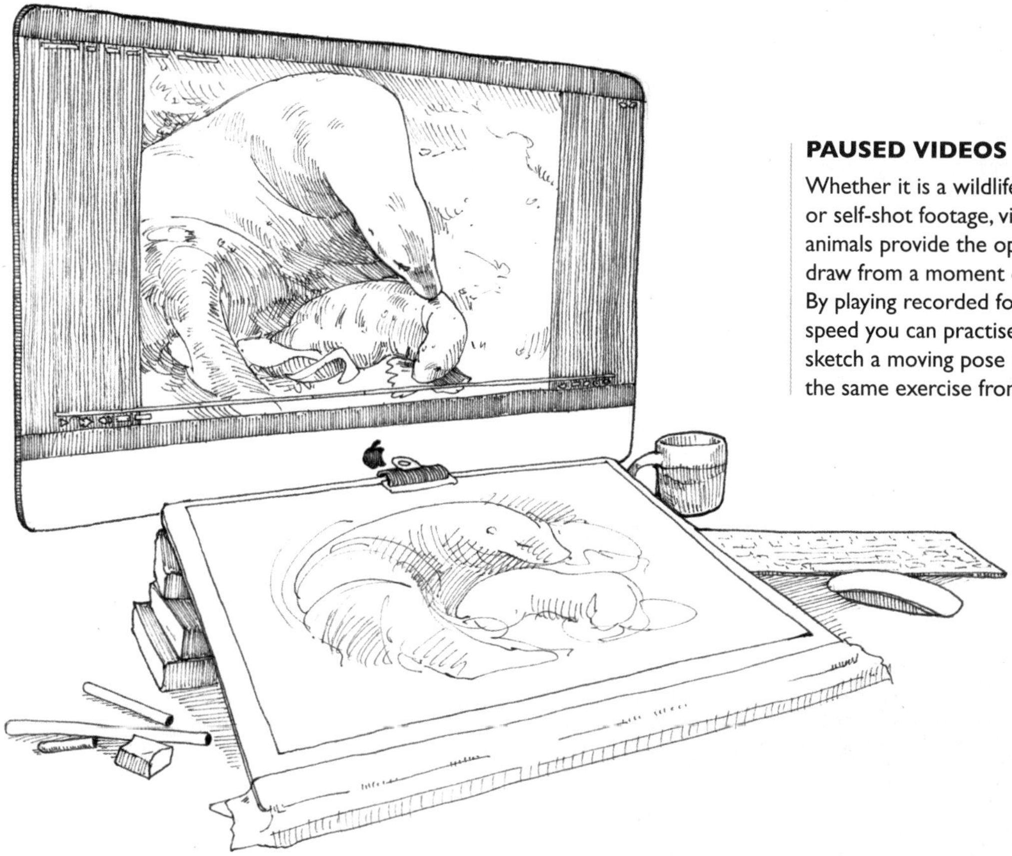

PAUSED VIDEOS

Whether it is a wildlife documentary or self-shot footage, videos of moving animals provide the opportunity to draw from a moment of paused action. By playing recorded footage at a slower speed you can practise your ability to sketch a moving pose before practising the same exercise from life.

STILL PHOTOS

Reference books and magazines of animal photography can provide detailed and beautifully lit material to draw from while internet searches yield a wide range of images. Dig through an image search to find less commonly used reference photos, and avoid photography that makes use of shallow depths of field, as this can obscure the structural qualities of an animal.

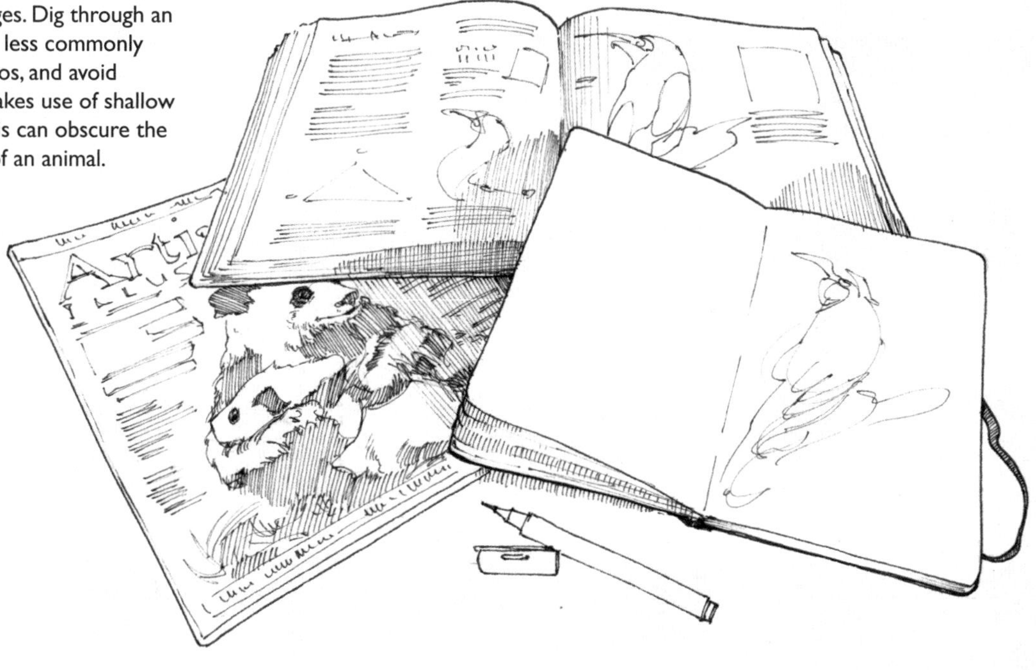

PART 01

OBSERVATIONAL DRAWING

A drawing made from observation is a conversation between you and your subject. When you are fully committed to it, the urgent process of looking and mark-making strings a thread of connection between you and the animal you are sketching, resulting in a drawing that records a moment of focused connection. This part will introduce some of the core skills that underpin observational drawing.

Drawing helps you to focus your observations of animals. You could sit at a window and watch seagulls cracking crab shells for two or three minutes, but it can be hard to maintain focus for very long. By drawing the birds as you watch them you rehearse the rough shapes of their bodies and the flow of their actions. Regardless of the quality of the drawing, the act of translating your observations into marks helps you look for longer and with greater intention. Later, when you flick back through your sketchbook, the drawing will transport you back to that moment of looking.

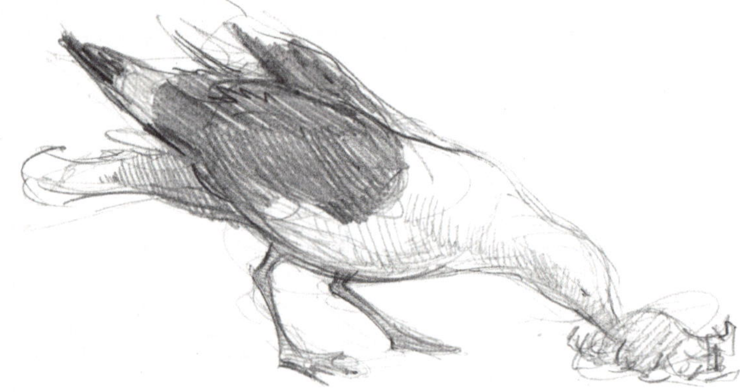

SOME ADVICE

- **Trust your eye** – your expectations of how you think an animal should look will stop you making clear observations of how it really appears. If you find you are surprised by the shapes you see in front of you, don't try to 'correct' your drawing, but trust what your eye has seen.
- **Make purposeful marks** – each mark you make should be a meaningful response to something you've perceived in your subject. As soon as you start to make marks without meaning, you will know you have stopped properly looking.
- **Find the answers in your subject** – spending more time looking at your subject will provide you with richer and more complete information to draw from. If there is something wrong with your drawing, then you might be tempted to stare at the drawing itself, but the answer to the problem will lie in the subject. You'll only solve that problem by looking back to the animal itself and comparing what you've seen to your study.

MINI-EXERCISE: BORROWING FROM OTHER ARTISTS

We learn to speak through imitation, repeating the sounds we hear until they take on meaning as learned words. Drawing is the same – through transcribing other artists' drawings you learn to imitate their vocabulary and borrow the visual phrases that most appeal to you. Enriching your drawings with marks borrowed from other artists is no less authentic than learning to speak by using the words spoken around you as a child – your originality will shine through in the subtleties of what your own eye notices and the inflections you lend to your drawn marks. When you see a drawing you like, make a copy of it with the following ideas in mind:

- Research the size and medium of the drawing you are copying and transcribe the drawing in the same medium and at its original scale.
- Think about how the artist made the marks in the drawing – were they made quickly or slowly, by pressing hard or lightly on the page? Were they standing or sitting when they made it? Rather than simply copying how the drawing looks, aim to make marks in the same way as the artist made their marks.
- Research the source that the artist worked from – did they draw from a moving animal? Taxidermy? A photograph? If the image was developed from their imagination, what supporting reference did they have to hand?
- Once you've made the copy, make your own original drawing from a similar reference, applying the lessons you have learned from the transcription.

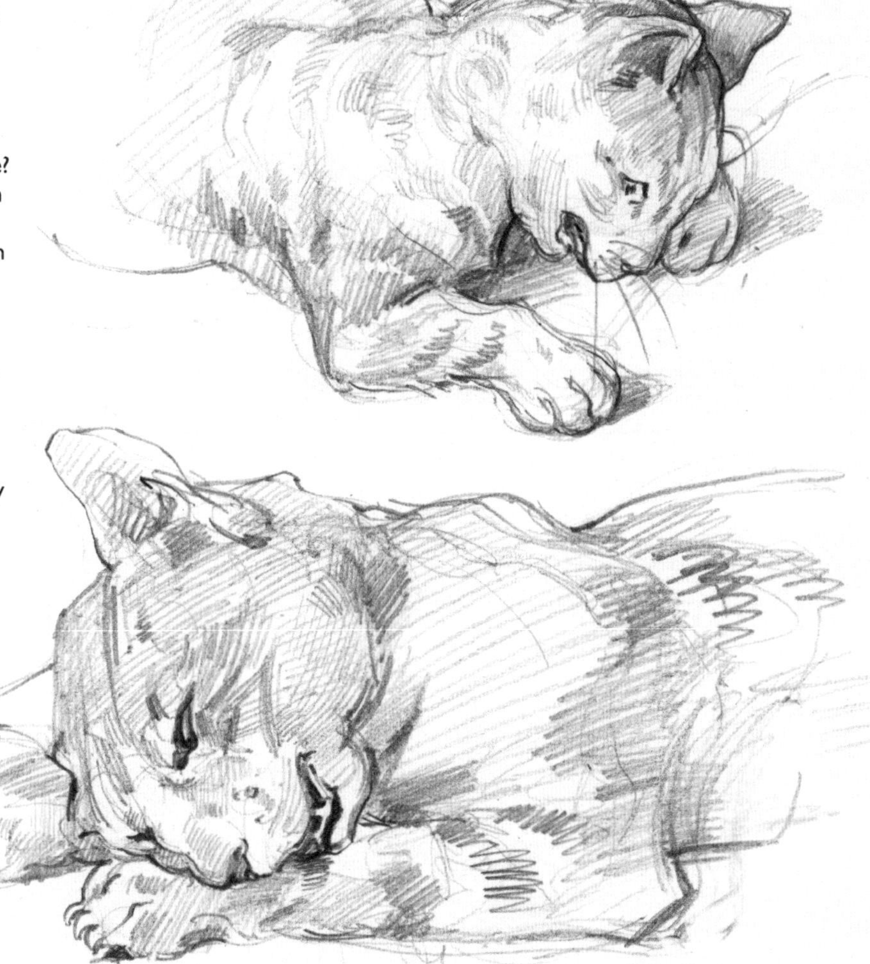

Transcriptions of drawings of cats by French artist Eugène Delacroix (1798–1863).

PART 01: OBSERVATIONAL DRAWING

MARK-MAKING

To draw is to make marks with meaning; the way in which you make marks in your drawing can be as important as the visual accuracy of the study. As you develop your observational skills, make time to explore the range of marks your materials can make, pursuing whims, enjoying the physicality of mark-making, and exploring the tactile relationship between medium and paper. The next few pages are all about playing with your chosen drawing material and exploring the marks you can make with it – use the suggestions as a starting point from which to launch into your own experiments.

EXTENSION & HOLDS

Drawn marks begin in your body, so the way you hold your medium will determine the range of marks you can make. Experiment by making abstract marks – then complete drawings – using different holds.

Explore the different lengths of marks made from your thumb and finger, elbow or shoulder.

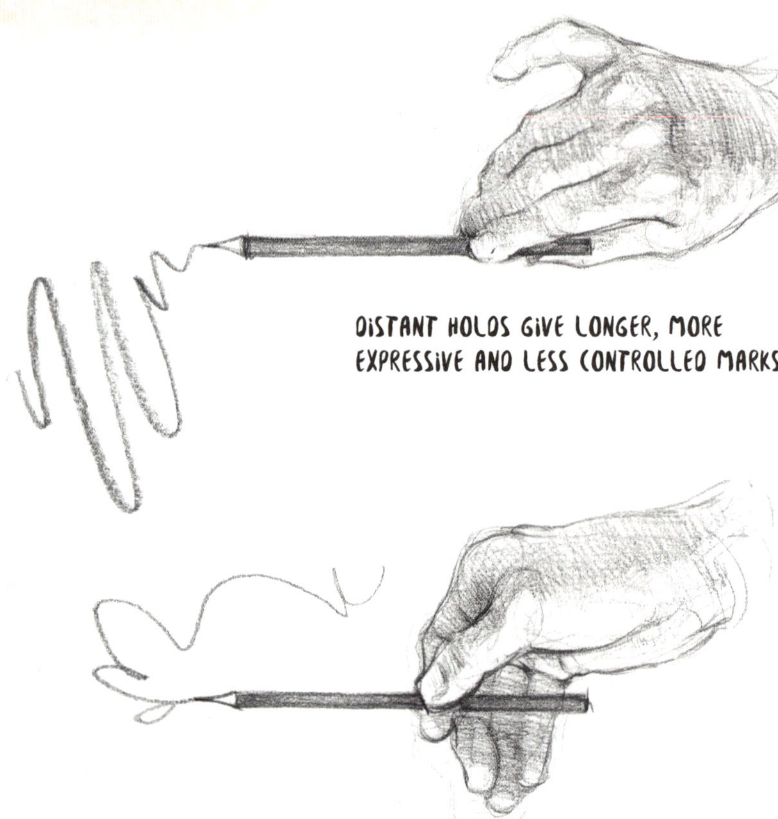

DISTANT HOLDS GIVE LONGER, MORE EXPRESSIVE AND LESS CONTROLLED MARKS

UNDERHAND HOLDS ARE MORE VERSATILE BUT LESS CONTROLLED

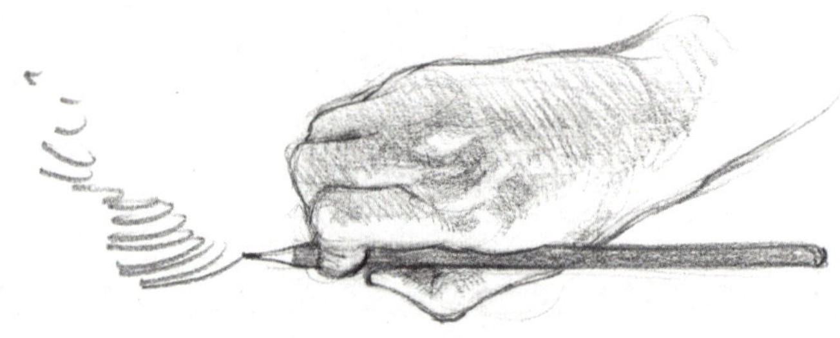

CLOSE, WRITING HOLDS CREATE SHORT, CONTROLLED MARKS

REPETITION

Repeated marks take on a meaning greater than the sum of their parts, implying the direction of flow in fur or feathers, the tessellating shapes that make up the texture of an iguana's skin, or the regular pattern of scales armouring a mackerel. Explore repetition by making a murmuration of marks: start with a short dash and follow it with another and another, leaving space between them and finding a direction of flow in the abstract mass of dashes.

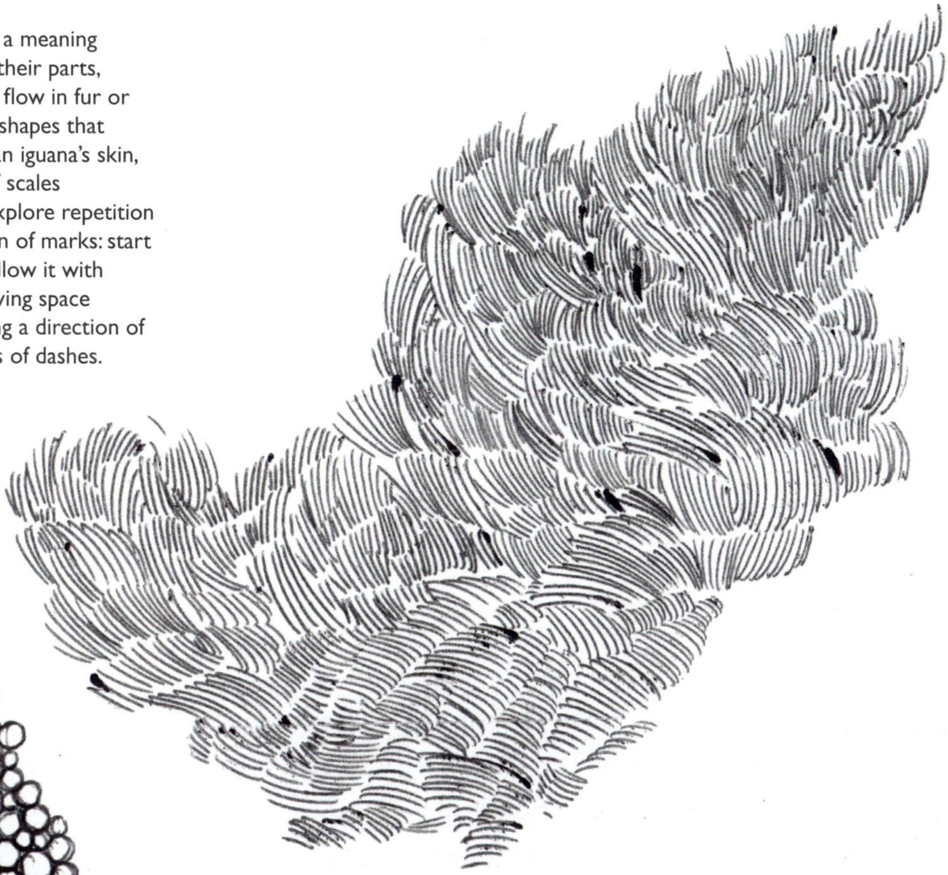

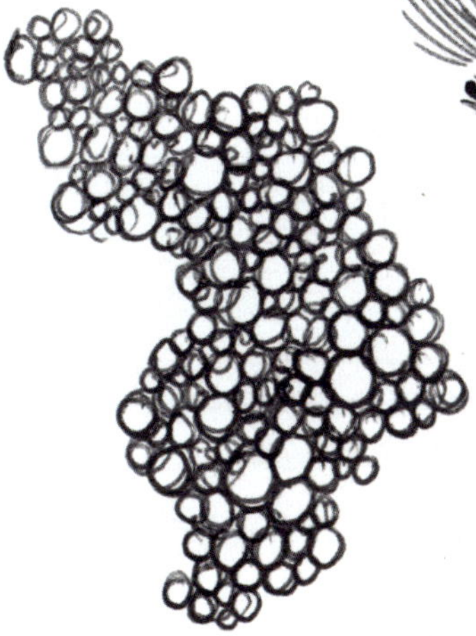

PRACTISE HERE

Think about how the mark and medium relate to your subject. What happens if you draw a fish in water-soluble pencil, or if you dip a feather in ink and use it to draw the bird that it fell from?

PRESSURE

The 'weight' of a mark describes both its width and the implication of pressure behind it. Heavy marks might hint at a weighty or muscular subject while the delicacy of lighter marks are suggestive of small animals, birds and insects. A distant grip will make it easier to mark the paper lightly while a close grip allows a heavier, more controlled mark.

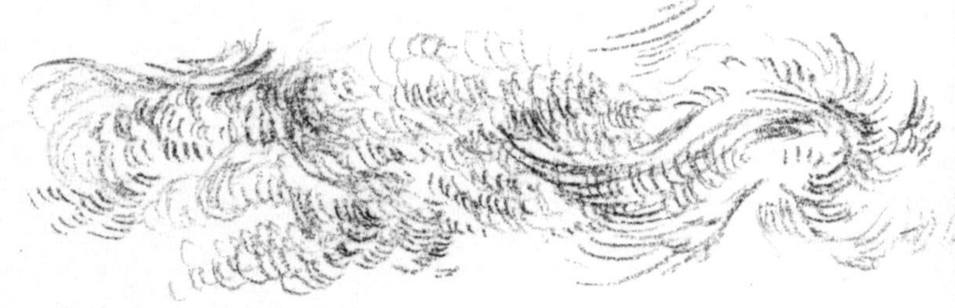

TICKLE THE SURFACE OF THE PAPER WITH A LIGHT, PLAYFUL MARK

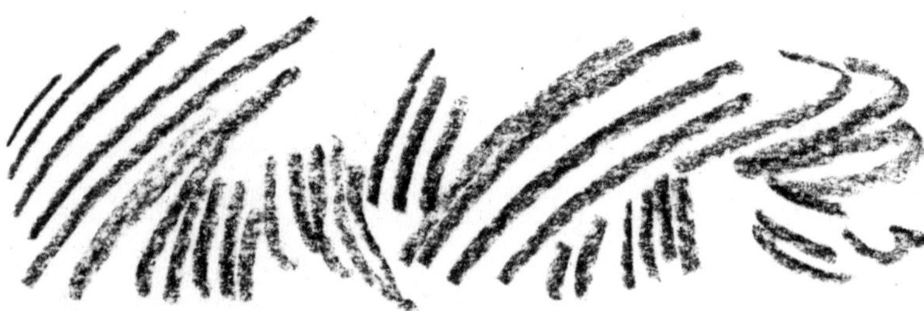

PRESS FIRM, HEAVY MARKS INTO THE PAGE WITH A BLUNT PENCIL

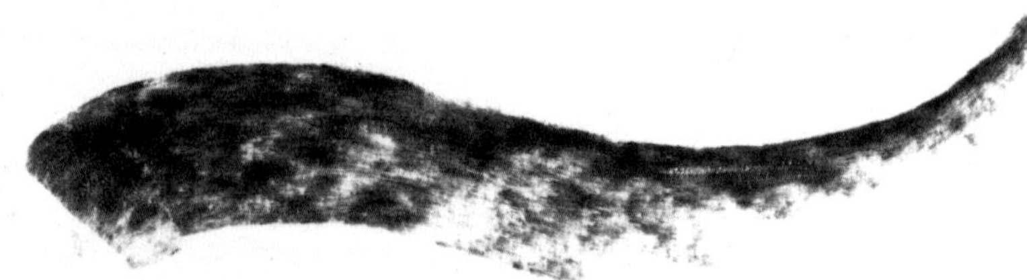

MAKE CALLIGRAPHIC MARKS THAT VARY IN WEIGHT ALONG THEIR LENGTH

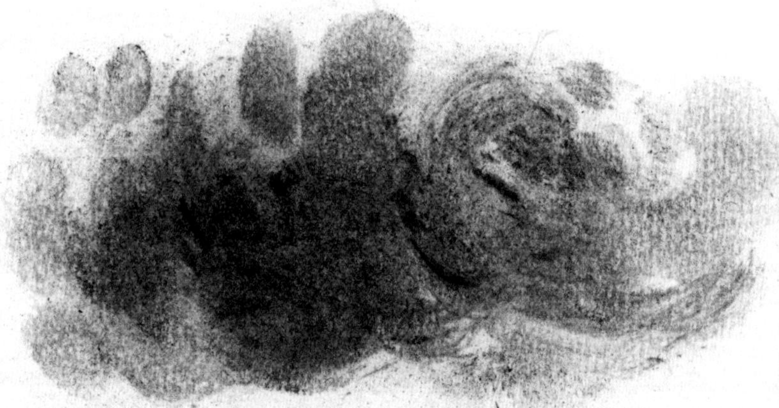

CRUSH CHARCOAL INTO THE PAPER WITH YOUR PALM AND WORK BACK INTO IT WITH YOUR FINGERS

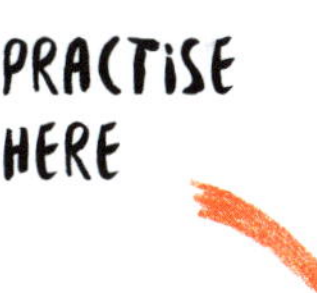
PRACTISE
HERE

SPEED

We read marks at the speed at which they were made, so that a fast drawing suggests a fleeting subject, and a drawing built up slowly suggests stillness. Sparrows darting to and from a window ledge might be recorded in a flurry of half-seen dashes, while a drawing of a dead robin found on a doorstep might be slow, delicate and detailed, drawn in marks that gently record its fragility over a long moment of looking.

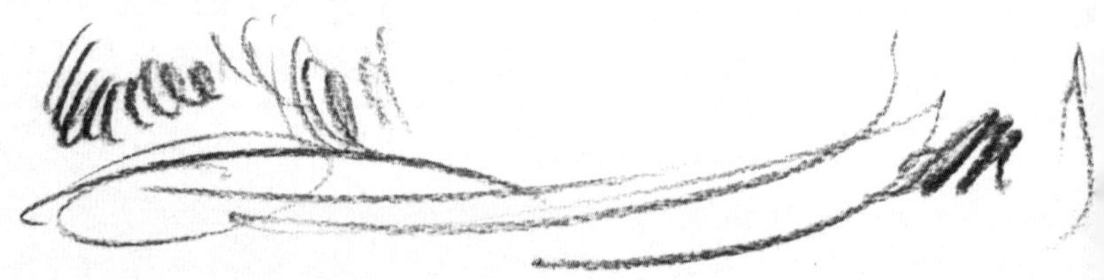

MAKE FAST DASHES AND SWEEPING LINES ON THE PAGE

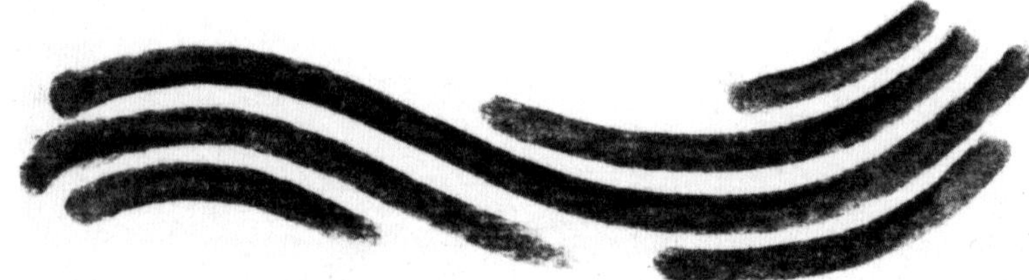

STROKE THE PAGE WITH STEADY, SLOW MARKS

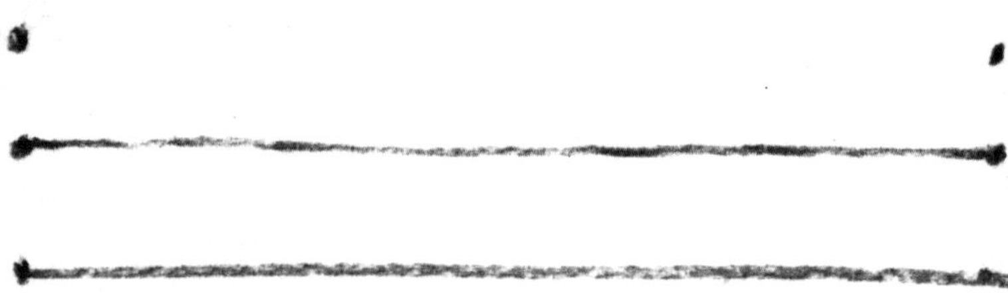

JOIN TWO DOTS WITH A FAST LINE AND NOTICE ITS SMOOTHNESS. JOIN TWO DOTS WITH A SLOW LINE AND NOTICE THE BUMPS IN THE MARK.

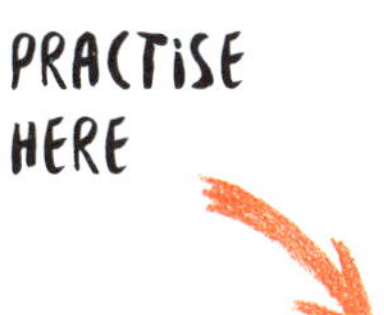
PRACTISE
HERE

SEEING WITH YOUR FINGERS – EXERCISE

WHAT YOU NEED

- A soft (2B–6B), well-sharpened pencil
- Any still animal subject
- 2–15 minutes

The best observational drawings are the result of relaxed and focused looking channelled through purposeful marks. This exercise will help you to cultivate that responsive process, resulting in a loose drawing that can serve as the foundation for a more considered study, or as an end in itself.

Start with a distant, underhand grip and make delicate contact with the page. Push all prior knowledge of your subject out of your head to focus only on what you see – make swift, loose marks to record the overall shape of the animal in its pose. Flick your eyes between subject and paper once every second, so that it feels as if you are looking at both at the same time. Explore the shapes and edges of your subject. Feel your way through the drawing intuitively, keeping your pencil on the page most of the time, and increasing the pressure behind your marks as you become more confident in your observations.

As the sharp tip of your pencil wears down, use the side to roughly block in reciprocating parallel hatching for the darker tones, using an eraser to rub light back into the dark marks.

Variation

As an alternative, make the entire drawing in pen – use a single continuous mark and never break contact with the paper.

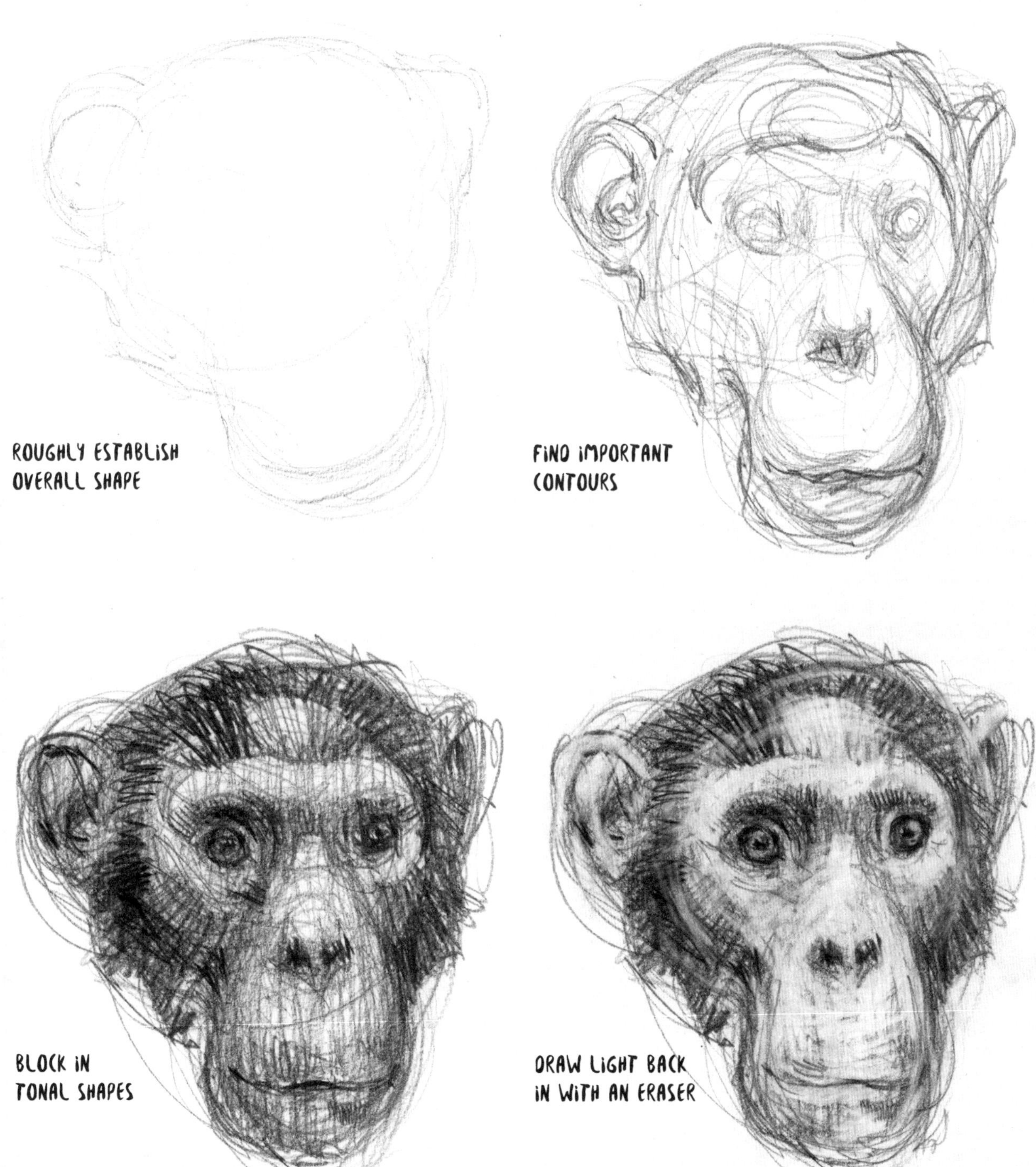
ROUGHLY ESTABLISH
OVERALL SHAPE
FIND IMPORTANT
CONTOURS
BLOCK IN
TONAL SHAPES
DRAW LIGHT BACK
IN WITH AN ERASER

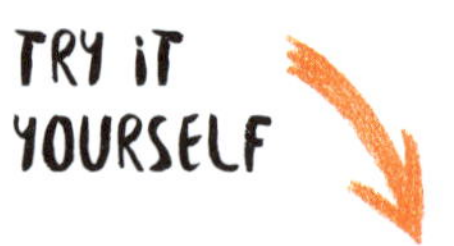
TRY IT
YOURSELF

PART 01: OBSERVATIONAL DRAWING

GESTURE

In drawing, gesture describes both the energetic quality that can be found within an animal's pose and the physical movements behind the marks you make. A drawing that focuses on gesture must speak about what an animal is doing, not just how they look. You are translating the physical gesture of the subject's pose into a physical gesture in your body.

Gesture is a felt quality, informed by an empathy for the subject, so gestural drawings will be individual to each drawer. Pure gesture drawings are often throwaway studies of action – preparatory exercises that help you better 'feel' the energy of an animal's pose, or underdrawings that are made to be drawn over. In the drawings on the right, you can see the difference between a contour drawing that focuses on the look of the subject and a gesture drawing of the same pose, which emphasizes action and focuses on the internal rhythms of the subject.

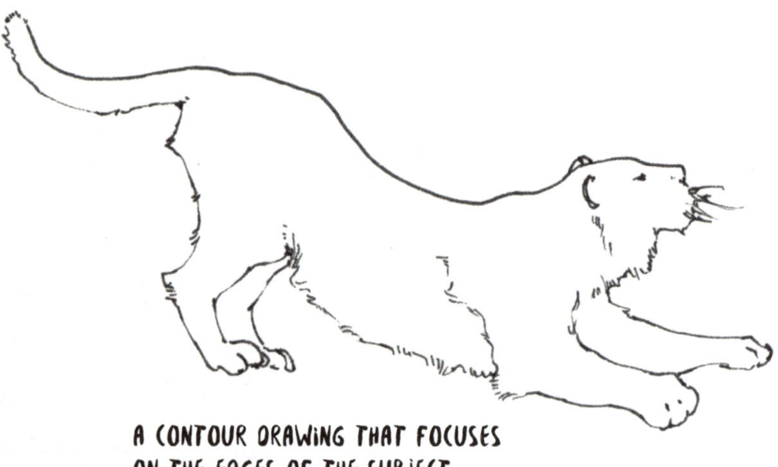

A CONTOUR DRAWING THAT FOCUSES ON THE EDGES OF THE SUBJECT

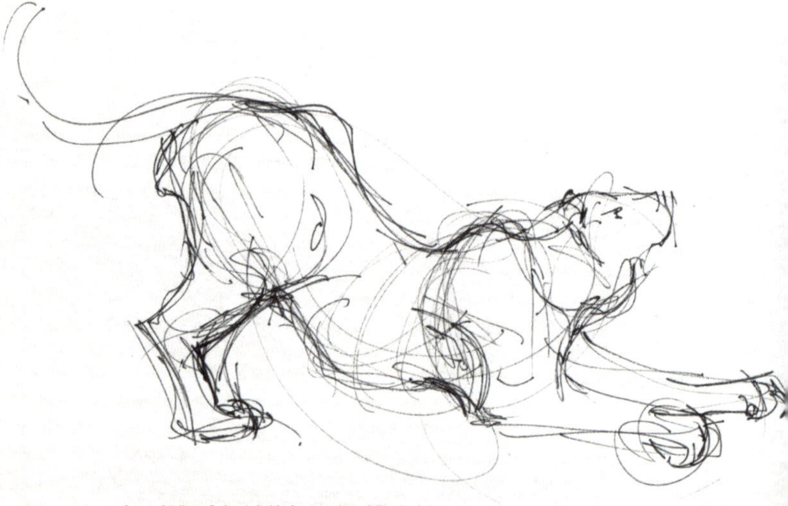

A GESTURE DRAWING THAT TAPS INTO ITS ENERGETIC QUALITIES

THE GESTURE BEHIND THE MARK

A gestural drawing is a metaphor for its subject, and the best drawings are the ones whose marks tap into the fundamental qualities of the animal they seek to represent. It is the physical gestures that you make with your own body – your arms, your fingers – that give rise to those marks on the page. You must consider how you make a mark as much as where that mark goes. If you are drawing a porcupine, how can you hold your medium and dash it onto the page so as to suggest the sharpness of its spines? If you are drawing a big cat, how can you make a mark that implies its sinuous power?

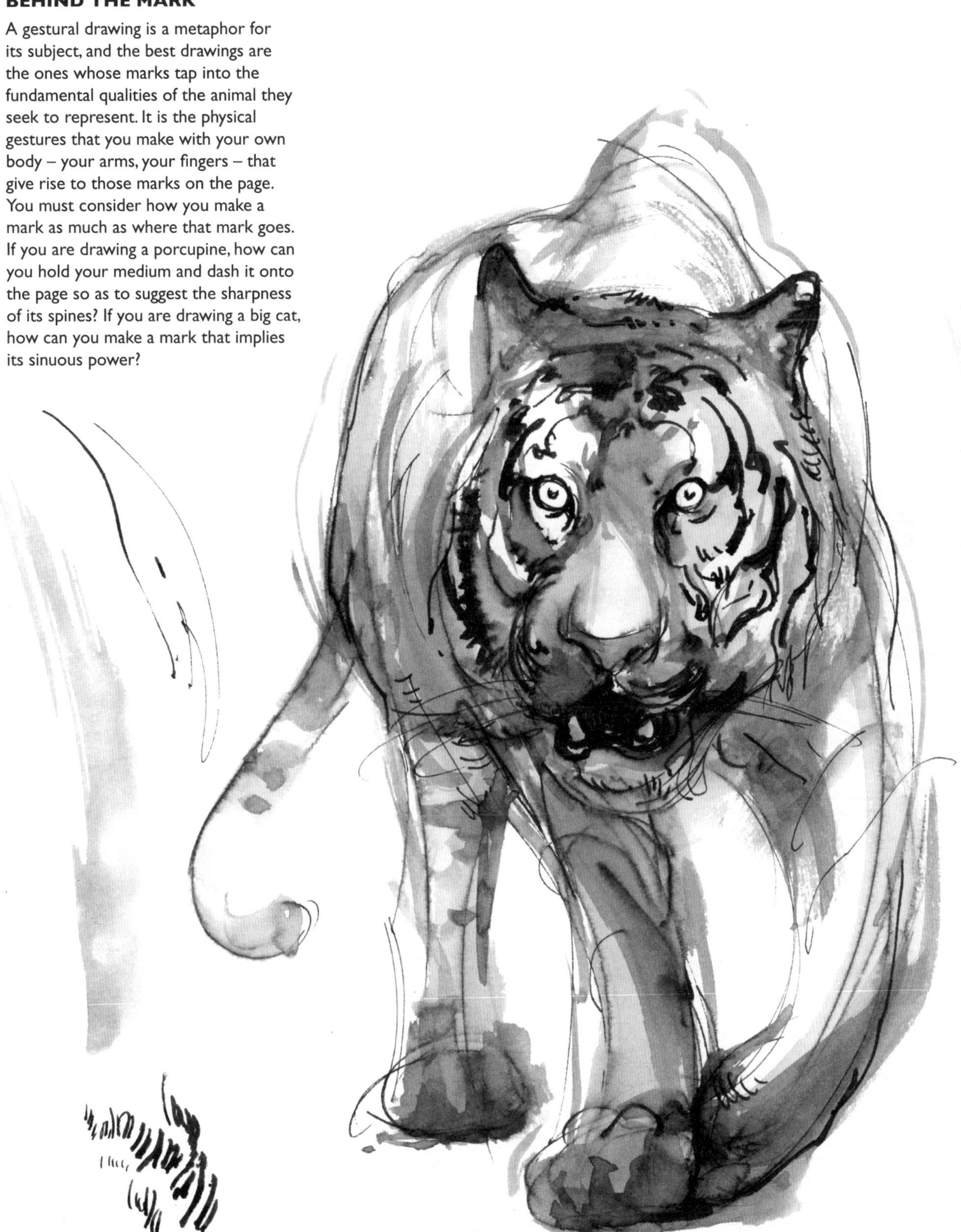

LINE OF ACTION

If you were to distil the gesture of an animal's pose into its simplest linear interpretation, you might arrive at a single line of action that runs through its body. That line often runs through the core of the animal, through its longest length – in a vertebrate it often follows the line of the spine, and in animals with tails it can run from head to tail-tip. A line of action can form the core of a gestural drawing, becoming a simple armature on which to build the rest of the pose.

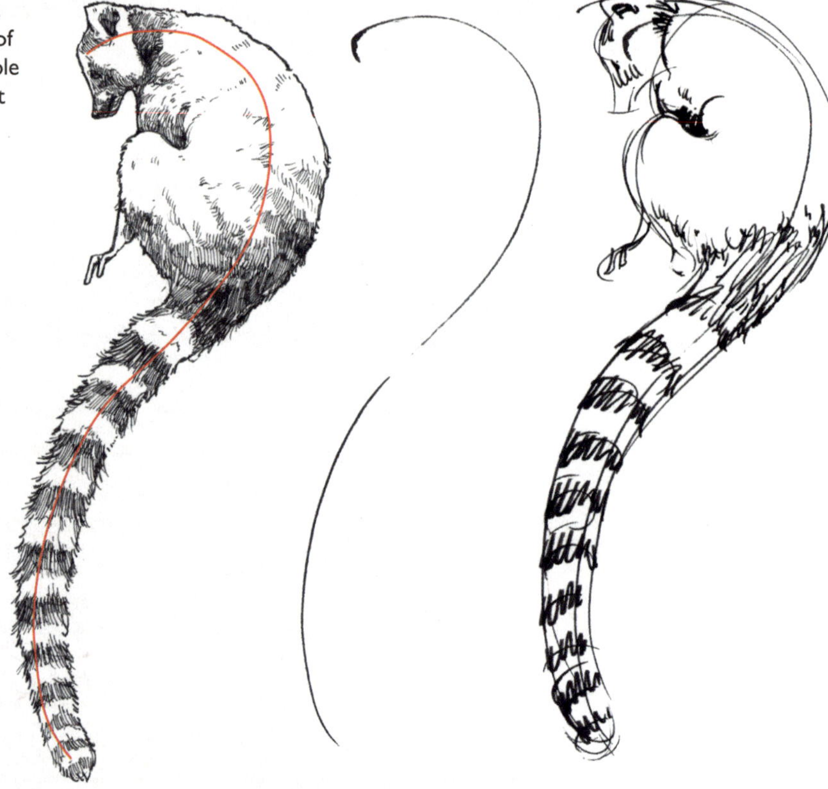

NOTICE HOW A LINE OF ACTION MIGHT CHANGE BETWEEN POSES

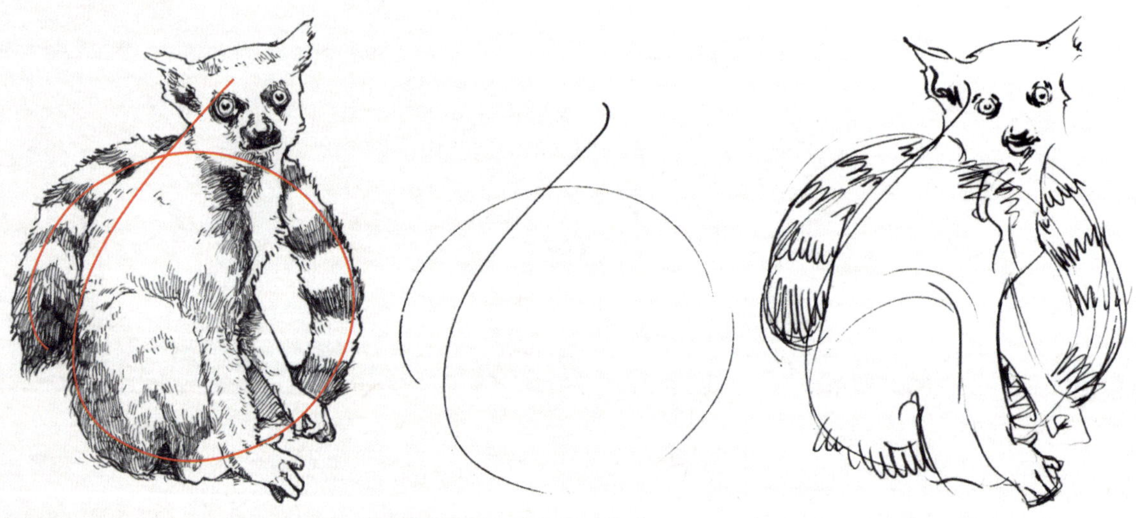

FIND LINES OF ACTION IN THESE POSES

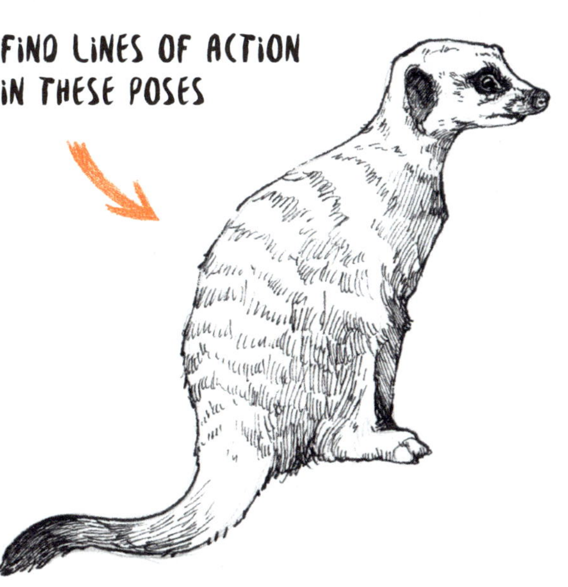

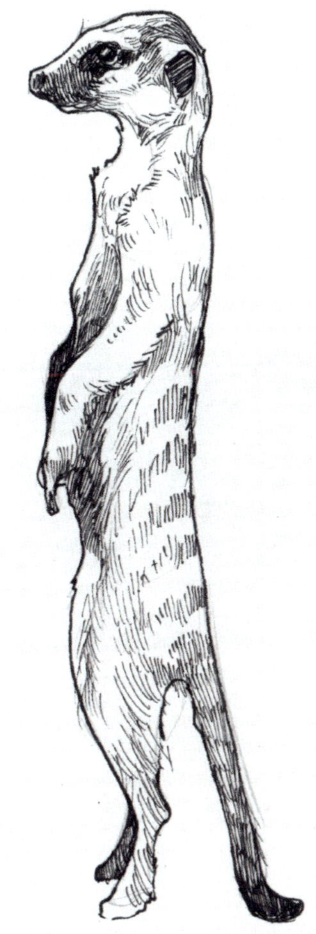

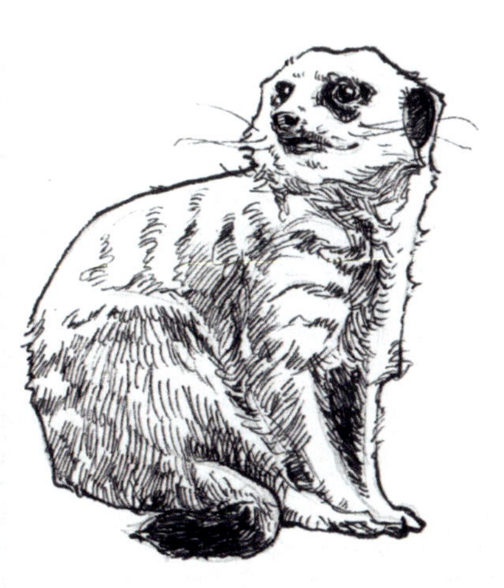

SIMPLE SHAPES

If you begin a drawing by working outwards from an area of concentrated detail, it can quickly fall out of proportion. Building a drawing up from simple shapes will help you to maintain good proportions, tackling the entirety of the pose in increasingly detailed passes over the subject.

The first shapes you draw should encompass the entire shape and flow of the subject. Just as a sculptor might begin a sculpture with a wire armature, you may want to begin with a line of action running through the pose. Then, just as a sculptor might shape a lump of clay over that armature, you can establish the overall dimensions of the animal you are drawing before going into any detail.

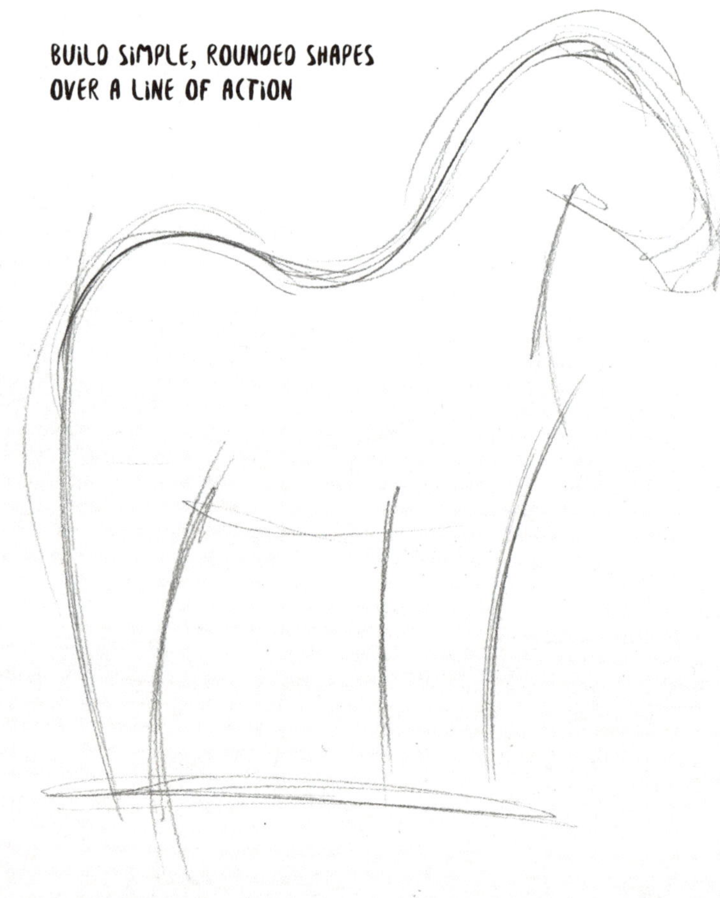

SECONDARY SHAPES

The next shapes you draw will relate to the major forms of the body – the shapes of the head and core. In animals with exoskeletons or shells, these shapes will be fixed and rigid, while in other animals they might relate to volumes of fur, feathers, fat or muscle. Although these shapes might be underpinned by the internal forms of skulls or ribcages, our approach here is purely observational, so you should draw the shape you see, rather than the structure underneath.

DRAW THE SIMPLE SHAPES UNDERPINNING THE BIG VOLUMES OF THE BODY

JOINTED LIMBS

While the joints of different animals work in different ways, points of articulation are always useful 'landmarks' to pinpoint. Use a rough circle to indicate the joint, extending it out to the edges of the limb.

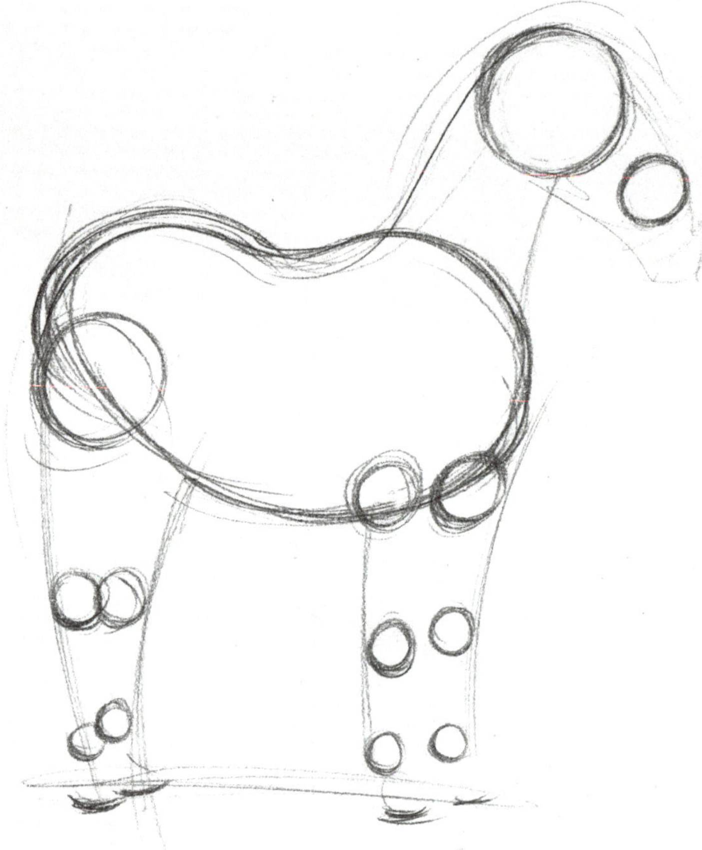

NOTICE HOW DIFFERENT JOINTS RELATE TO EACH OTHER ACROSS THE POSE – IS ONE JOINT ABOVE OR BELOW, OR TO THE LEFT OR RIGHT OF ANOTHER? WHAT IS THE DIAGONAL RELATIONSHIP BETWEEN JOINTS?

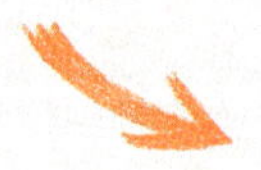

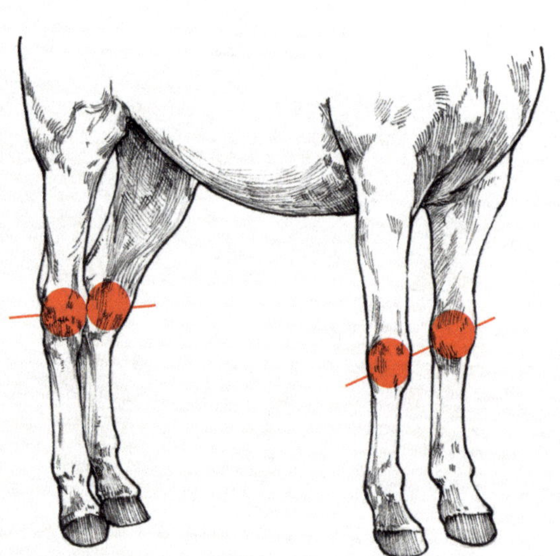

BRIDGING LINES

Join the rounded volumes of secondary shapes and the landmarks of jointed limbs with tangential bridging lines to create the final rough shapes the body. Average any surface textures into a single line, noting its direction, length and tilt. Whether it is a straight line or a curve, each line should be made as a clear and distinct mark.

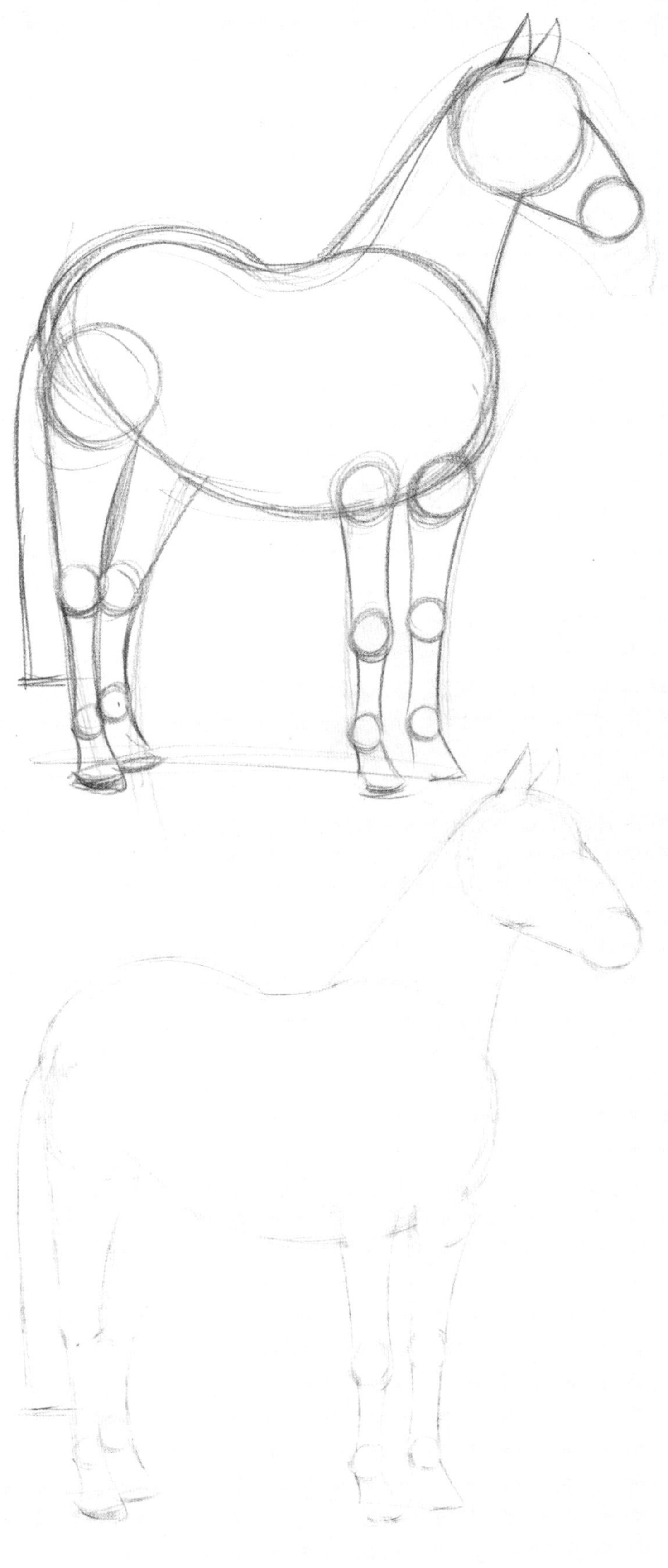

CONTOURS

Once you have built a scaffold of supporting shapes, you can add your observations of the surfaces of your subject over the top, starting with the contours of the animal. Contours are the physical edges that you see; unlike the borders of shadows, contours are edges that you could trace your finger over – the horizon lines of the animal's body.

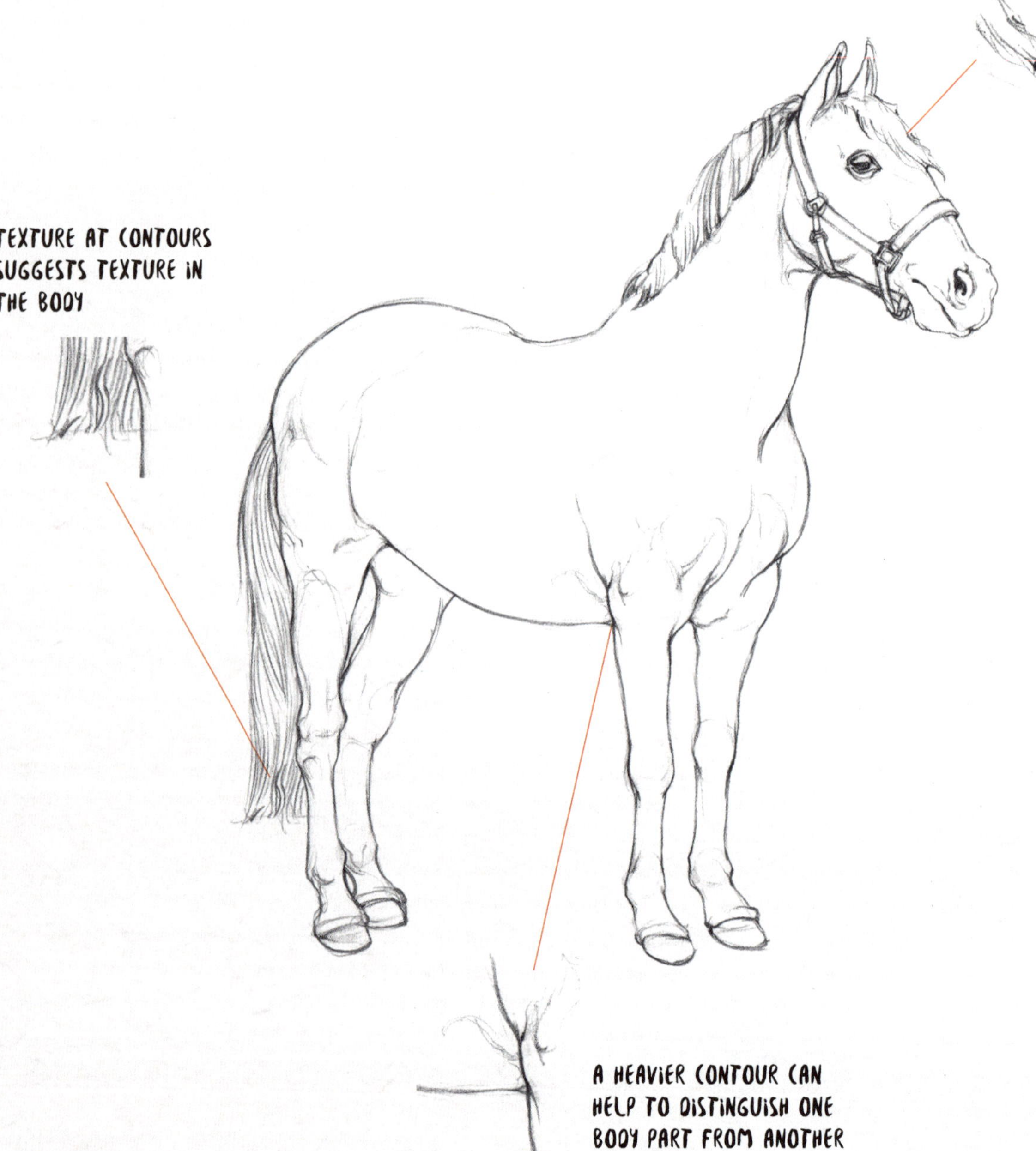

PRACTISE HERE

ANIMAL EXAMPLES

Here are some different examples of simple shapes that could be used to underpin animals in different poses. On the following spread, apply the process to reference images of your own.

PRIMARY SHAPES

SECONDARY SHAPES

LIMB JOINTS

BRIDGING LINES

CONTOURS

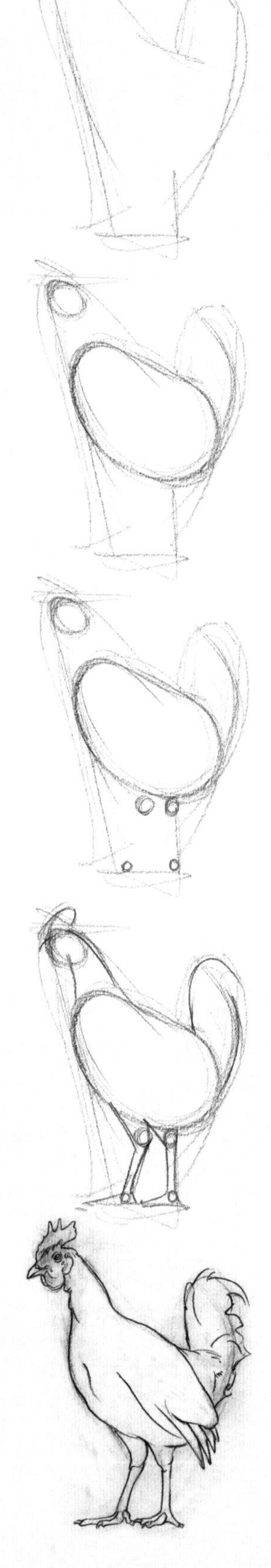

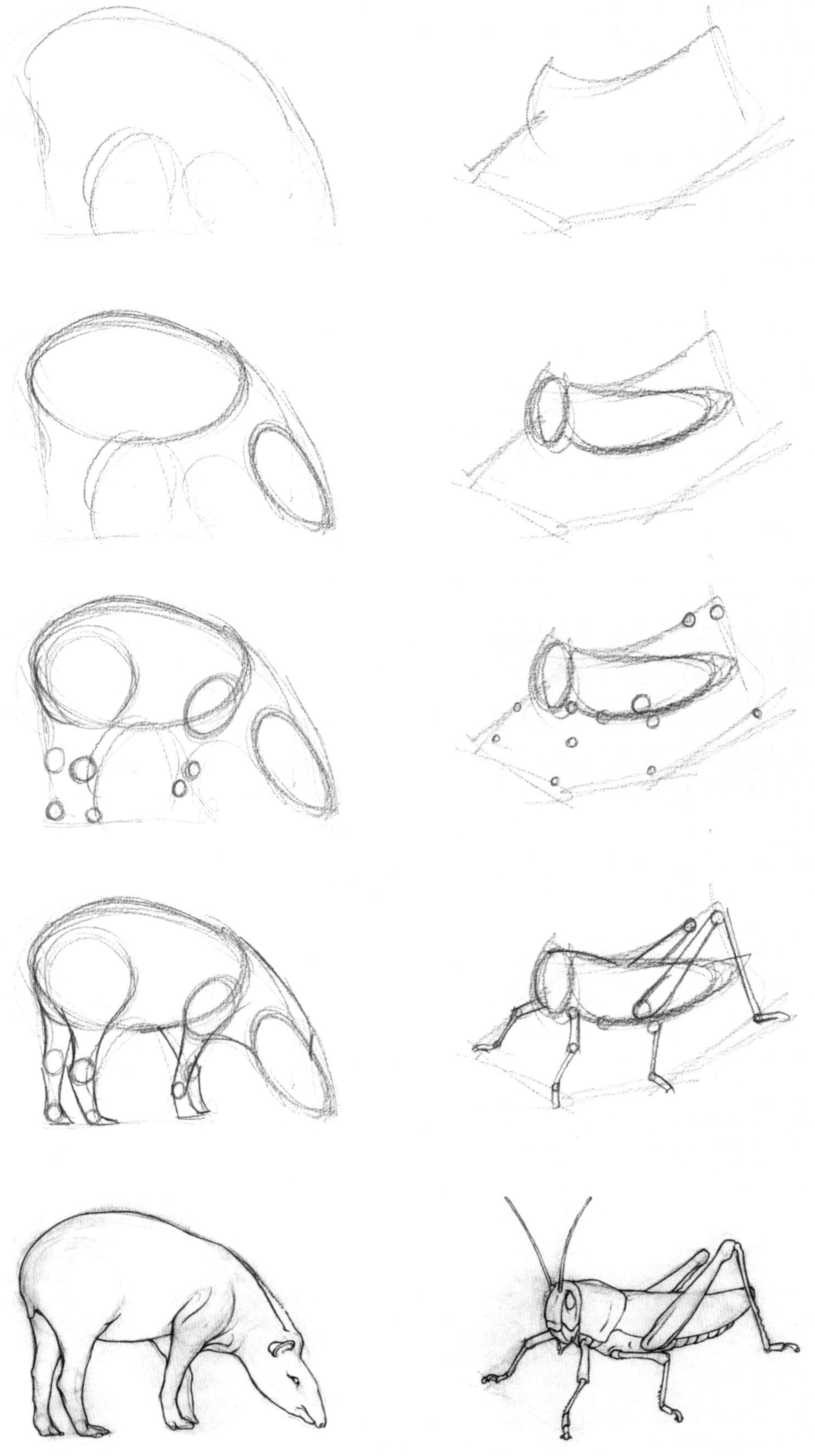

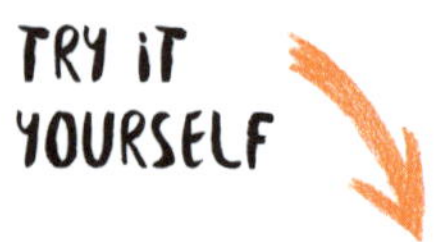
TRY IT
YOURSELF

NEGATIVE SPACE

'Negative space' describes the space around a positive subject. Because we don't bring the same preconceptions to shapes we see around the animal as we do to the animal itself, they are an excellent tool for helping us to see the subject more objectively. Early in a drawing you can use negative spaces to help you establish the shapes of your animal's pose, and later you can use them to check proportions.

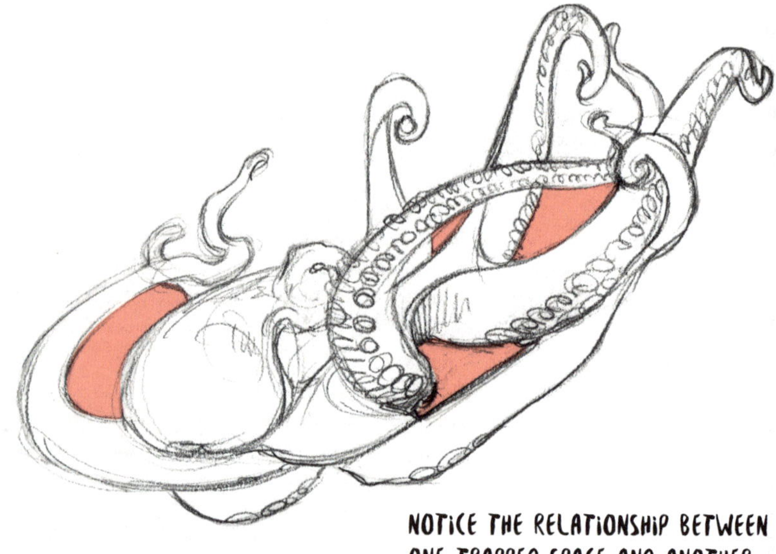

NOTICE THE RELATIONSHIP BETWEEN ONE TRAPPED SPACE AND ANOTHER

TRAPPED SPACES

Trapped spaces are self-contained negative spaces that are bounded on all sides by the subject. They are particularly present in animals with lots of complex, interacting body parts. Every now and again look at a trapped negative space in your subject, then look at the same shape in your drawing – do they match? If they don't match and the subject hasn't moved, you'll need to check your drawing.

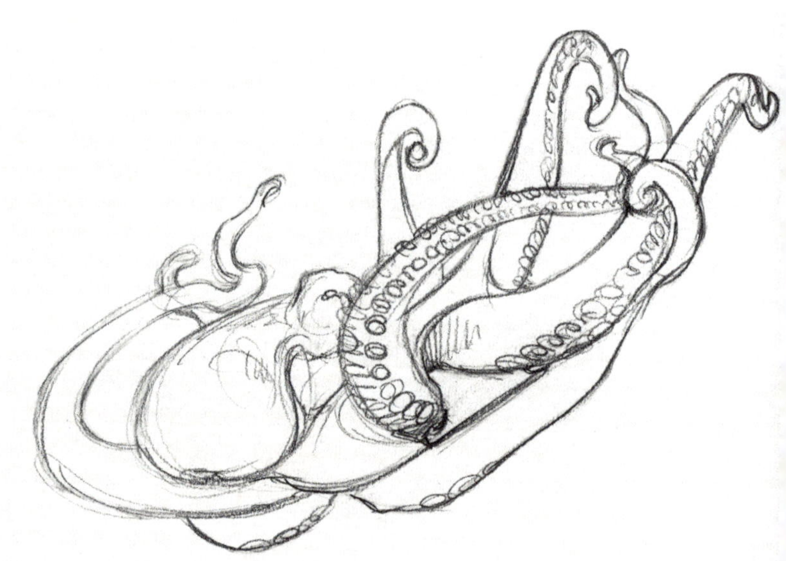

OPEN SPACES

The negative spaces around an animal are open to the visual world that surrounds them, making it more difficult to define their shape. To see them more clearly, you'll need to introduce your own boundaries to help define them. You can use two methods to help isolate open negative spaces: tangents or crates.

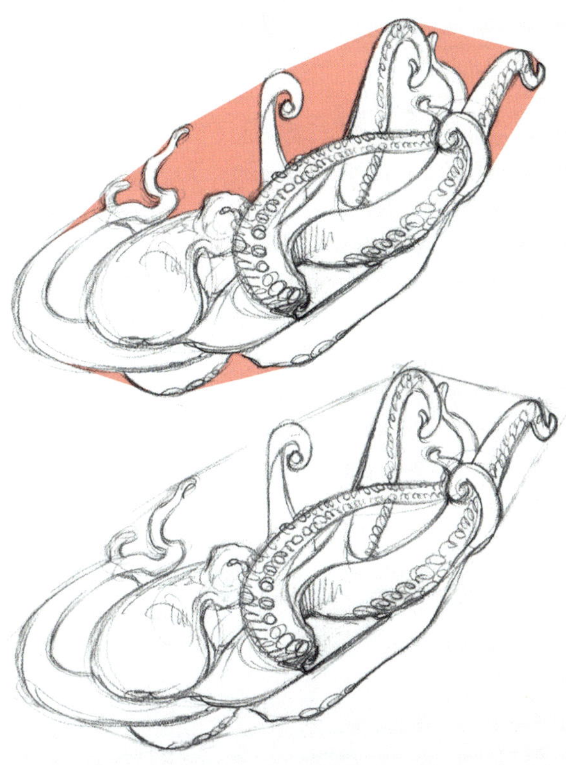

Tangents

To define negative spaces using tangents, imagine that the animal you are drawing is caught inside an elasticated bag, lines stretched tight between each of their extremes. Notice the particular shape of each negative space created between the animal and its connecting tangents.

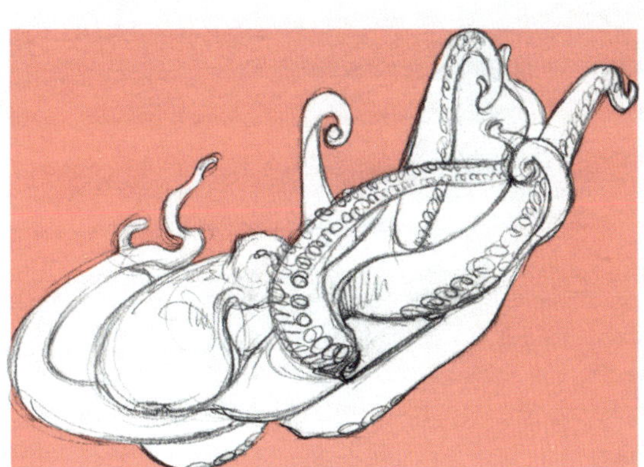

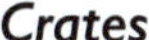

Crates

We are used to thinking within a box, with cameras, screens and sketchbooks all framing our view with four edges and four right-angled corners. Imagine a tight-fitting crate around your animal, and draw in the tangential horizontals and verticals. The spaces between the imaginary crate and your subject can be treated as negative spaces.

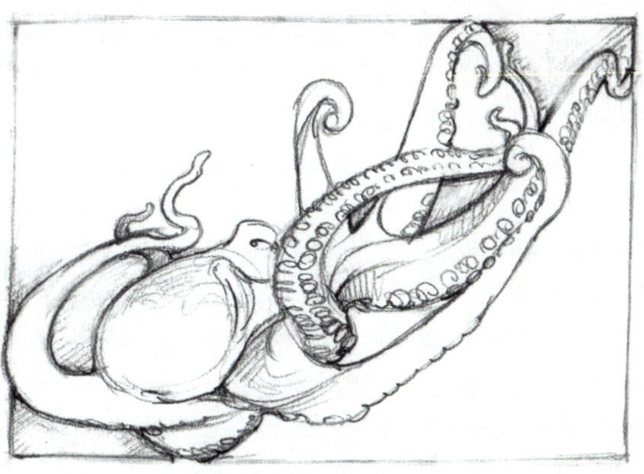

PART 01: OBSERVATIONAL DRAWING

SILHOUETTES – EXERCISE

WHAT YOU NEED

- Charcoal
- A still subject
- Large paper
- Masking tape
- An eraser

INSPIRATION

- The prehistoric cave drawings at Lascaux

An evolutionary need to distinguish predator from prey at a distance has made us particularly receptive to the shapes of silhouetted animals. This exercise will help you to hone that sensitivity further by drawing the filled-in outline of your subject. It works best from static reference – photographs, film stills or taxidermy. Although the exercise can work with a pencil and a sketchbook, it is most satisfying on a large scale, using a malleable medium like charcoal.

Tape a large piece of paper to a wall or a drawing board on an easel and stand back, drawing with charcoal held out at arm's length and allowing your whole arm to participate in the mark-making. Begin by blocking in the large, rough shapes of the animal like a sculptor hewing rough chunks from a block of marble, constantly flicking your eyes back and forth between subject and drawing, remaining aware of the negative spaces that surround the animal. Allow your awareness to zoom in and out between the shape of the subject as a whole and the detail at the boundary of the outline. Fill the body in with black, ignoring all detail and using an eraser to reshape the borders of your drawing.

Variation

Reverse the exercise and draw in the negative spaces only, leaving the subject as a white cut-out space in the centre of your paper.

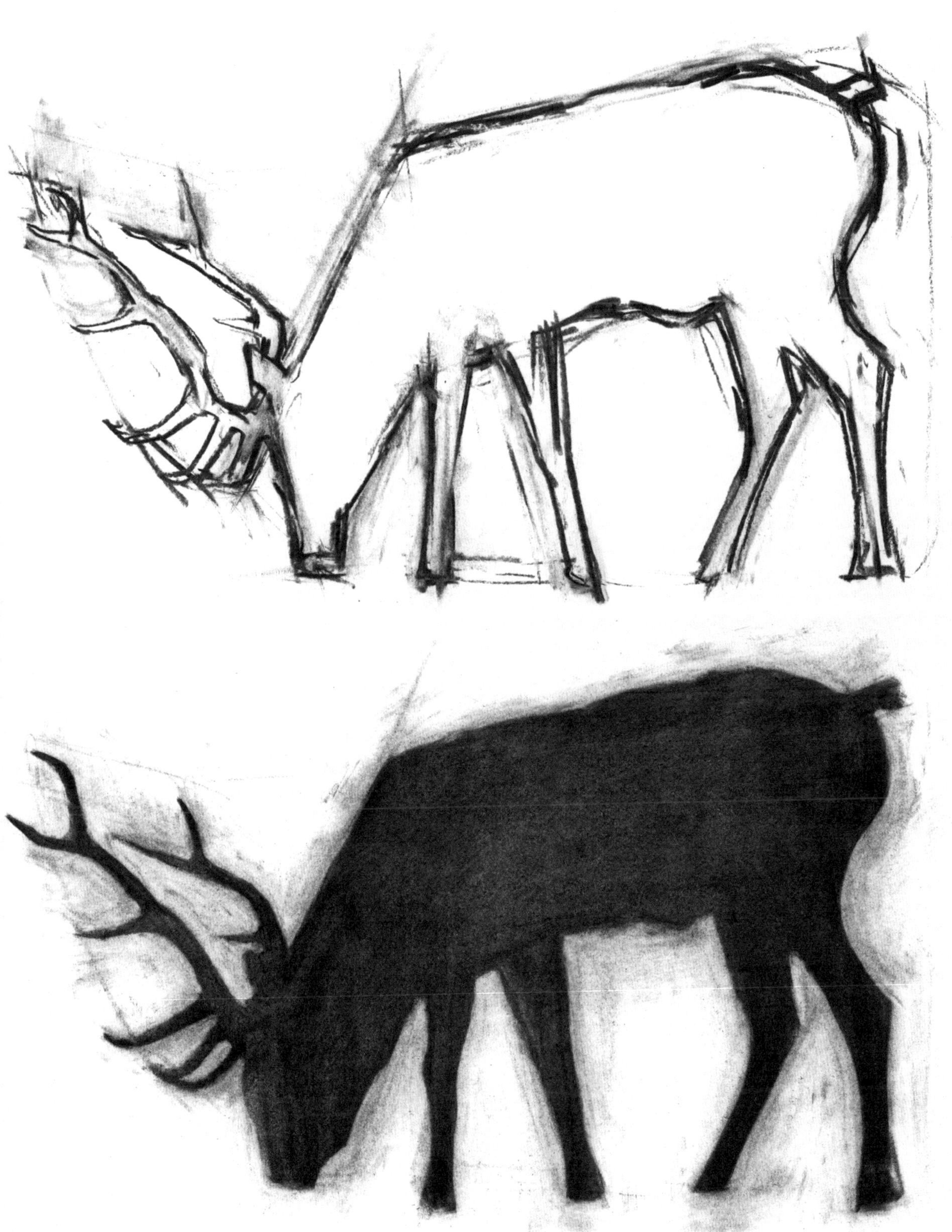

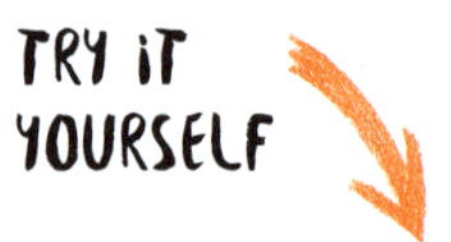
TRY IT
YOURSELF

FORM

Form describes the three-dimensional character of a subject, its roundedness, the idea that something else exists around the other side of what you can see. Drawing with an awareness of form requires both observation and empathy. Your own physical experience of the world should help you to empathize with an animal's physicality and inform the marks you make in your drawings.

So far we have focused on translating animals into flat shapes – over the next few pages we'll look at how to introduce the illusion of three-dimensional form to those two-dimensional drawings. If you're working from a photograph, then your subject has already been flattened into two-dimensions; that makes it easier to translate into a two-dimensional drawing but harder to intuit the animal's form. Live subjects or paused video will make better reference for exploring form, as they allow you to see the shape of the animal from several angles.

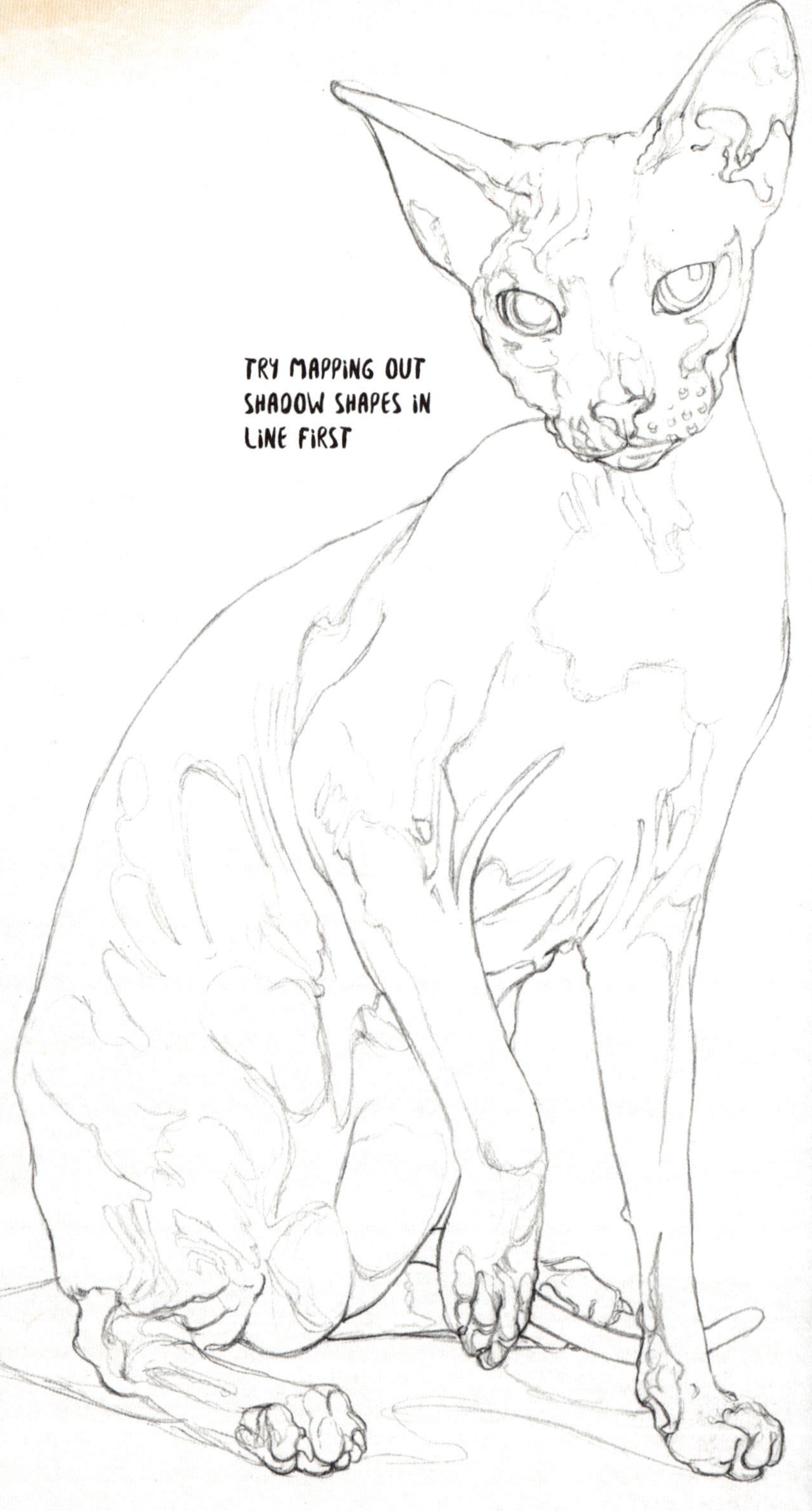

TRY MAPPING OUT SHADOW SHAPES IN LINE FIRST

LIGHT & SHADOW

The pattern of light and shadow that plays over an animal's body and the shadows that it casts on surrounding surfaces all help to reveal its form. Sometimes those dark shapes of shadows will have harder or softer edges; sometimes they will resolve as smooth gradients of tone. Explore methods of mark-making to describe those different edges.

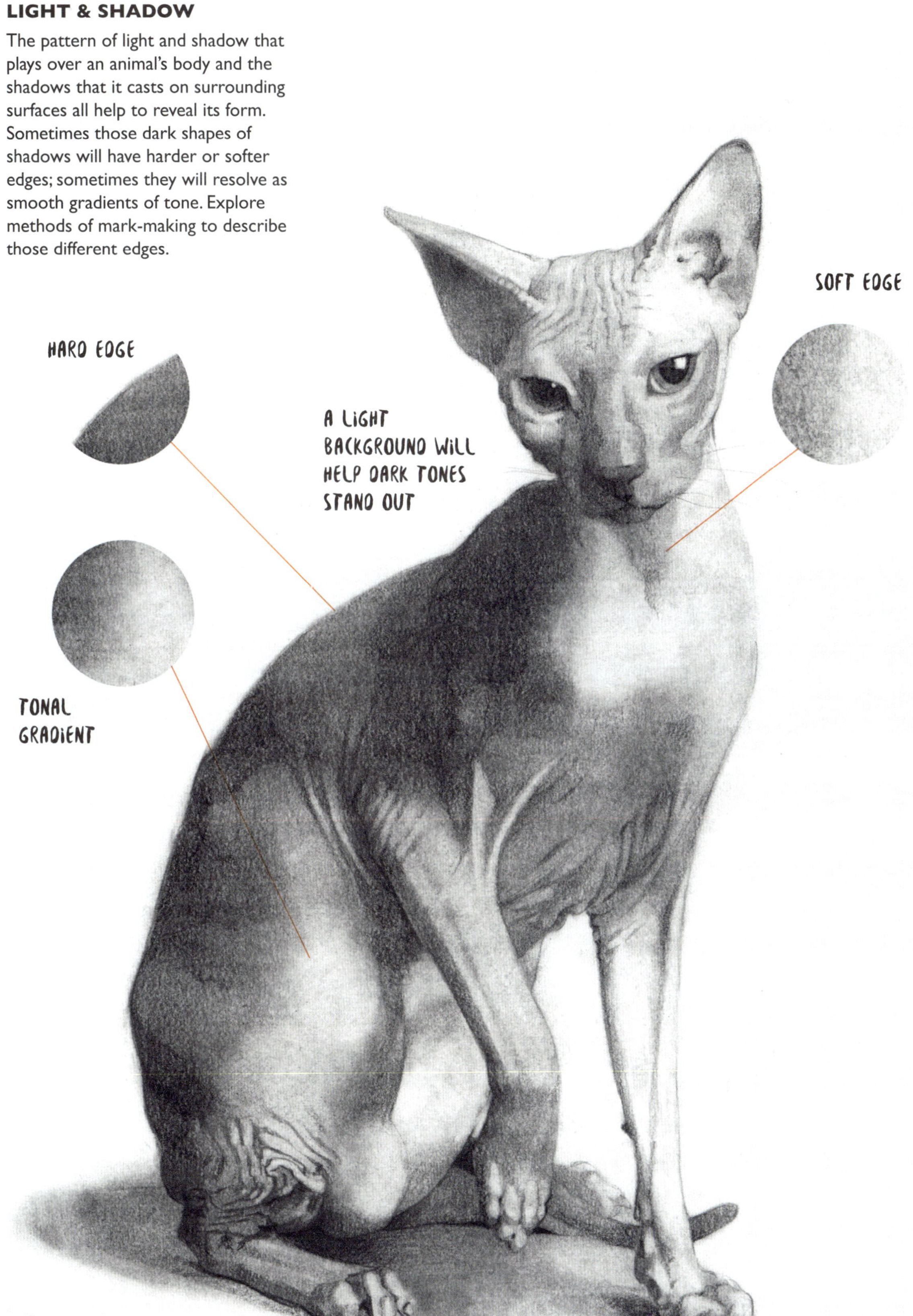

CROSS-CONTOUR

A cross-contour is an imagined line that bridges the contours of a subject, running over its surface to help describe its form. We don't see cross-contours, but we can look for marks, creases and patterns that suggest their direction. Imagining these lines can help inform the direction of our mark-making and to emphasize form without relying on shadows alone.

CROSS-CONTOURS AROUND A FORM DESCRIBE WIDTH

IMAGINE CROSS-SECTIONS TO HELP YOU VISUALIZE CROSS-CONTOURS

CROSS-CONTOURS ALONG A FORM DESCRIBE LENGTH

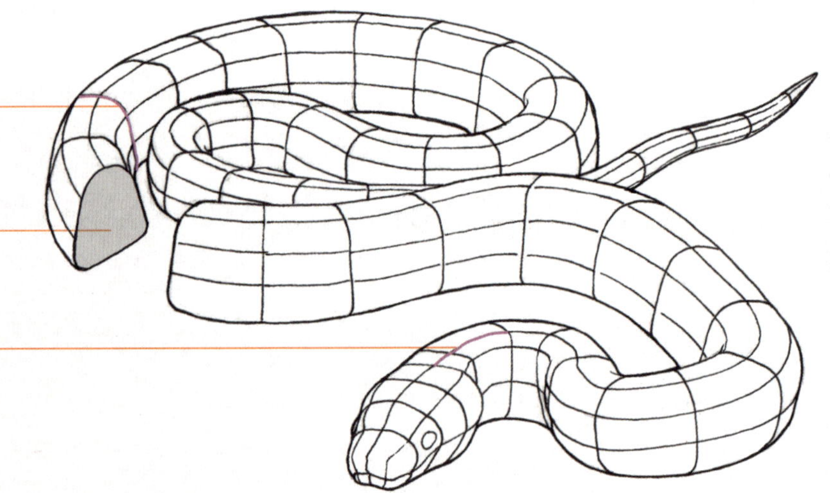

MARKINGS AND SURFACE TEXTURES MIGHT FOLLOW CROSS-CONTOURS

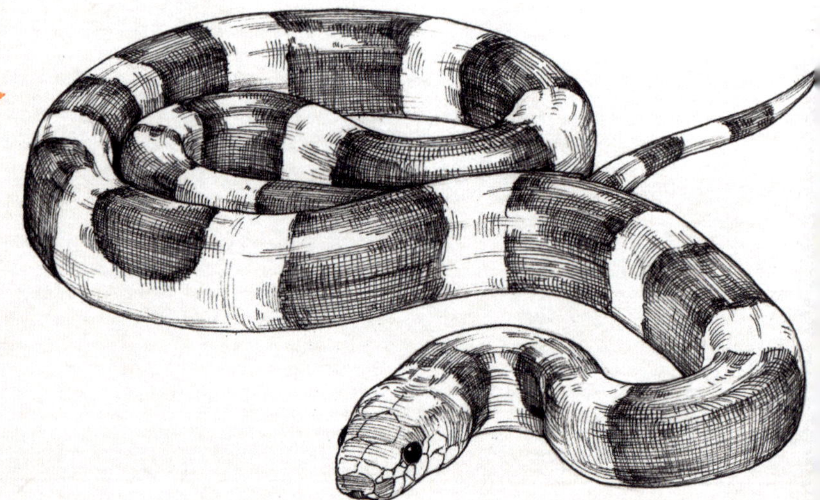

FORESHORTENING

Visual distortions of depth mean that nearer parts of an animal appear larger than more distant parts of the same size. Your brain will try to correct the distortion in your drawing, so it is important to remain true to your observations of your subject and to trust your eye, drawing from the shapes that you see, not what you imagine should be there. You'll find other cues in the subject that help you to replicate and emphasize depth in an animal's pose.

NOTICE THE DIMENSIONS OF THE CRATE (PAGE 45) THAT THE ANIMAL WOULD FIT INTO – IS IT SQUARE, LANDSCAPE OR PORTRAIT FORMAT?

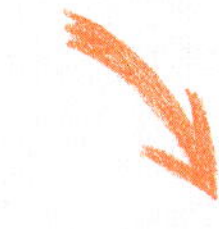

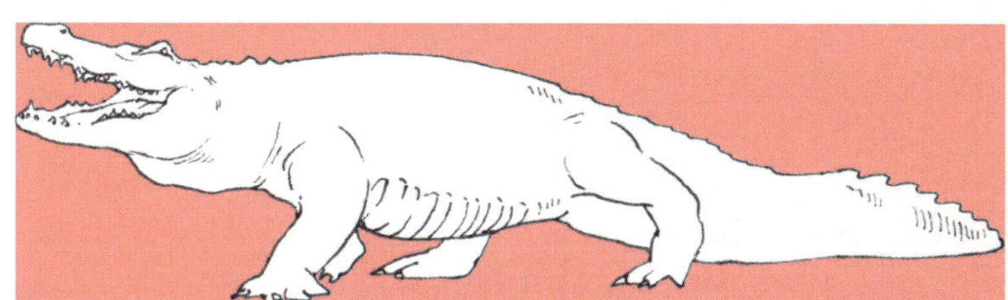

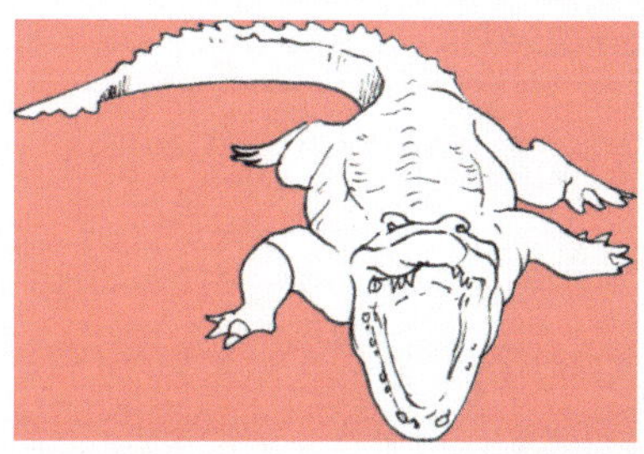

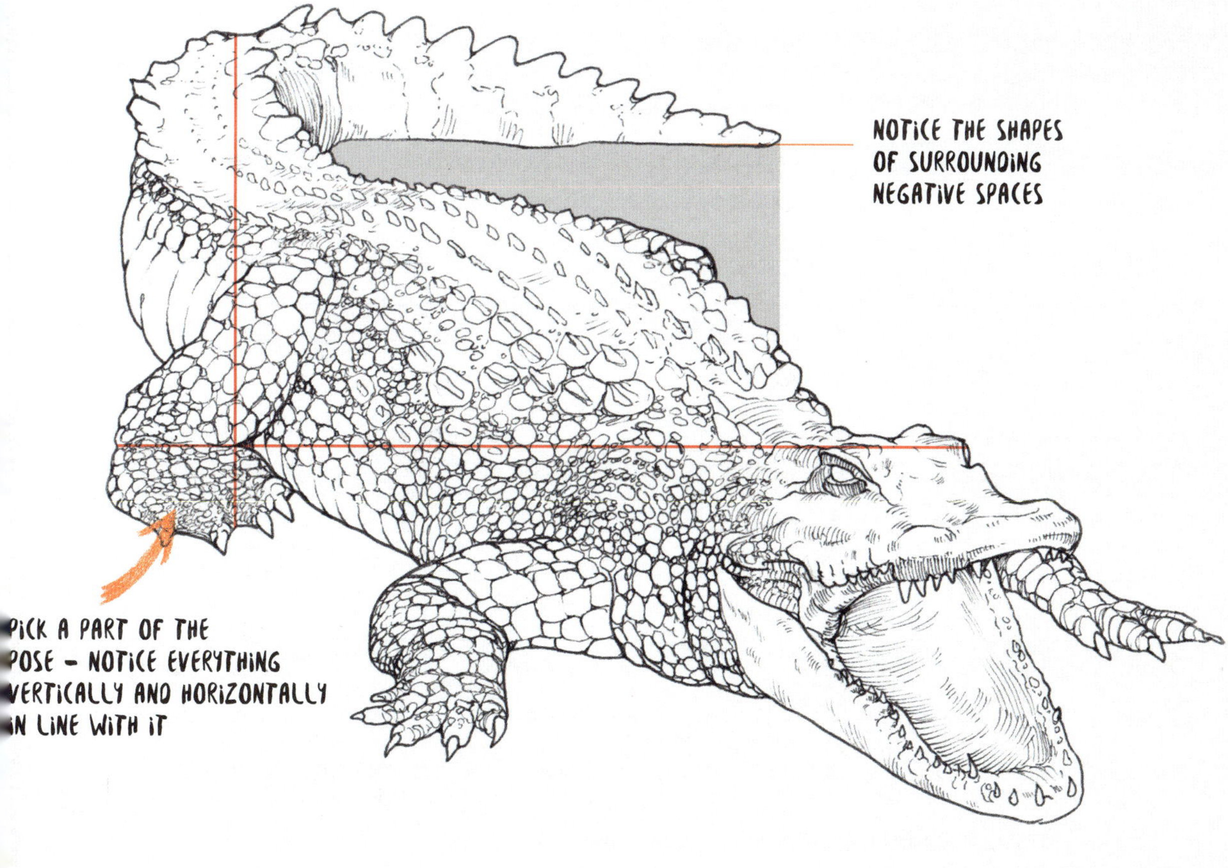

NOTICE THE SHAPES OF SURROUNDING NEGATIVE SPACES

PICK A PART OF THE POSE – NOTICE EVERYTHING VERTICALLY AND HORIZONTALLY IN LINE WITH IT

MODELLING

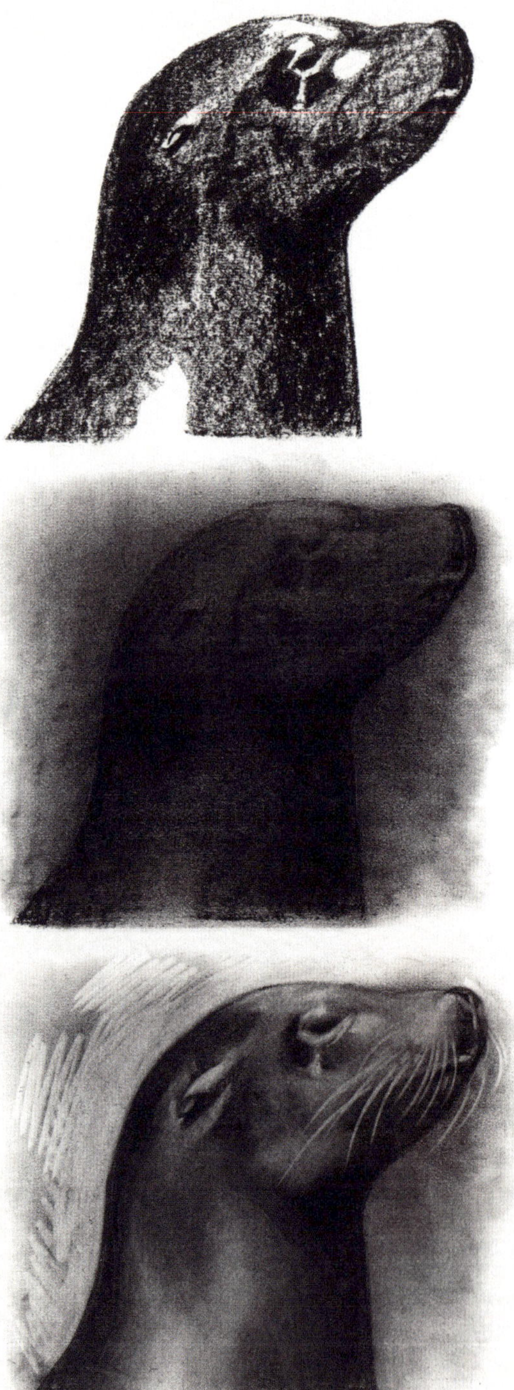

'Modelling' describes mark-making that creates an impression of form – modelled marks can be expressive or controlled and might respond to shadow shapes, cross-contours, or both at once. The memory of touch is an important part of the modelled mark. For example, when you pet a dog and feel its ribcage beneath its fur, your tactile awareness of that form can find its way into any drawing you make of it in the pressure or direction of your marks.

ADDITIVE & SUBTRACTIVE TONE

If you're working in a medium that can be rubbed out, an eraser will allow you to draw light back into an area of dark. Think of your eraser as a drawing tool and cut it to a sharp edge to help you control your mark-making.

HATCHING AND CROSS-HATCHING

Hatching and cross-hatching use line to suggest tone. Hatched marks can follow cross-contours, curving across a perceived surface to further model form.

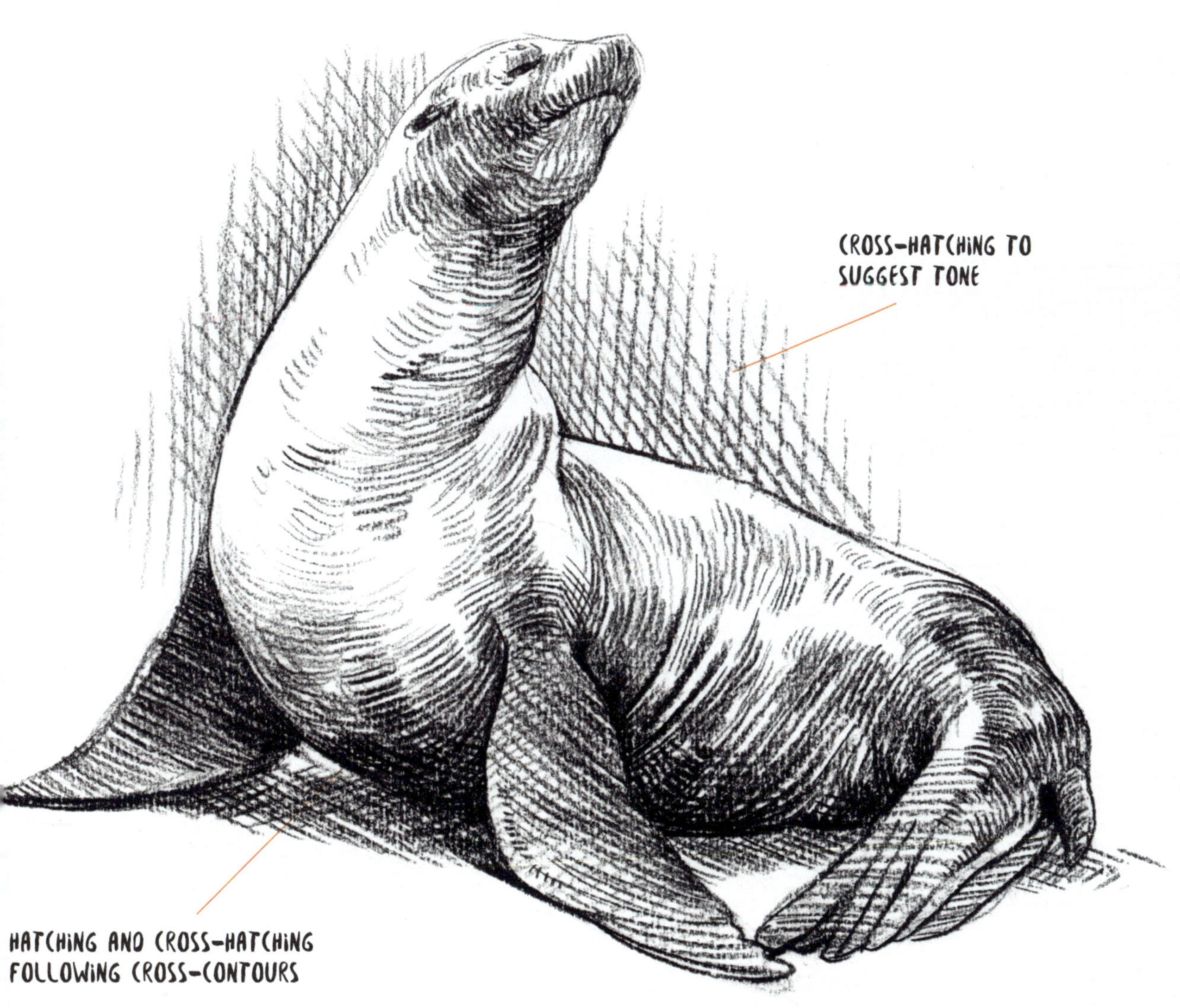

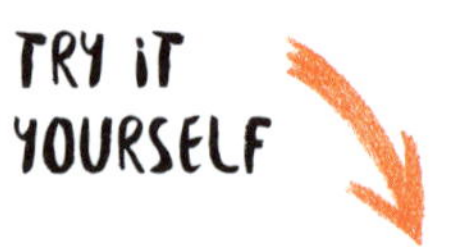
TRY IT
YOURSELF

WEIGHT

Just like gesture, 'weight' in drawing can describe both a quality you perceive in your subject and the physical pressure behind your drawn mark. Drawing with an awareness of the weight of your animal subject will mean picking up on the visual cues that indicate its weight and cultivating a sympathetic awareness of how that heaviness or lightness feels.

What kind of pressure would you feel if a robin alighted on your finger? How heavy does your cat feel as it nestles in your lap? What pressure does a hippopotamus exert on its surroundings? There is no single, correct way to interpret weight in a drawing, but bringing an awareness of that quality into your process can mean the difference between a drawing that just looks like your subject and one that really *feels* like it.

INDICATORS OF WEIGHT

Weight is often expressed in the relationship between surfaces – some surfaces will bow with weight, while others remain unmoving. Notice how the contours of your subject change when it comes into contact with a surface and how marks that follow cross-contours can be used to emphasize the distortion of form that pressure creates.

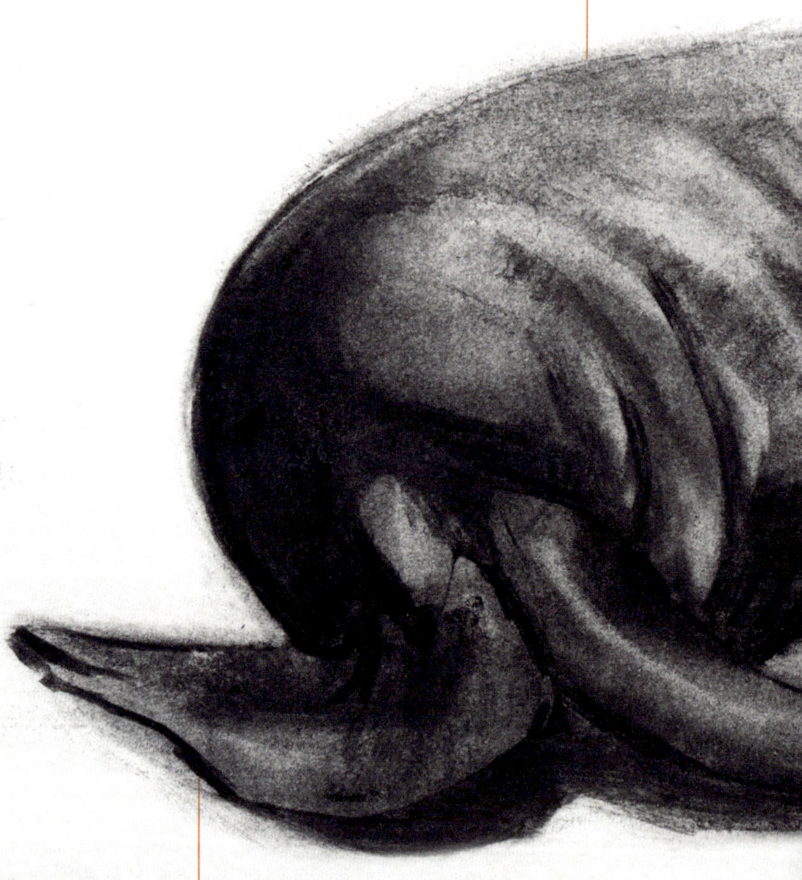

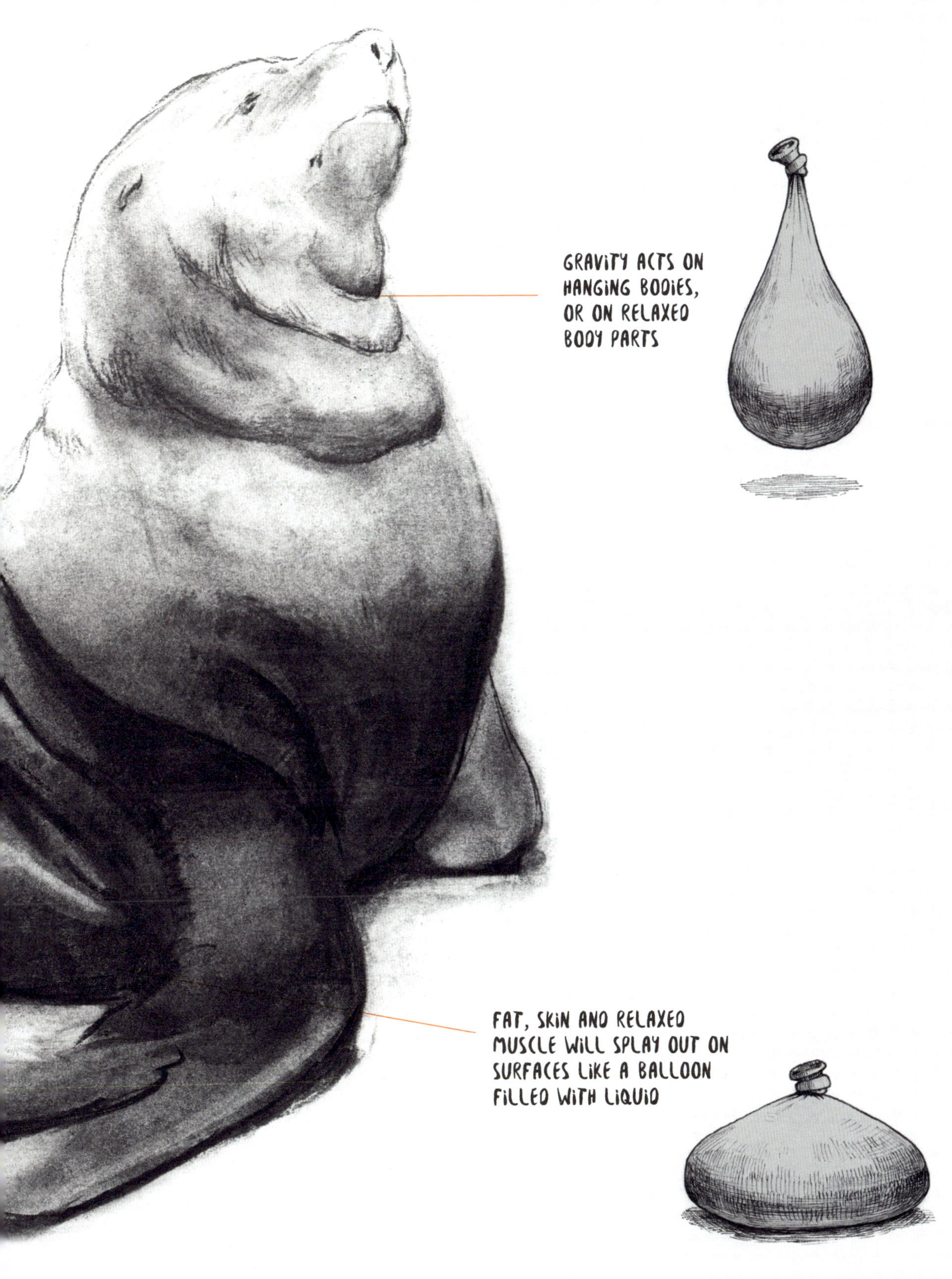
GRAVITY ACTS ON HANGING BODIES, OR ON RELAXED BODY PARTS
FAT, SKIN AND RELAXED MUSCLE WILL SPLAY OUT ON SURFACES LIKE A BALLOON FILLED WITH LIQUID

PART 01: OBSERVATIONAL DRAWING

A COMPLETE PROCESS (i)

The next few pages lay out an observational drawing process that unites all of the ideas explored in Part 01. Practise it until it becomes an intuitive process, and adapt it to suit your subject and your preferred method of working. If you're working in pen, you might find it helpful to draw lightly at first, and if you are working in pencil or charcoal, you can partially erase your evolving drawing between steps to push earlier layers back and build stronger observations over the top. This process should form the foundation of all your observational drawing.

Parts 02–03 will elaborate on qualities you might encounter in particular animals.

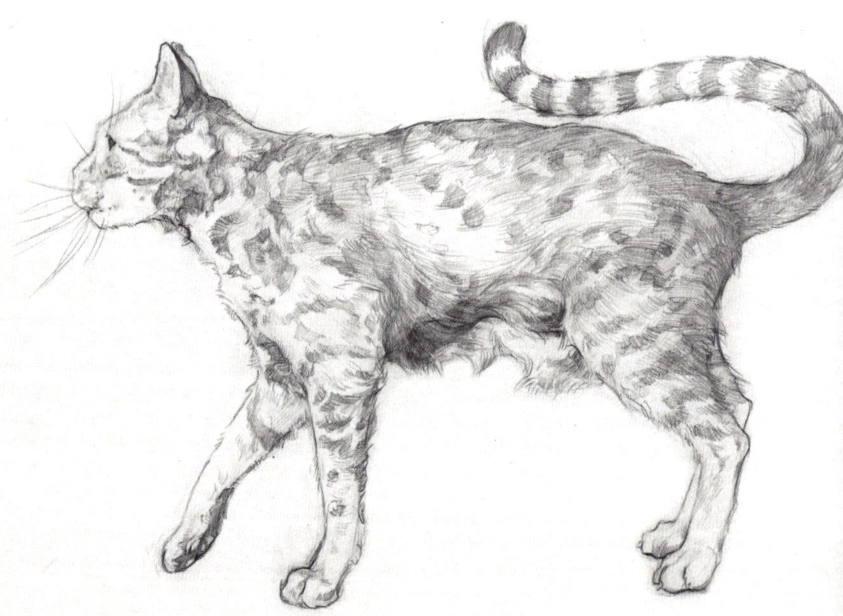

PRIMARY SIMPLE SHAPES
(PAGE 34)

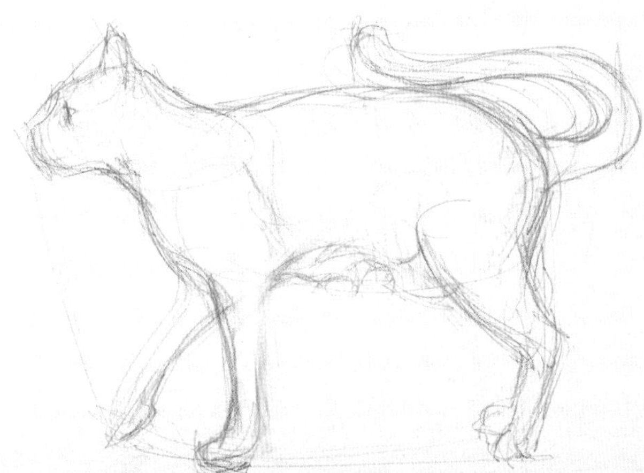

SEEING WITH YOUR
FINGERS (PAGE 26)

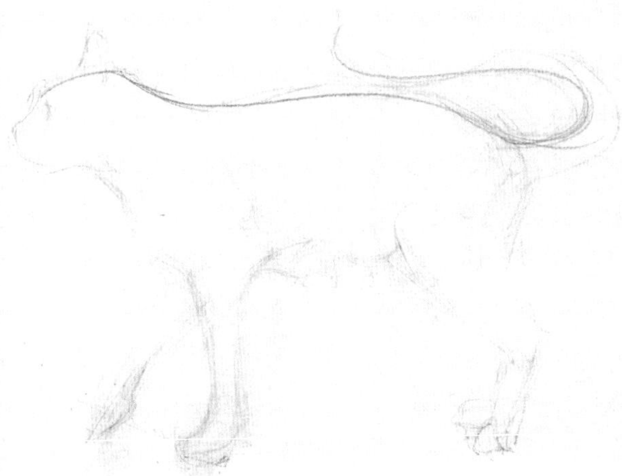

LINE OF ACTION
(PAGE 32)

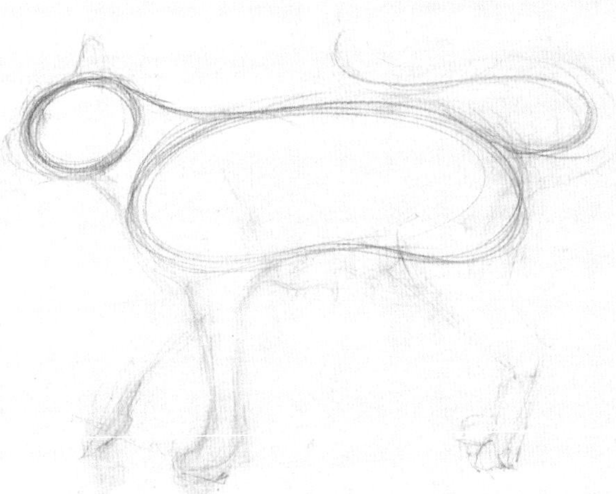

SECONDARY SIMPLE SHAPES
(PAGE 35)

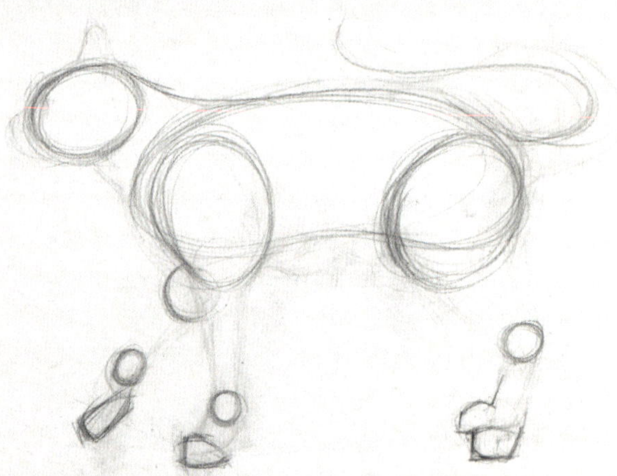

JOINTS
(PAGE 36)

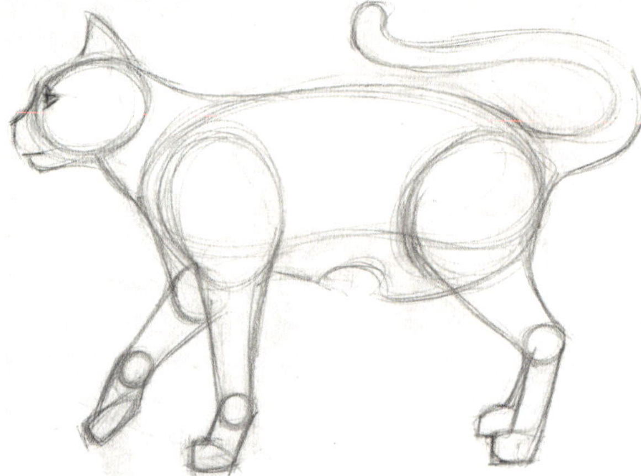

BRIDGING LINES
(PAGE 37)

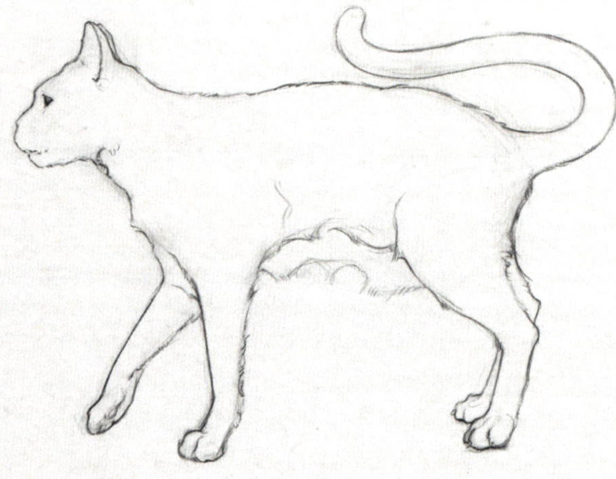

CONTOUR
(PAGE 38)

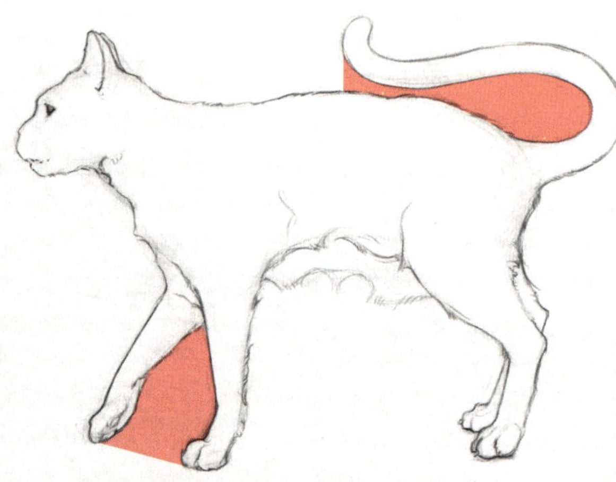

DOUBLE CHECK YOUR NEGATIVE SPACES (PAGE 44)

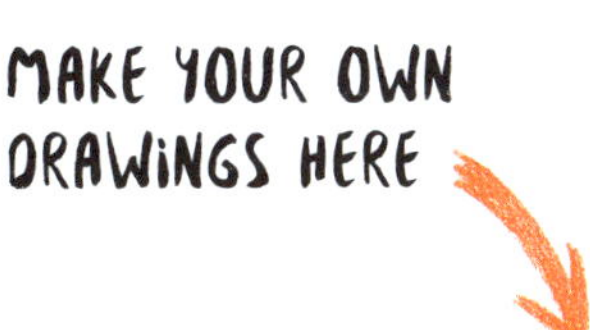
MAKE YOUR OWN
DRAWINGS HERE

PART 02

STRUCTURES

While Part 01 laid down the foundations of looking and mark-making that inform observational drawing, this part will help you to build on those practical skills, helping you overcome the drawing challenges that particular body parts might introduce.

Rather than taking a biological approach to this part and grouping animals by their genetic similarities, we'll look at the body parts of animals that share the same visual characteristics, tackling the body of a snake and an elephant's trunk on the same page. That will mean that, even if this book doesn't deal with your animal of choice, you'll still be able to find ideas that will help you draw it.

MAKING STUDIES

While you might make some drawings for the outcome, the majority will be studies – drawings that help you to look at and makes sense of the animal you are drawing. You will be following in the footsteps of early naturalists who, before cameras became ubiquitous, used drawing as their primary method of recording and communicating the new species that they had discovered. You will need to bring their attitude of curiosity and discovery to your studies, allowing yourself to be surprised by what you see and to make new, personal discoveries as you draw. While you can make an instantaneous record of an animal by snapping a photograph of it, drawing requires you to process what you see through a tactile process of mark-making, helping to embed your understanding more deeply.

GETTING TO KNOW AN ANIMAL

If you're planning to draw a new animal, you'll need to make a range of different studies to develop a complete picture of how it looks and behaves. Your drawings should vary from long studies that help you to reflect on the nuances of your subject to more energetic and responsive studies that help you understand it from all angles.

The search for reference material that features your chosen animal will introduce you to new books and documentaries. It will also help you to have encounters with the animals in real life. Here are a few of the different kinds of study you can make to get to know your animal of choice:

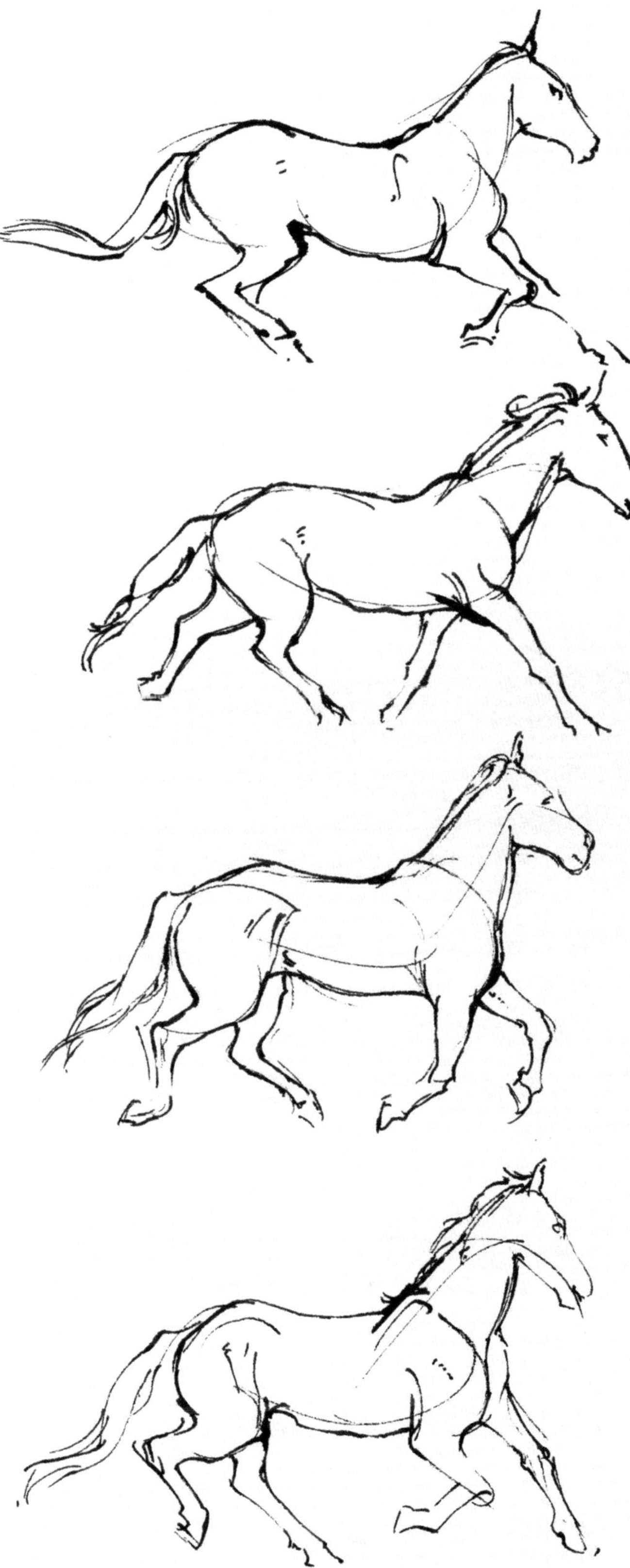

1.

STUDIES OF ACTION

To understand your chosen animal in action, make sequential drawings of movement from life or from video. Keep the studies quick and gestural to maintain a sense of energy and explore variations on a simple study: draw one pose over another or make the drawings as separate, sequential studies, as if creating movement cycles for animation.

2. STUDIES OF BODY PARTS

Making studies of discrete body parts will help you make more focused observations, free from the concerns of maintaining accurate proportion across the whole body.

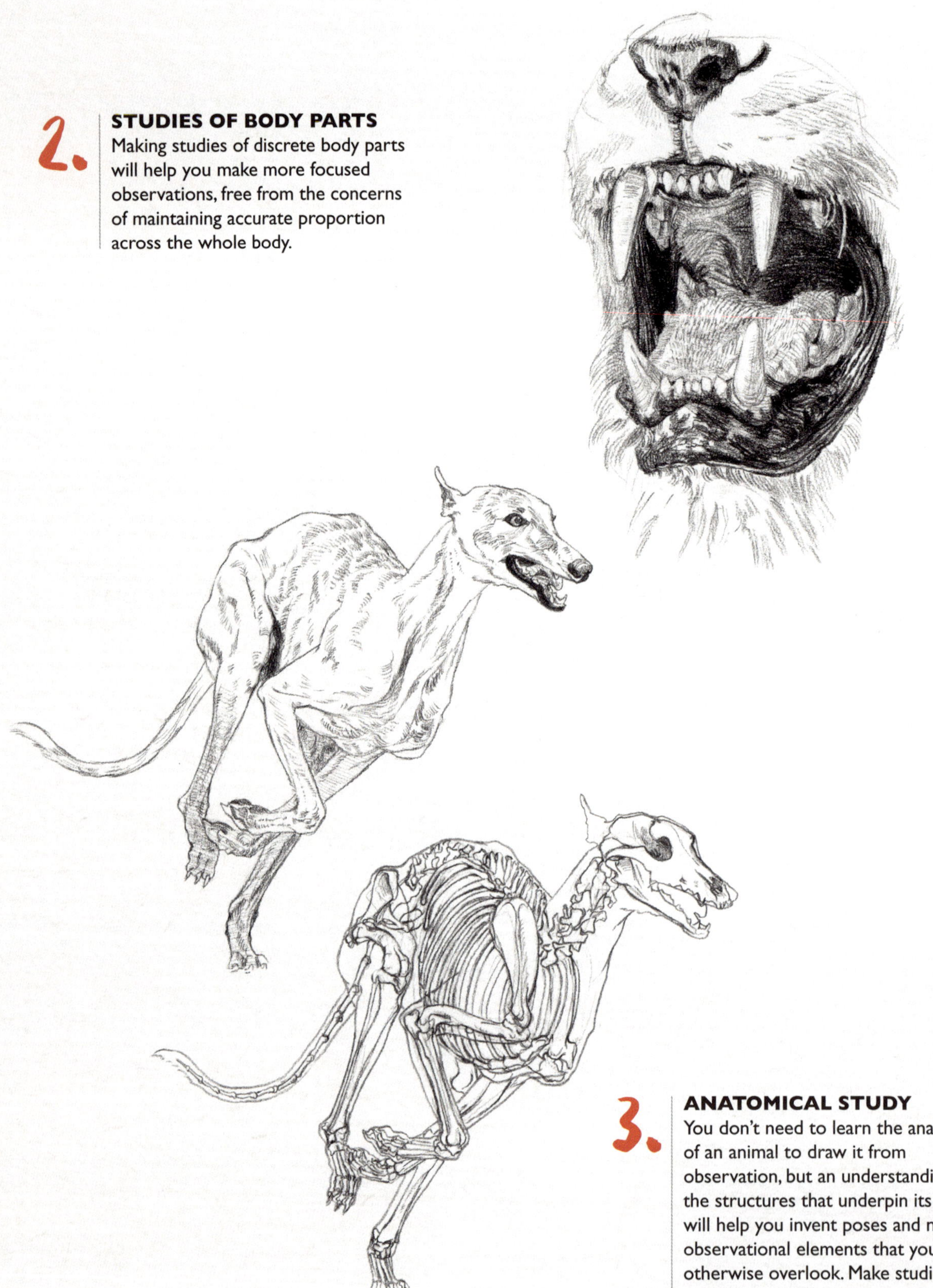

3. ANATOMICAL STUDY

You don't need to learn the anatomy of an animal to draw it from observation, but an understanding of the structures that underpin its body will help you invent poses and notice observational elements that you might otherwise overlook. Make studies to support your observations, not to replace them.

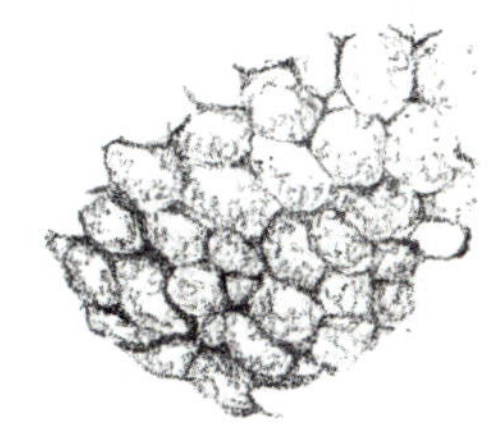

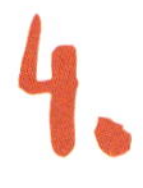

SURFACE STUDIES

Fill a page with up-close studies (page 130) of your chosen subject's skin, fur, feathers or scales. Use tactile studies (page 118) to generate new marks, and make maps of the animal's markings (page 136). Take a look at Part 03 for more ideas.

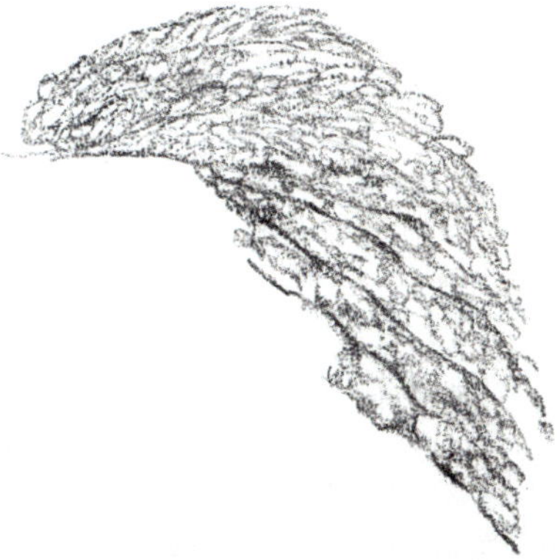

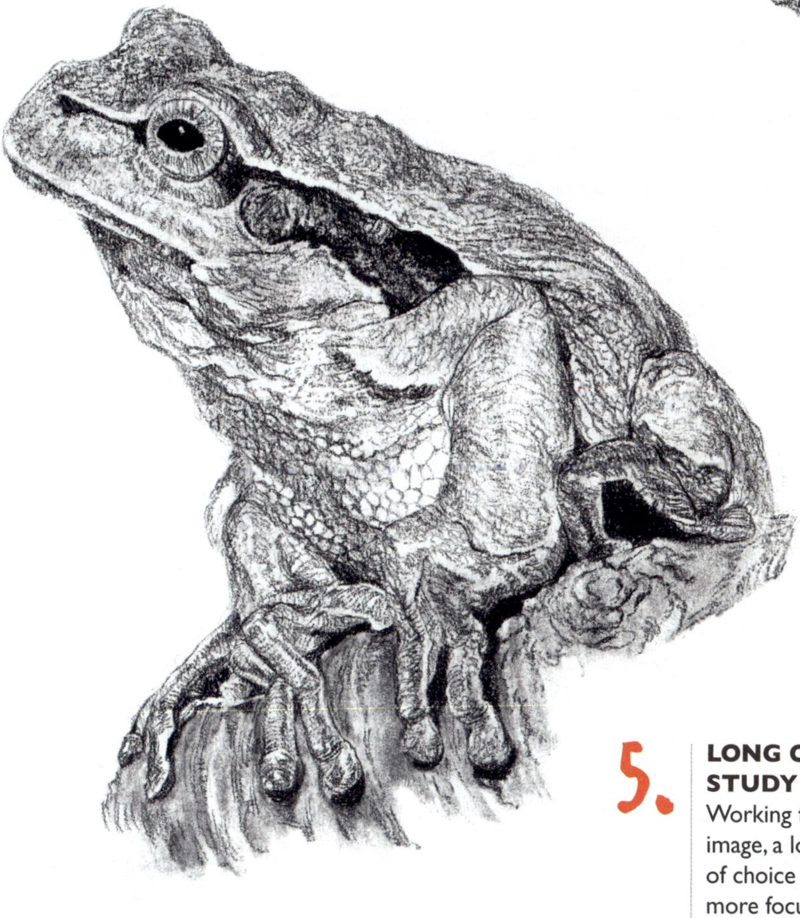

5. LONG OBSERVATIONAL STUDY

Working from a static subject or image, a long study of your animal of choice will help you develop a more focused appreciation of the subject. These longer studies will both borrow from and contribute to more energetic and exploratory studies of surface, movement and anatomy.

FILL THE PAGE WITH STUDIES OF YOUR ANIMAL OF CHOICE

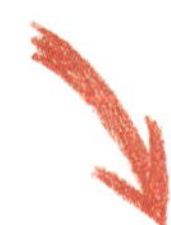

HEAD

A CROSSHAIR THAT CUTS THROUGH THE EYES AND THE MUZZLE CAN INDICATE THE DIRECTION AN ANIMAL IS LOOKING

The next few pages will help you to improve the simple, underlying shapes explored in Part 01. First, establish the shape of the head as a whole without fixating on the features of the face and notice how it can direct the animal's entire pose. Check where it sits in relation to the rest of the body – is it above, below or in line with the core? Which body parts sit vertically and horizontally in line with the head?

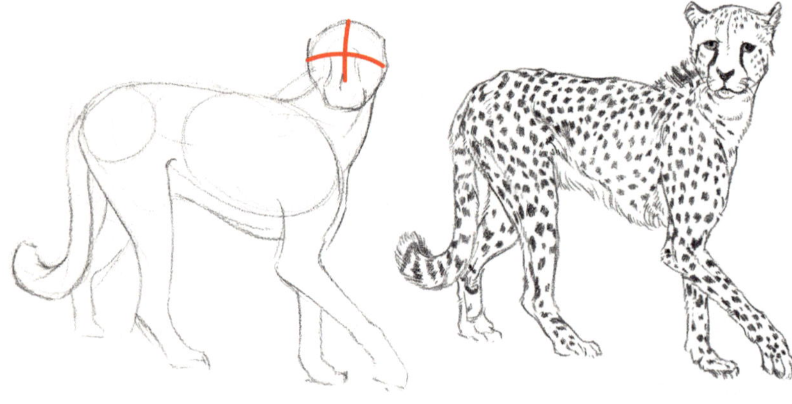

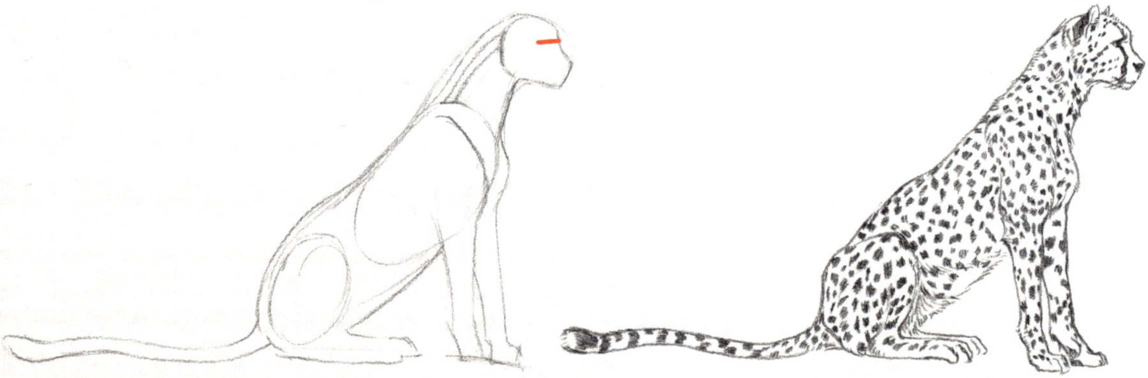

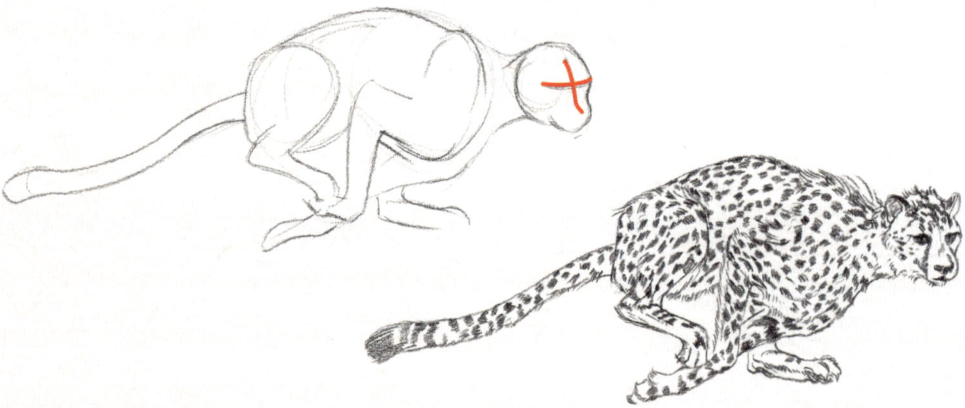

When you are drawing the head, notice its position in relation to the core of the body – is it horizontally aligned, vertically aligned, or at a diagonal to its main volume?

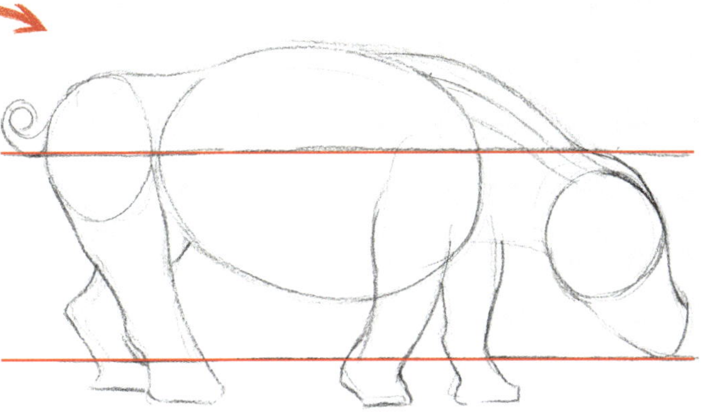

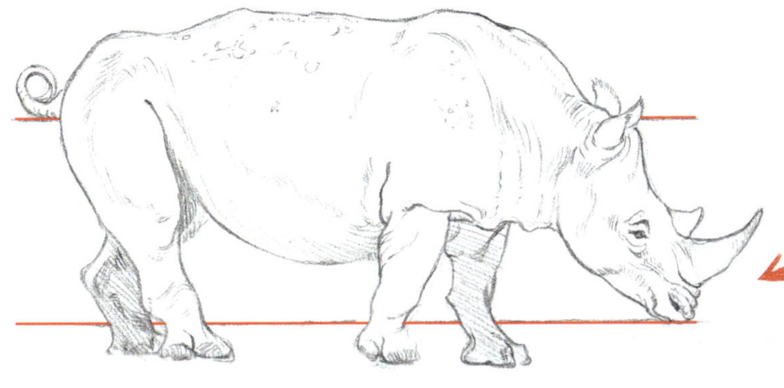

USE HORIZONTAL LINES TO COMPARE WHICH PARTS OF THE BODY THE TOP AND BOTTOM OF HEAD LINE UP WITH

FOR MORE UPRIGHT ANIMALS, USE VERTICAL COMPARISONS TO CHECK THE POSITION OF THE HEAD AGAINST THE BODY, AND NOTICE THE NEGATIVE SPACES THAT JOIN THE HEAD AND TORSO.

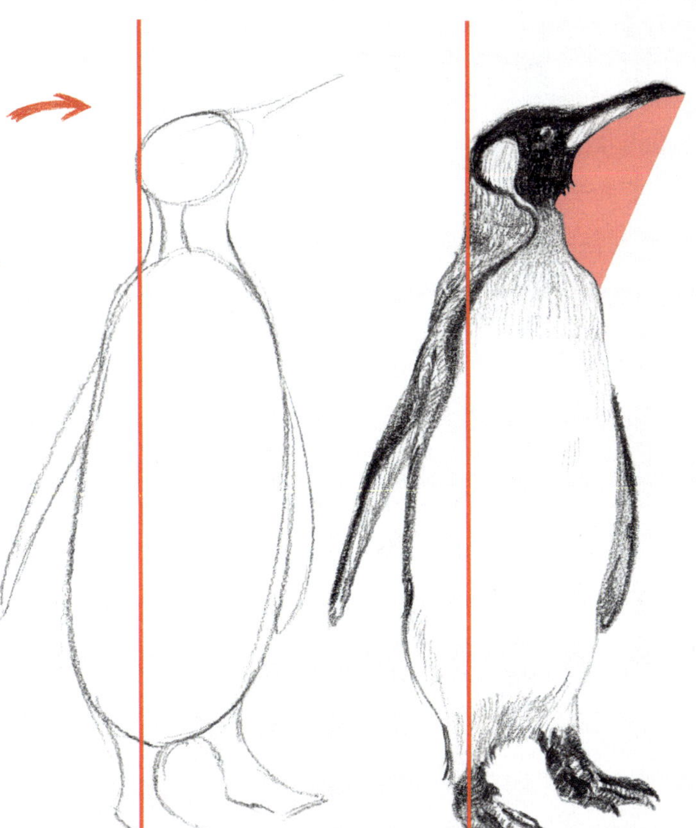

PART 02: STRUCTURES

CORE

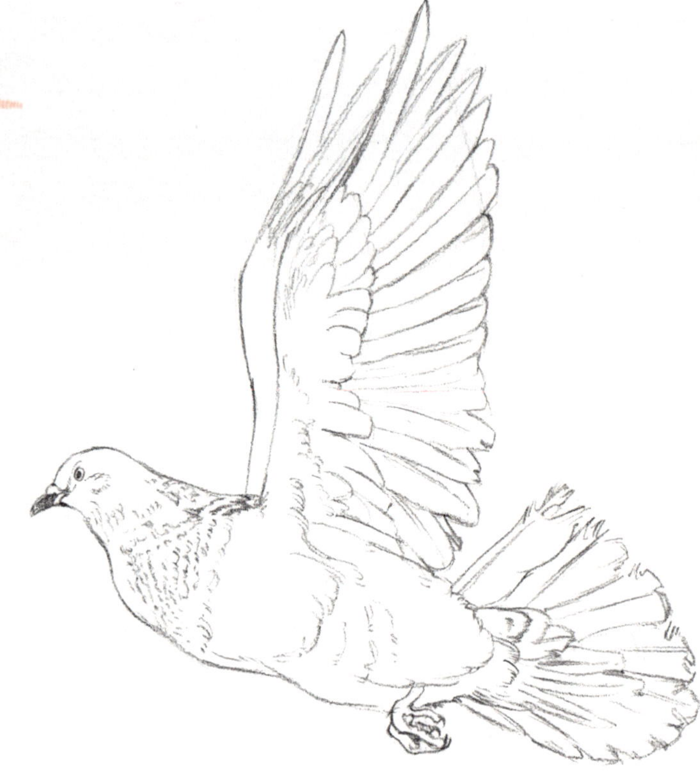

While it finds wildly different expression in different animals, the core of the body will be the anchor of the pose, with the line of action invariably running through it. Get to know the anatomical volumes that make up the core of your chosen animal – what balance of bone, muscle and fat sit beneath its skin? How do feathers, fur, skin or shells add bulk to its form?

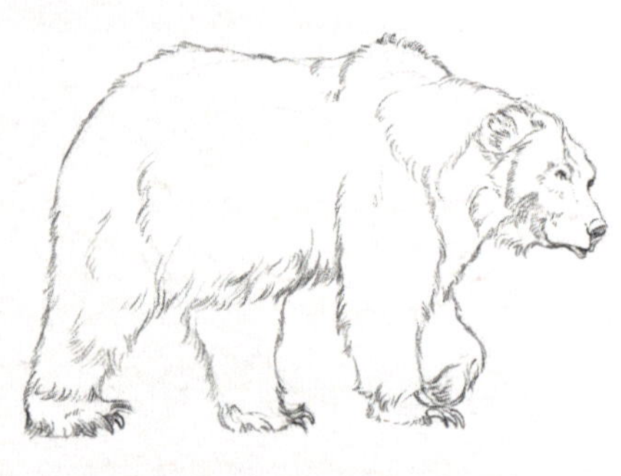

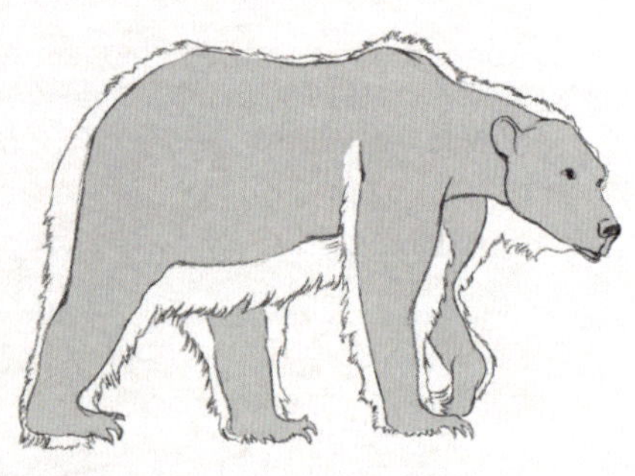

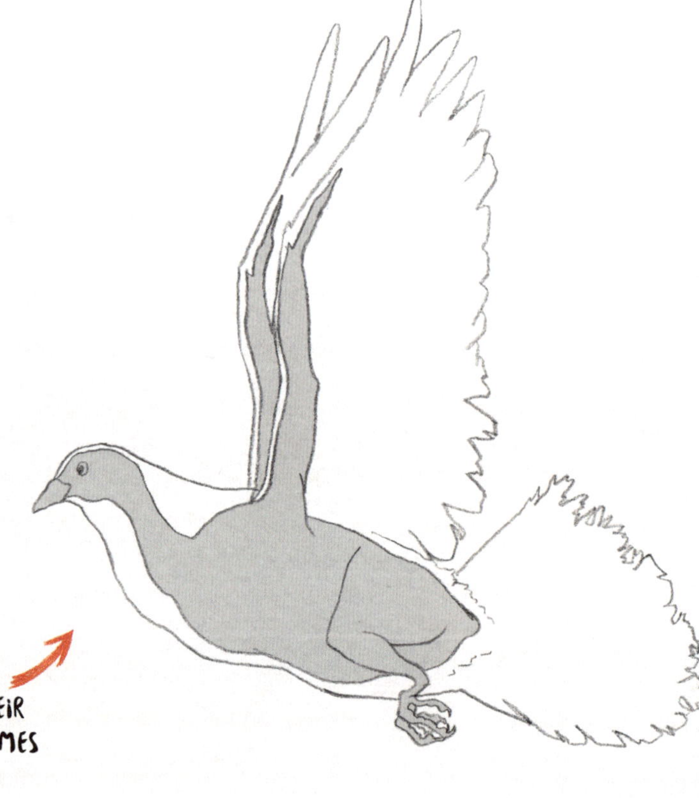

SOLID FORMS MIGHT BE HIDDEN BY FUR AND FEATHERS, BUT THEY ARE STILL VISIBLE IN THEIR EFFECTS ON THE SURFACE. ANATOMICAL VOLUMES DICTATE THINGS WE CAN SEE SUCH AS FUR DIRECTION AND THE PLACEMENT OF FEATHERS.

A line of action supports the core forms of each of these animals. Action lines should be simple curves that the core shapes of the body can hang from, like beads on a string.

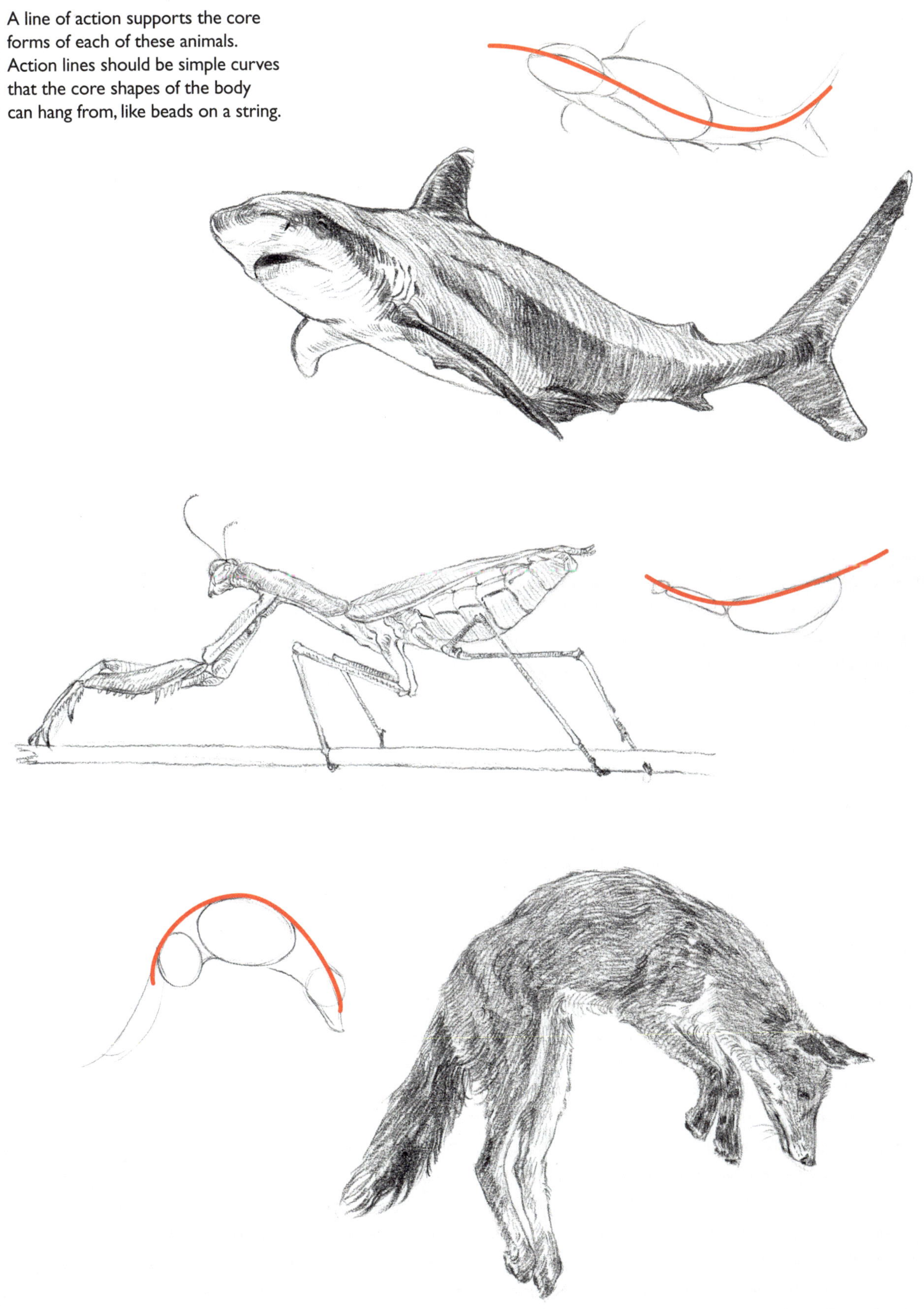

PART 02: STRUCTURES

JOINTED LIMBS

To understand the limbs on an animal you'll need to recognize the position of their joints, the volume of the limb around that joint, and the negative shape that surrounds the limb. It is the function of a limb that leads its form, so getting to know how an animal moves will give you an insight into the qualities you see.

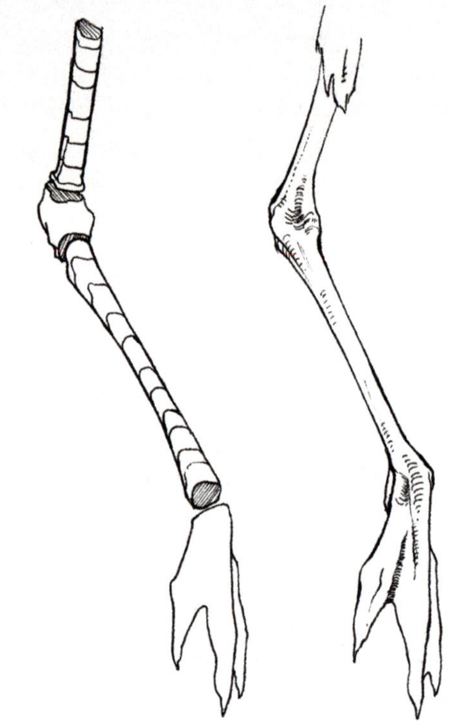

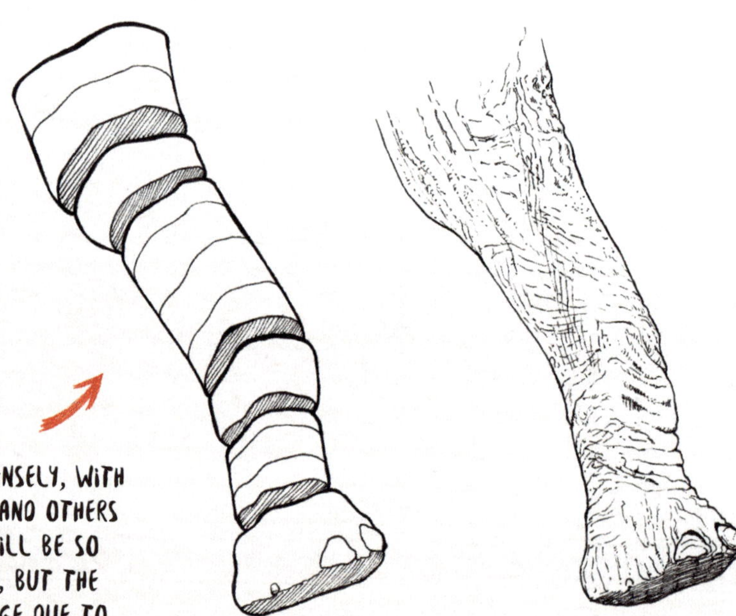

THE VOLUMES AROUND JOINTS VARY IMMENSELY, WITH SOME LIMBS BEING RELATIVELY SLENDER AND OTHERS MUCH BULKIER. SOMETIMES THE LIMBS WILL BE SO STOCKY THE JOINTS ARE HARD TO DISCERN, BUT THE CROSS-SECTION WILL STILL SUBTLY CHANGE DUE TO UNDERLYING MUSCLE AND BONE.

EACH JOINT HAS A LIMITED RANGE OF MOVEMENT AND WILL BEND ONLY IN CERTAIN DIRECTIONS. THIS EXAMPLE OF A DEER'S FOOT CANNOT BEND FORWARDS, ONLY BACKWARDS.

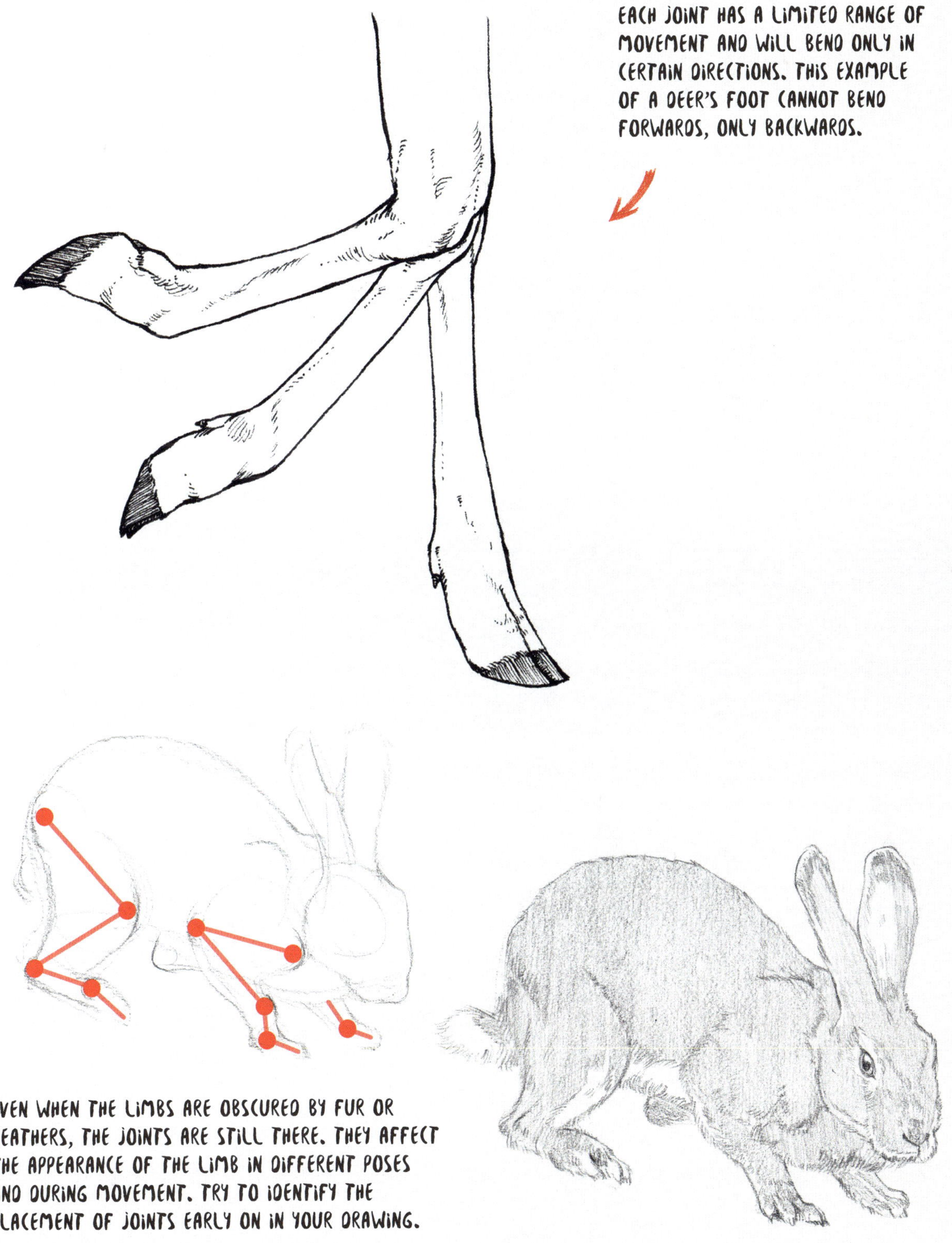

EVEN WHEN THE LIMBS ARE OBSCURED BY FUR OR FEATHERS, THE JOINTS ARE STILL THERE. THEY AFFECT THE APPEARANCE OF THE LIMB IN DIFFERENT POSES AND DURING MOVEMENT. TRY TO IDENTIFY THE PLACEMENT OF JOINTS EARLY ON IN YOUR DRAWING.

MAKE SOME STUDIES
OF LIMBS

PART 02: STRUCTURES

TAILS, TRUNKS & TENTACLES

Long, looping body parts like tails and trunks and the bodies of snakes or slugs have very different evolutionary roots but share similar visual characteristics. Their cylindrical forms are characterized by gesture and cross-contour and defined by the extent of their tapering and the shape of their cross-sections. The bodies of animals like slugs and worms are all tail, and drawing them can help you practise the principles you might apply to the isolated body-part of another animal.

ESTABLISH A LINE OF ACTION

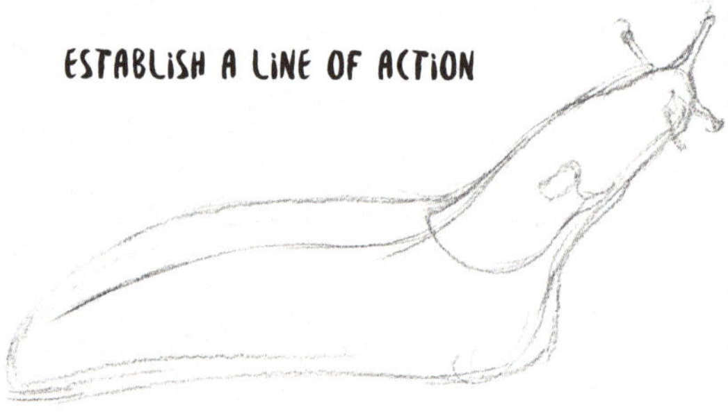

BLOCK IN SIMPLE SHAPES

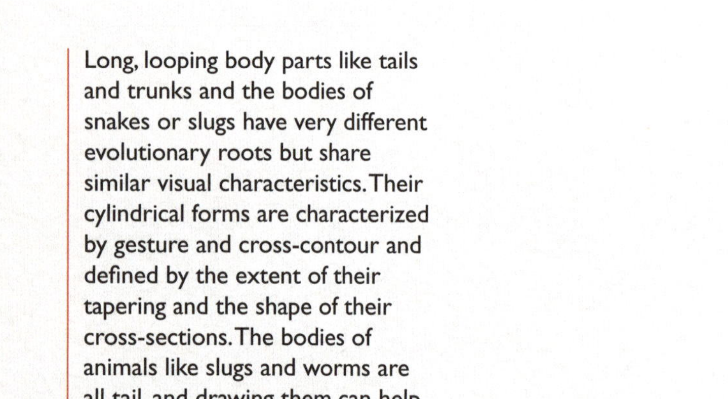

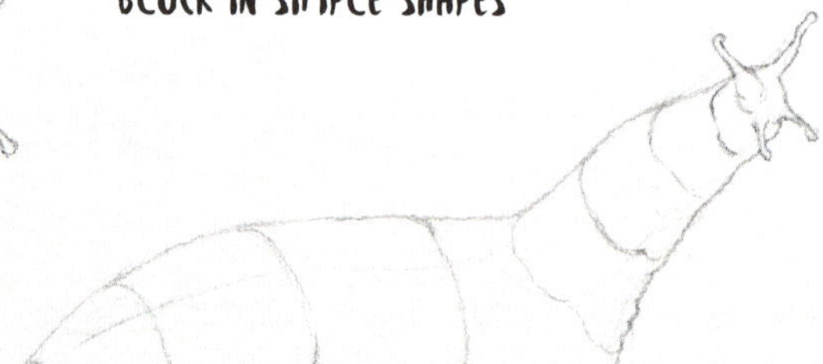

DRAW THE CROSS-CONTOURS

When you are drawing a tail, trunk, tentacle or an animal like a slug, imagine how its cross-section might look – is it completely cylindrical, or does it flatten out on one side? To help, imagine how the cross-contours would continue around the other side of your subject.

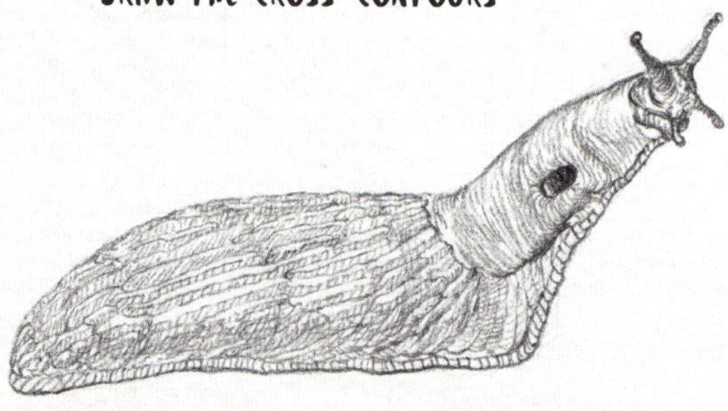

ELABORATE ON SURFACE TEXTURE

NOTICE HOW THE WIDTH OF A TAIL, TRUNK OR TENTACLE VARIES ALONG ITS LENGTH. SOME TAPER, BECOMING SLIMMER TOWARDS THE TIP.

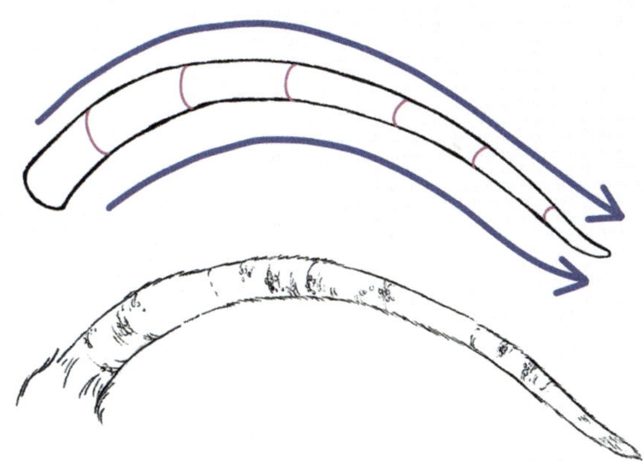

NOTICE HOW THE VOLUME OF HAIR CAN CHANGE THE OUTLINE OF A TAIL – WHILE ITS CORE STILL TAPERS THE FURRY END OF THIS TAIL MAKES IT FLAIR OUT BEFORE ITS TIP.

WHEN A TAIL IS COVERED IN FUR, WOOL OR FEATHERS, IT IS THE VOLUME OF THAT MASS THAT DEFINES ITS SHAPE MORE THAN THE CORE OF THE TAIL. NOTICE THE FLOW OF THE SURFACE TEXTURE AS YOU DRAW.

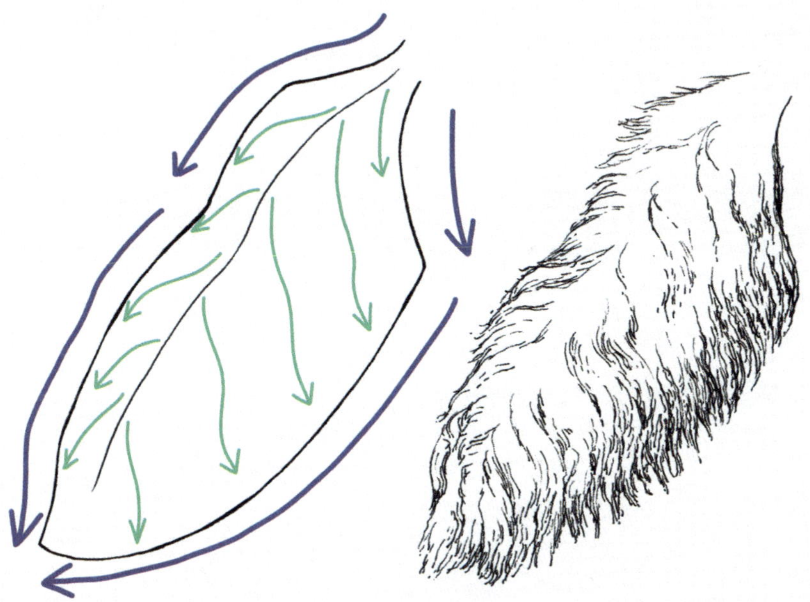

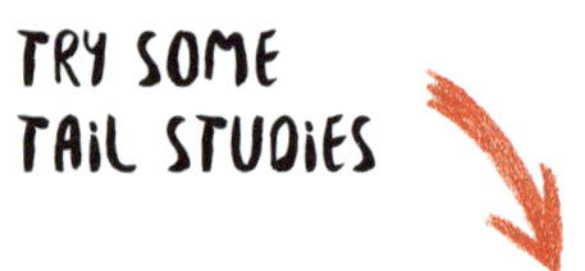
TRY SOME
TAIL STUDIES

PART 02: STRUCTURES

WINGS

From the delicate wings of insects to the expansive feathered extensions of birds and the membraned limbs of bats, all wings express themselves differently when they are tucked away compared to when they are outstretched in flight.

INSECT WINGS

Most insects have two pairs of wings, but these can be adapted into a range of shapes and forms. Often it is enough to imply the direction and structure with a few key lines rather than including everything.

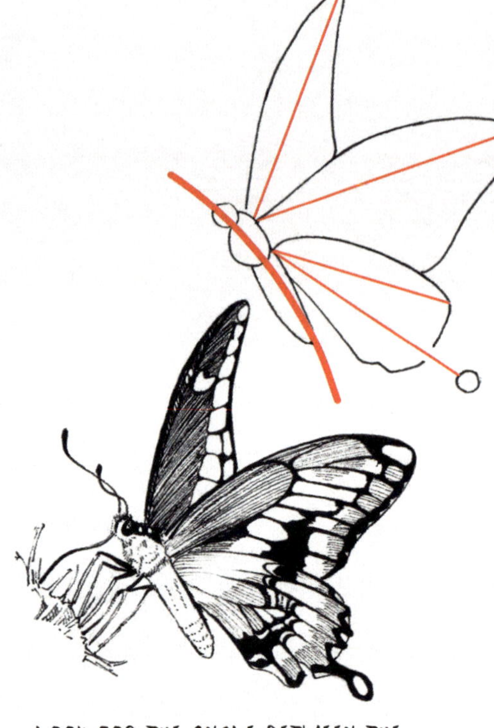

LOOK FOR THE ANGLE BETWEEN THE BODY AND THE TIP OF THE WING BEFORE DRAWING ITS SHAPE

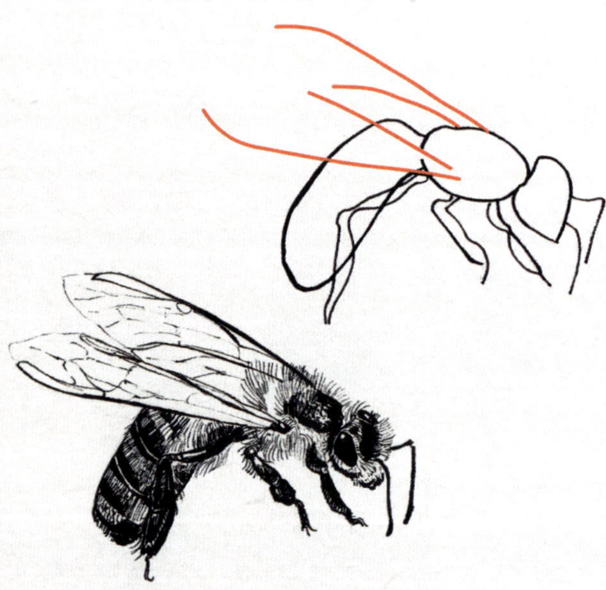

START WITH THE FRONTMOST EDGES OF THE WINGS BEFORE ADDING DETAILS OR PATTERNS

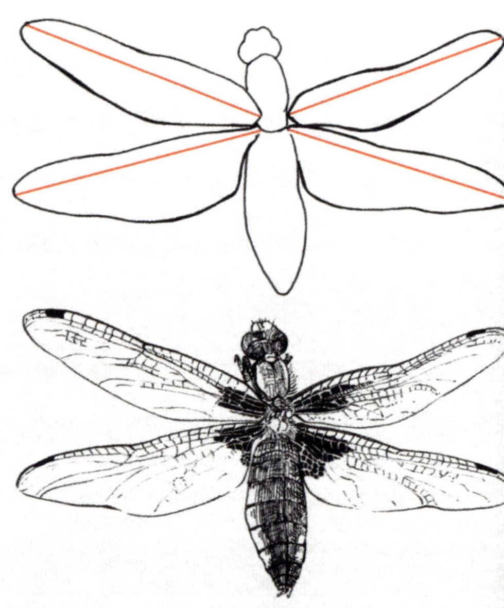

WHEN ADDING VEINS, DRAW THE LONG RADIATING LINES FIRST BEFORE ADDING BRANCHING ONES

BIRD WINGS

Bird wings are adapted arms, with shoulder, elbow and wrist joints – the 'hand' is fused. Even fully extended, the wing joints are not quite fully straight. As the wing folds, the sections of feathers overlap. When fully folded, the wing comes down and sits against the side of the bird.

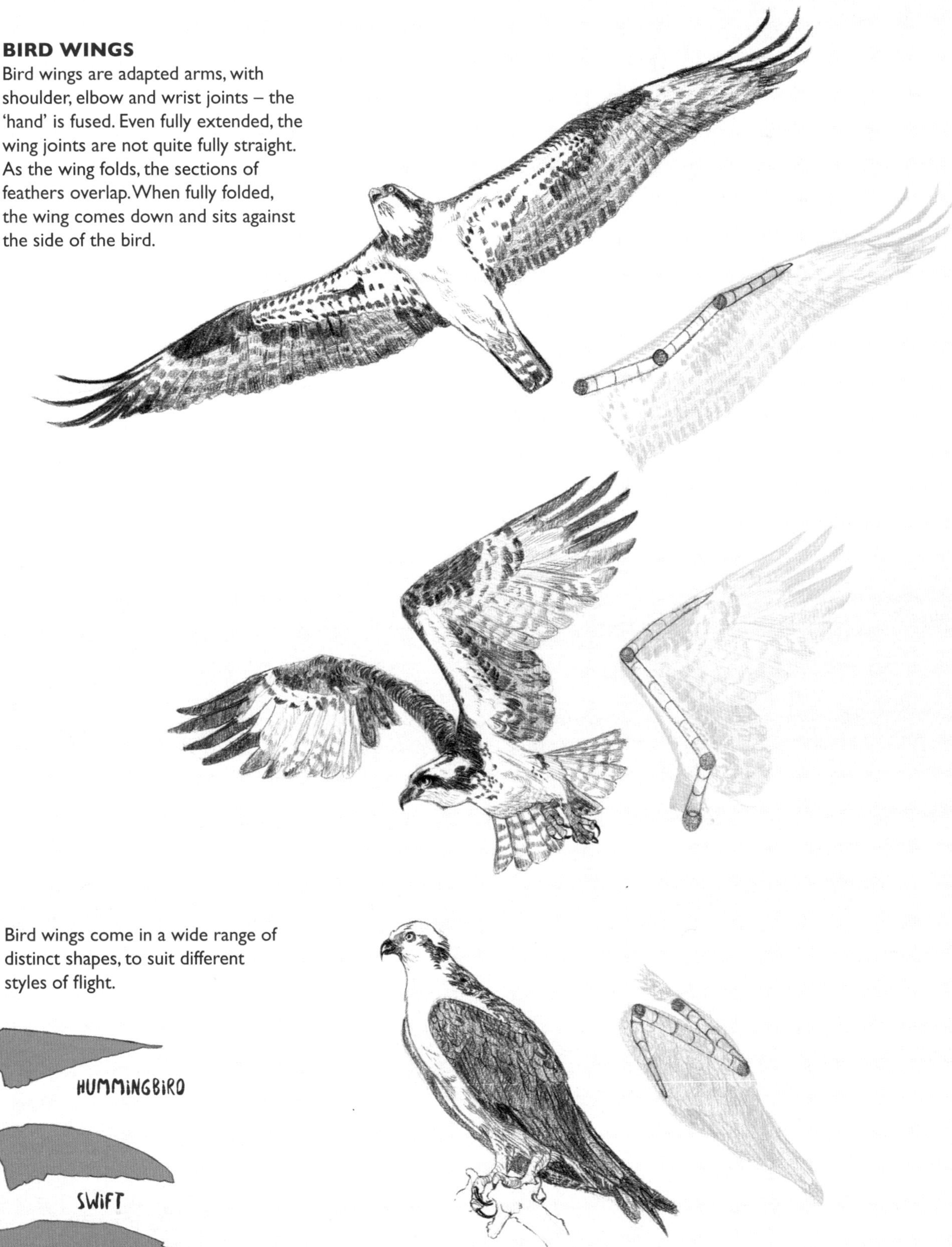

Bird wings come in a wide range of distinct shapes, to suit different styles of flight.

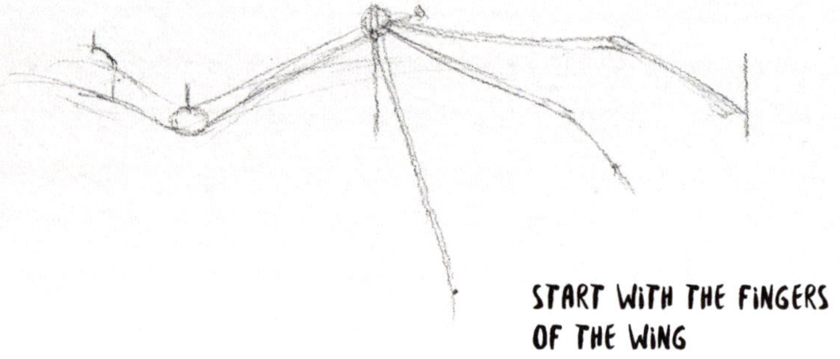

START WITH THE FINGERS OF THE WING

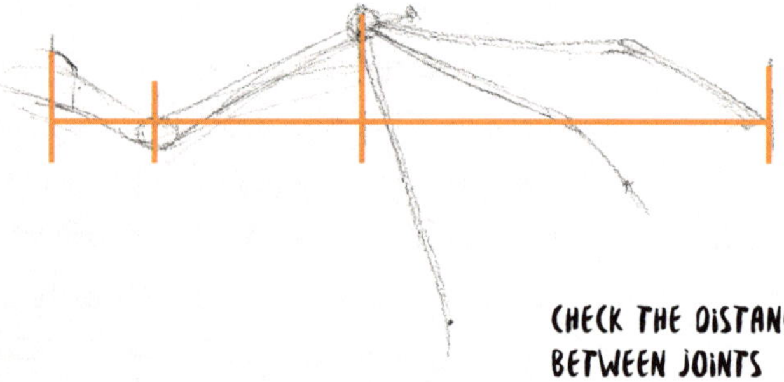

BAT WINGS

Bat wings are also adapted arms, their extended fingers providing a framework for the membrane of the wing, which is stretched between them. When you are drawing bat wings, start with the fingers, checking the distance between the joints before you join their tips with the curved contours of the membranes edge to create the shape of the wing.

CHECK THE DISTANCE BETWEEN JOINTS

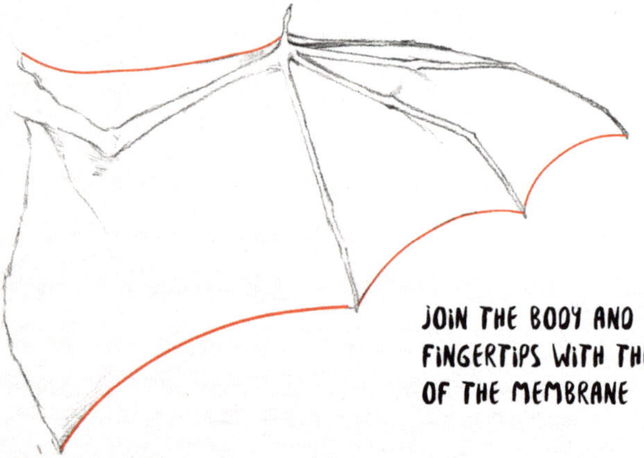

JOIN THE BODY AND FINGERTIPS WITH THE CURVE OF THE MEMBRANE

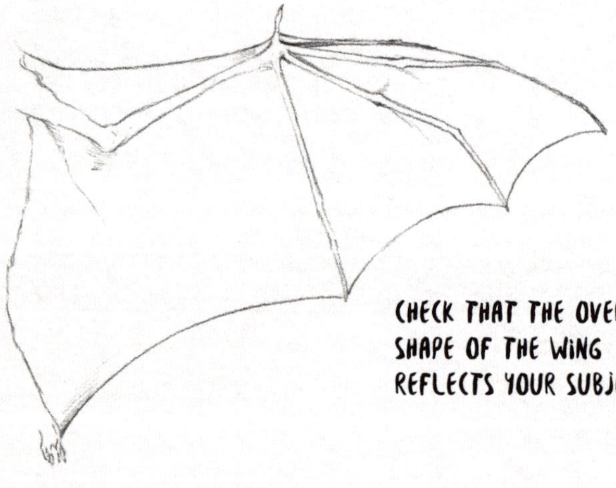

CHECK THAT THE OVERALL SHAPE OF THE WING REFLECTS YOUR SUBJECT

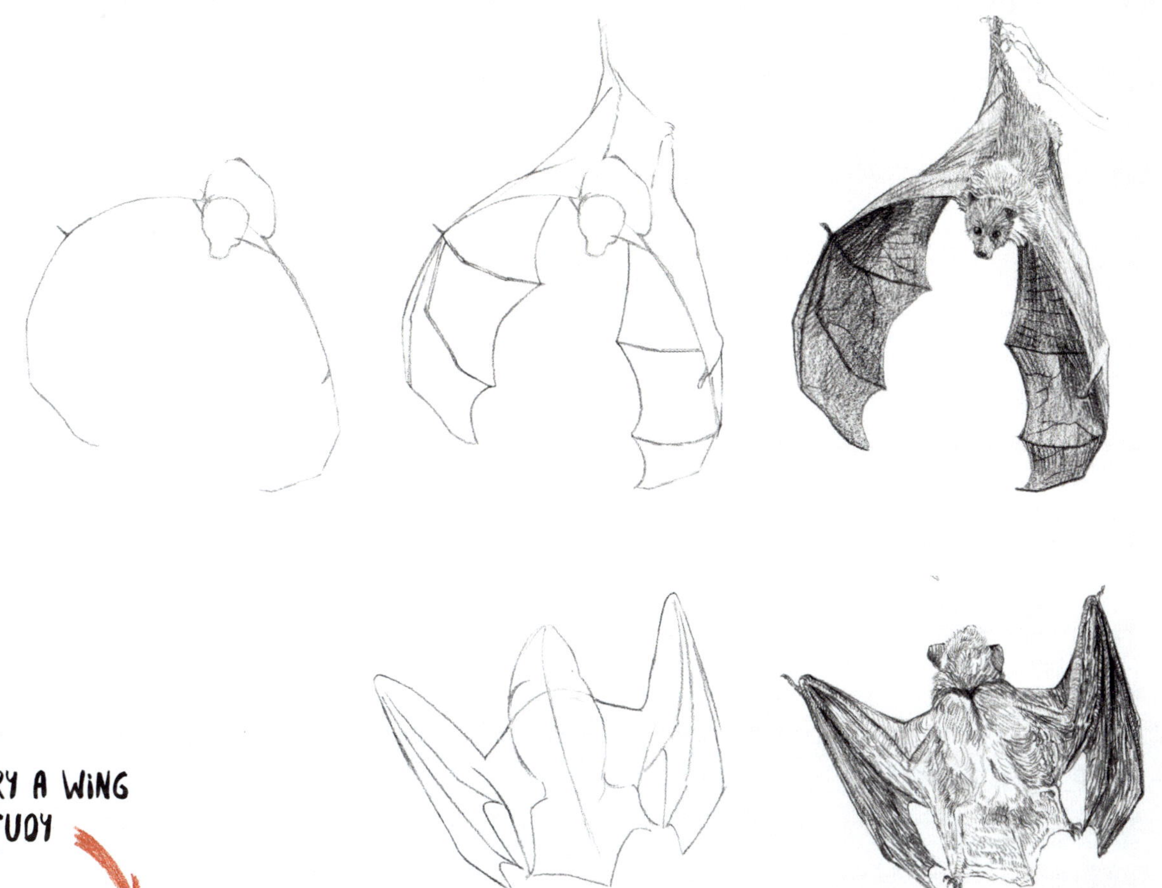

RY A WING
TUDY

PART 02: STRUCTURES

FINS & FLIPPERS

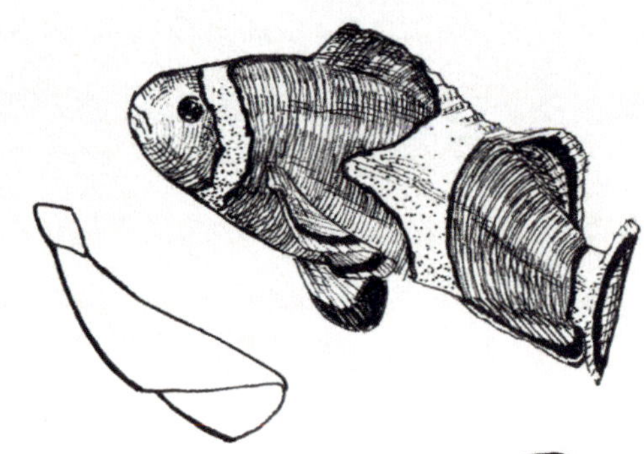

Fins, flippers and the powerful tails of aquatic animals serve to propel and direct them through the deep. They can range from the thin, delicate fins of small fish through to the powerful flippers of dolphins and whales, underpinned by bone structures inherited from their land-dwelling ancestors.

FISH FINS COME IN A WIDE VARIETY OF DIFFERENT TYPES – SOME ARE THIN AND FLEXIBLE, LIKE THOSE OF THE CLOWNFISH

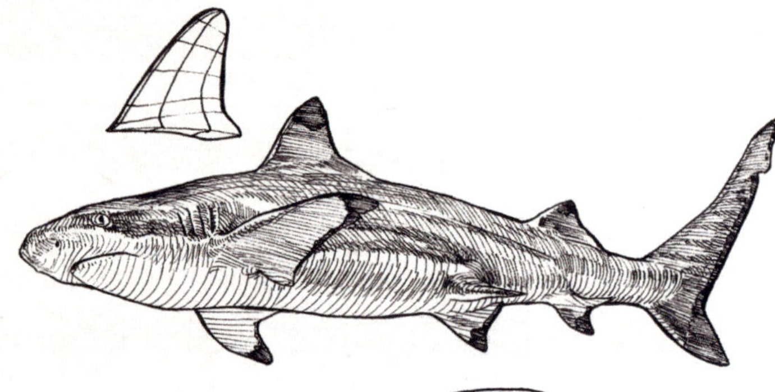

CARTILAGINOUS FISH, LIKE SHARKS AND RAYS, HAVE FINS WITH A MORE DEFINED THICKNESS AND VOLUME

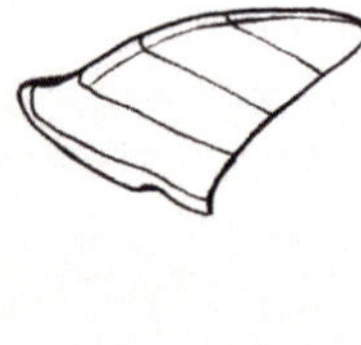

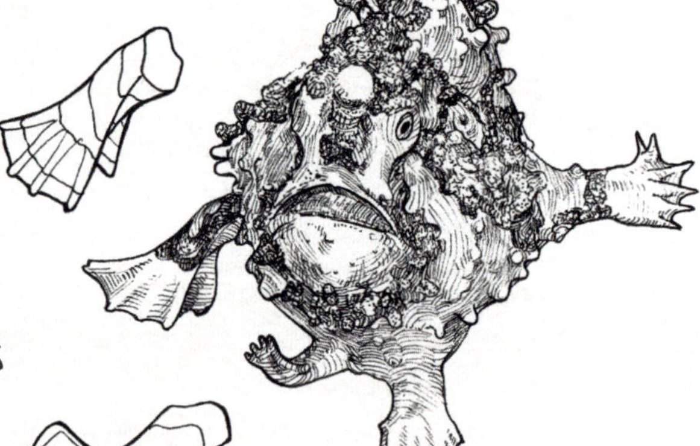

LOBE-FINNED FISH, LIKE THIS FROGFISH, HAVE BULKIER FINS

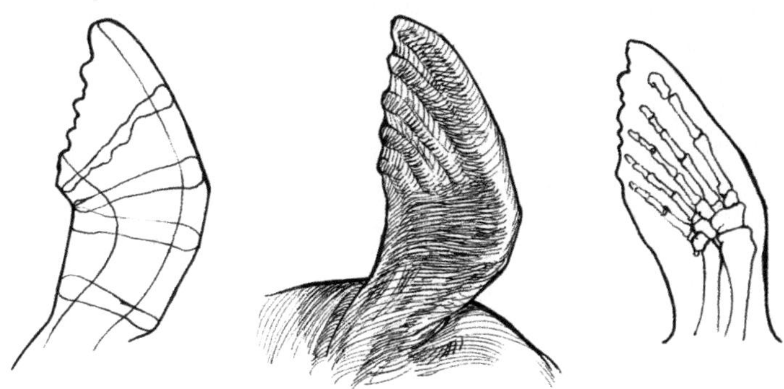

AQUATIC MAMMALS HAVE FLIPPERS THAT ARE ADAPTED FROM HANDS. INDIVIDUAL DIGITS ARE FUSED TOGETHER INTO A BROAD, FLATTENED FORM

PINNIPEDS LIKE SEALS AND SEA LIONS HAVE FLIPPERS THAT CAN BEND AT THE WRIST, SUPPORTING THEM ON LAND

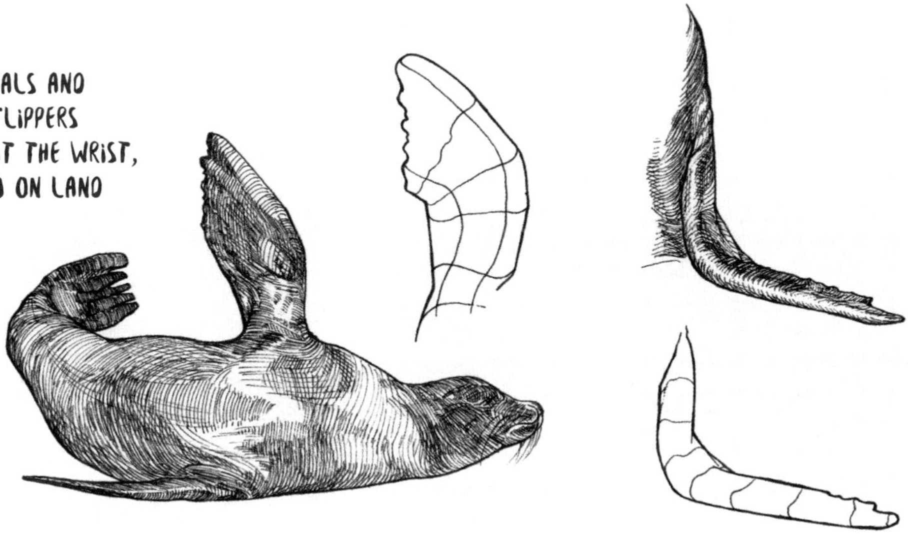

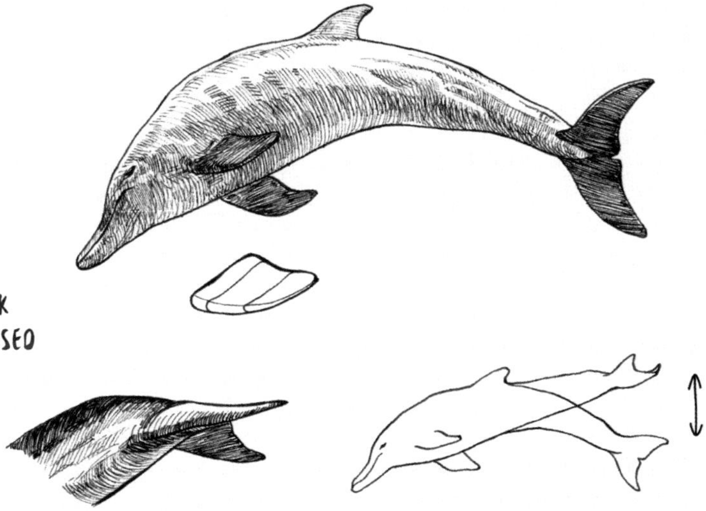

ANOTHER DISTINCTIVE FEATURE OF AQUATIC MAMMALS IS THAT THEIR BACK FLIPPERS MOVE UP AND DOWN, AS OPPOSED TO THE SIDEWAYS MOTION OF FISH

FACES

While we cannot help viewing animals through the lens of our own humanity, we should also careful not to anthropomorphize them. Each species has its own set of behaviours, expressed through its body as much as through its facial features.

Most animals have symmetrical faces, so when you are drawing the face of an animal, start by finding the centreline, then create a crosshair with lines which connect the position of features like the eyes, nostrils, mouth and ears.

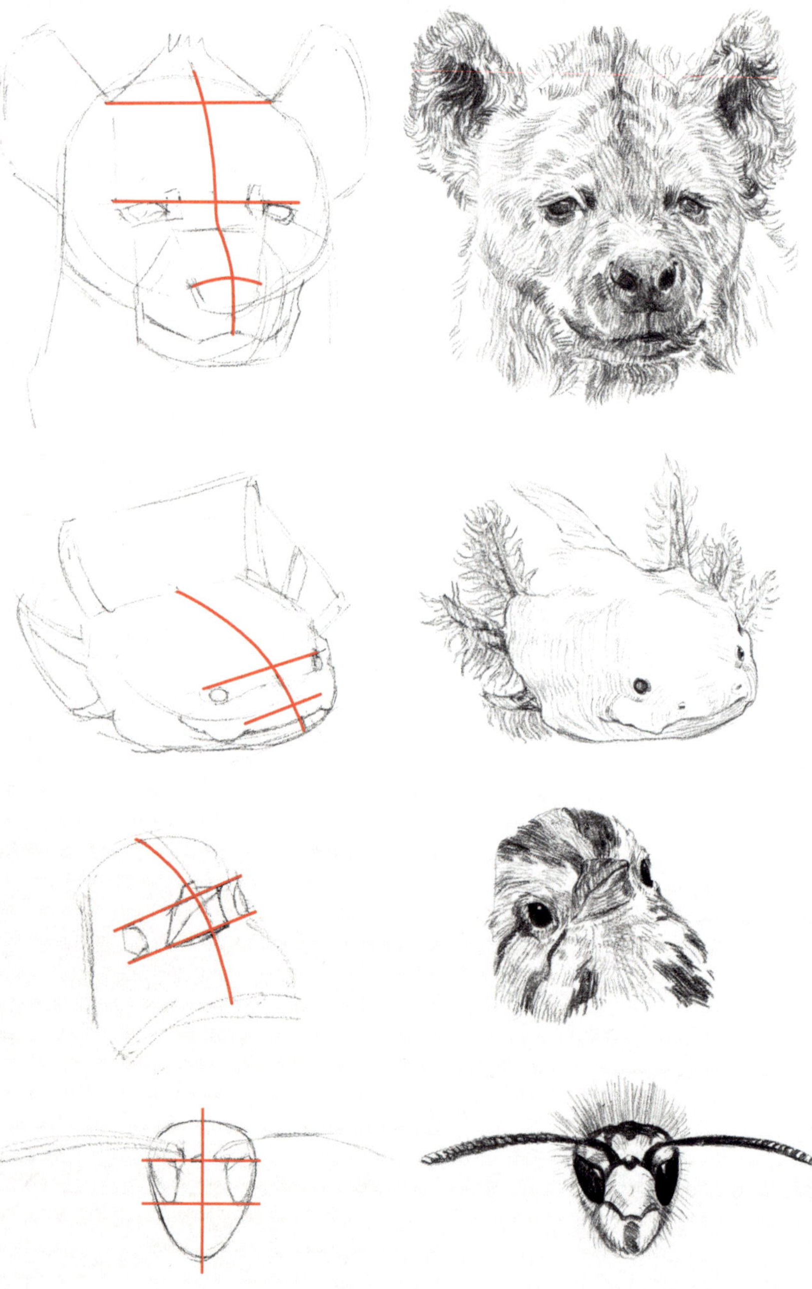

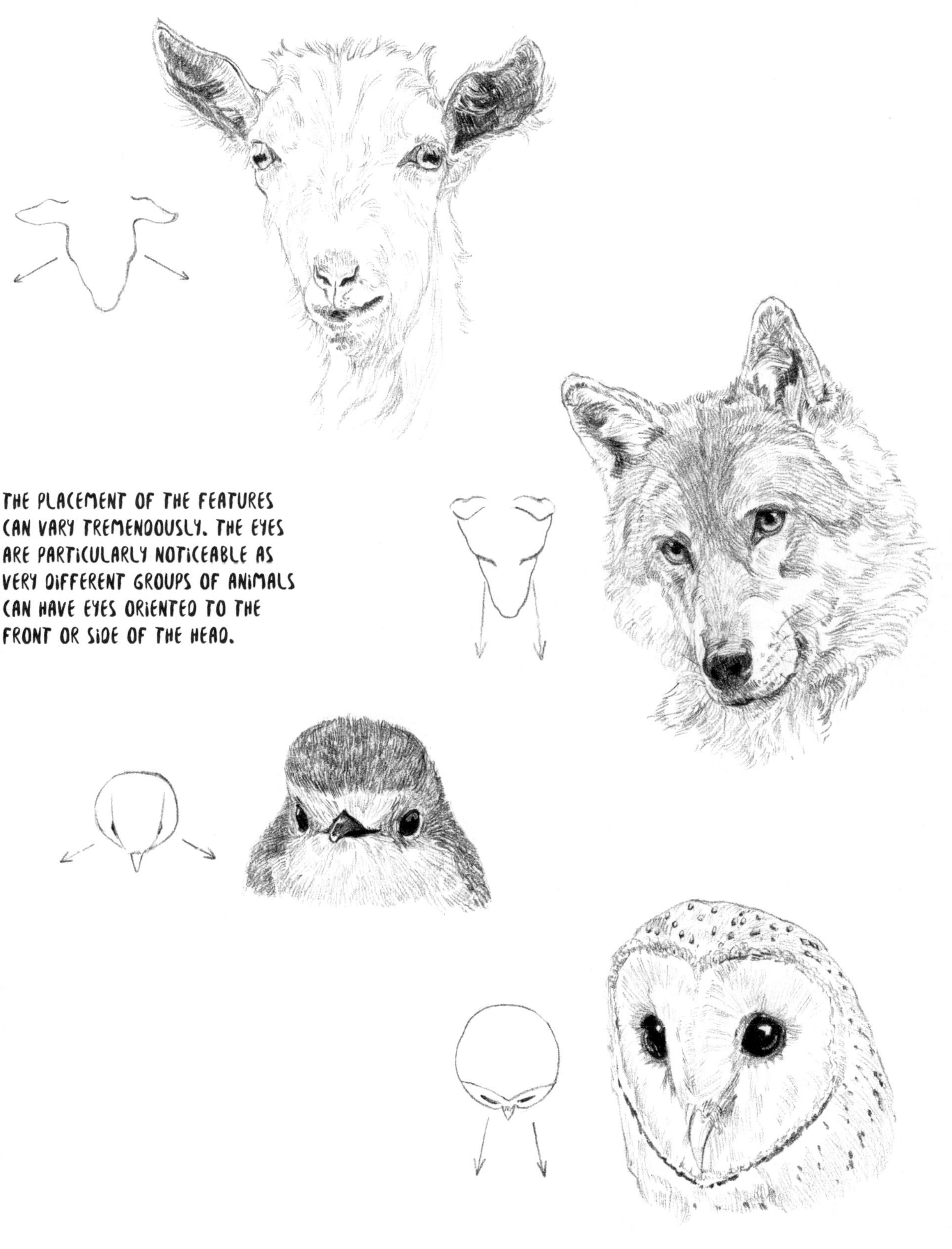

THE PLACEMENT OF THE FEATURES CAN VARY TREMENDOUSLY. THE EYES ARE PARTICULARLY NOTICEABLE AS VERY DIFFERENT GROUPS OF ANIMALS CAN HAVE EYES ORIENTED TO THE FRONT OR SIDE OF THE HEAD.

PART 02: STRUCTURES

PINPOINTING FEATURES

Eyes, nostrils and the edges of the mouth all make for useful fixed 'landmarks'. So long as you are working from a still subject, those features can be used as reference points for checking the proportions of the face, and the body as a whole.

As well as using a crosshair for the vertical centre of the face and the features, you can look for other relationships between the features, like the lines here that join the ears, eyes and nostrils of the cat's head.

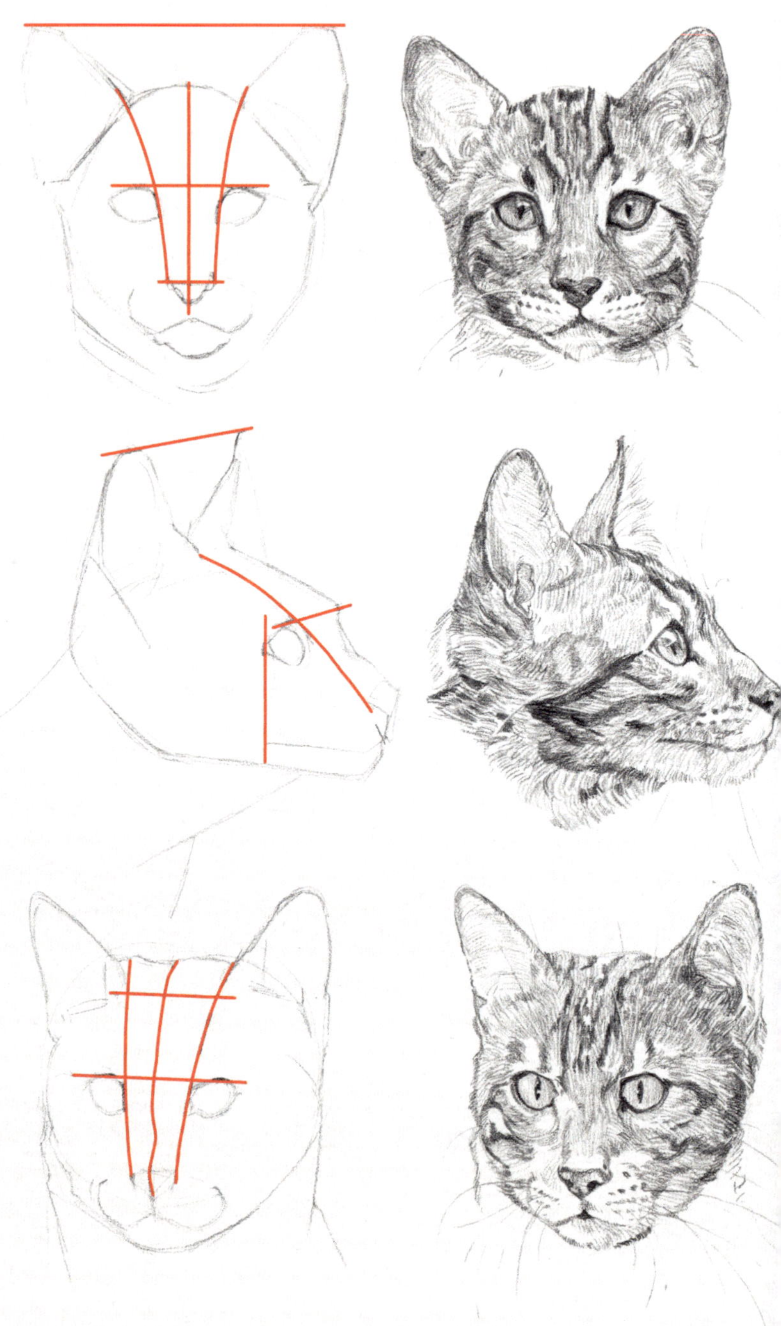

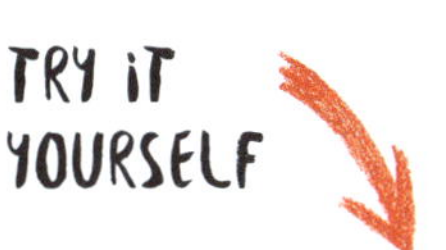
TRY IT
YOURSELF

PART 02: STRUCTURES

MUZZLES

While the eyes, nose and mouth often draw our attention, it is the landscape of the space in-between that often defines how we recognize the shape of an animal's face. The rhythm of the muzzle seen in profile is critical for achieving a convincing likeness.

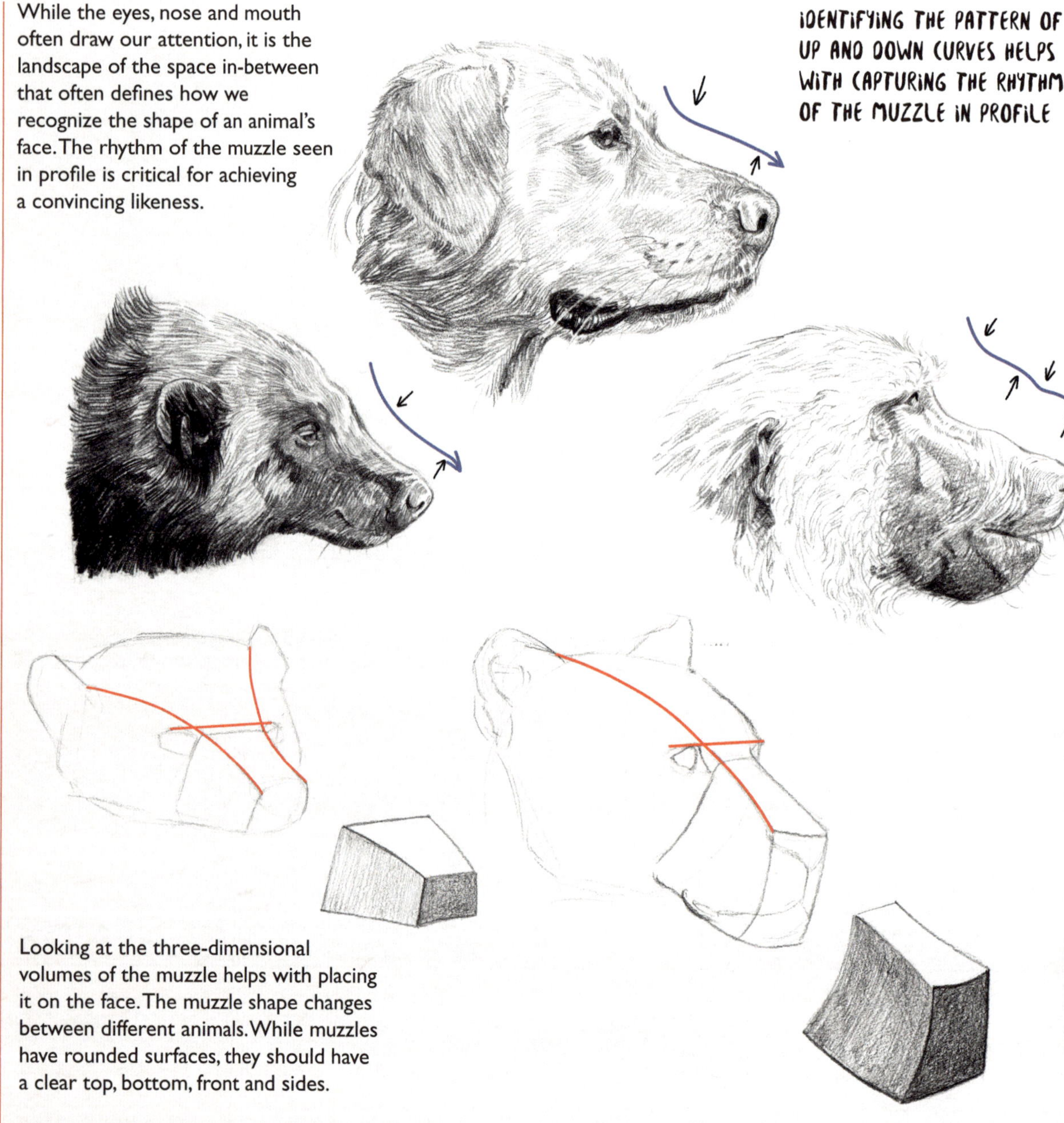

Looking at the three-dimensional volumes of the muzzle helps with placing it on the face. The muzzle shape changes between different animals. While muzzles have rounded surfaces, they should have a clear top, bottom, front and sides.

WHISKERS

It is easy to draw long, delicate whiskers too heavily. They should be drawn lightly and confidently, using different approaches depending on whether they are sitting against a dark or light background.

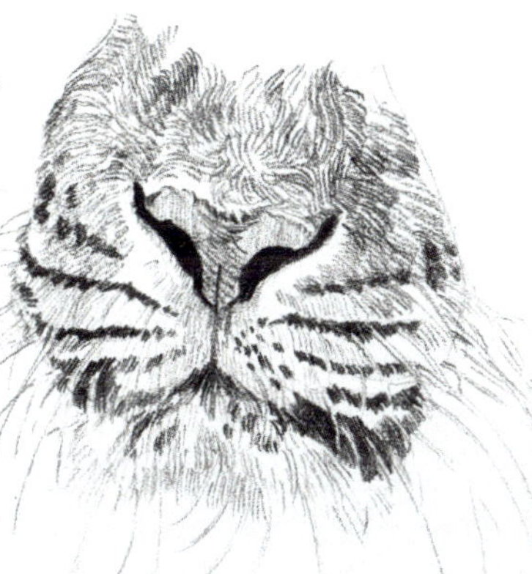

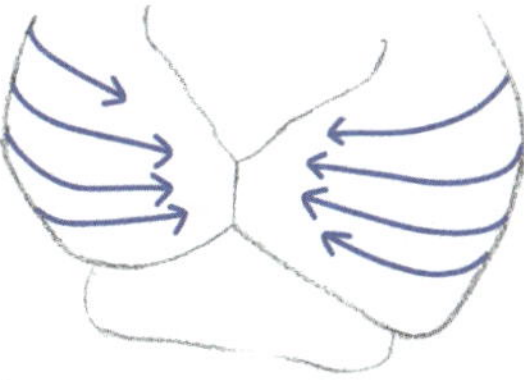

Whiskers sprout from the lip in rows. They tend to point at varied angles, so try to let them cross over each other, and give them uneven negative spaces.

Each whisker tapers down its length. This can be portrayed by varying the line thickness. You can suggest the delicate tip of the whisker with a broken line, or a single dot where the light catches the end.

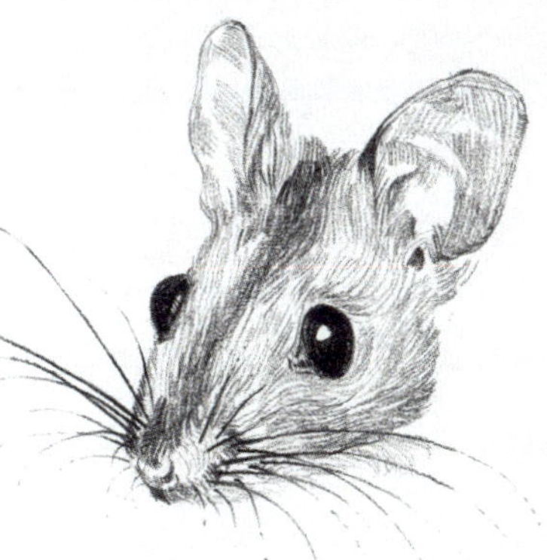

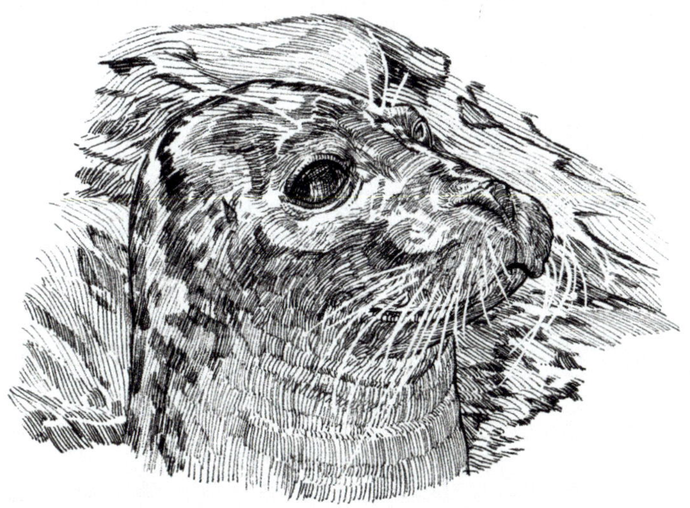

Pale whiskers can be challenging to draw. You may want to draw around them, leaving the white of the paper, or you can draw them on top in white using mediums like white pen, gouache or chalk.

NOSES

The shapes of noses vary from simple slits to significant visual characteristics on an animal's face. The dark shapes of the nostrils will be the most useful reference points to focus on, while the surrounding flesh will differ from animal to animal.

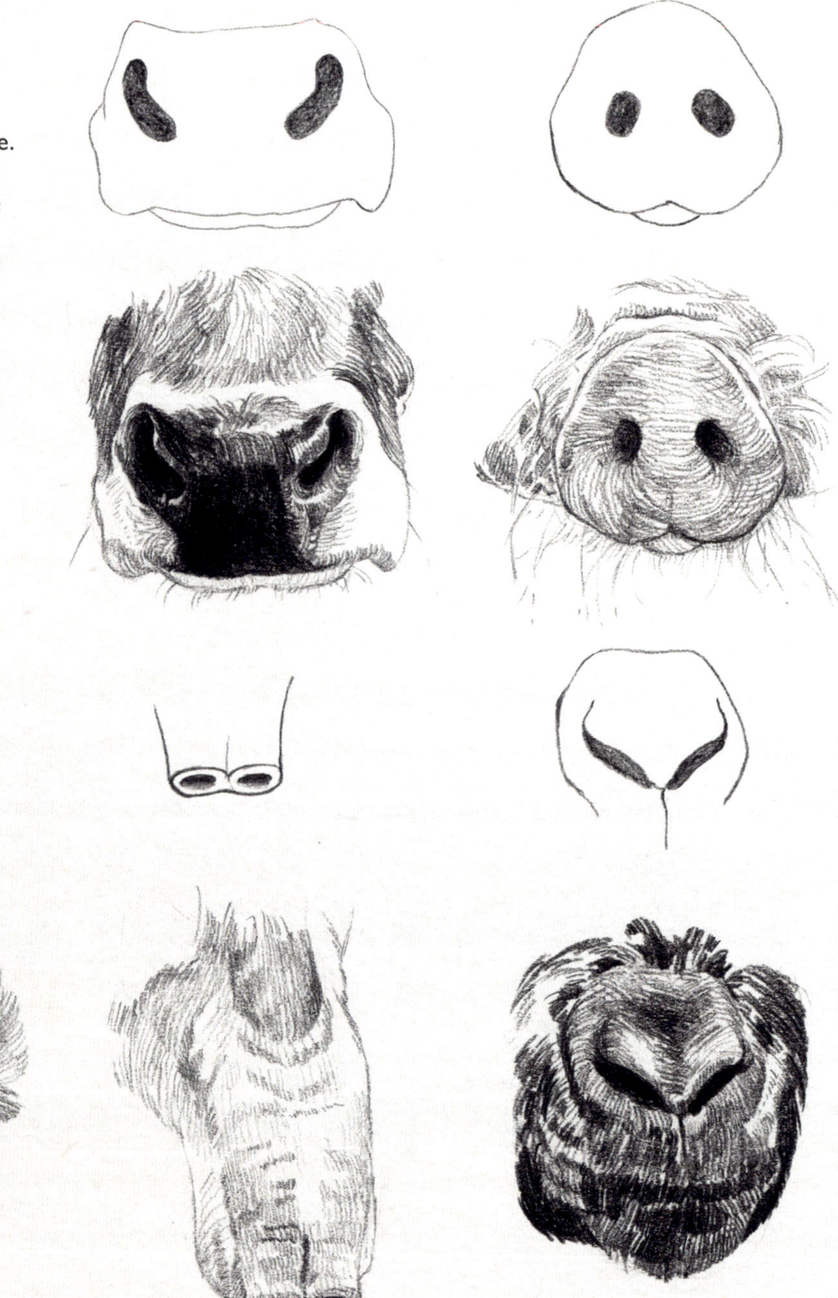

START A NOSE WITH ITS OVERALL SHAPE AND THE LINES THAT JOIN THE NOSTRILS

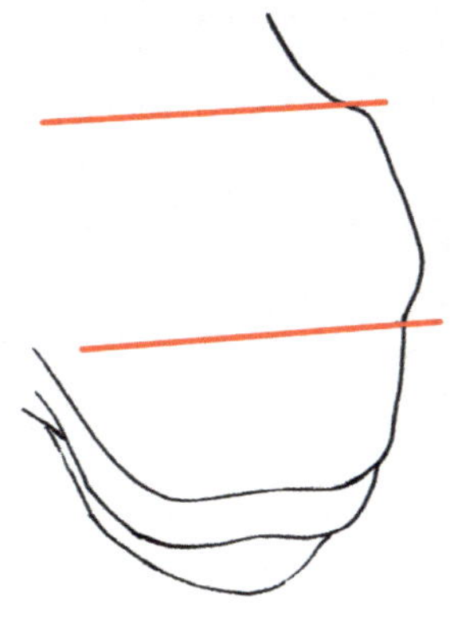

PLACE THE NOSTRILS, DRAWING THEIR DISTINCT SHAPES AND CHECKING THE DISTANCE BETWEEN THEM

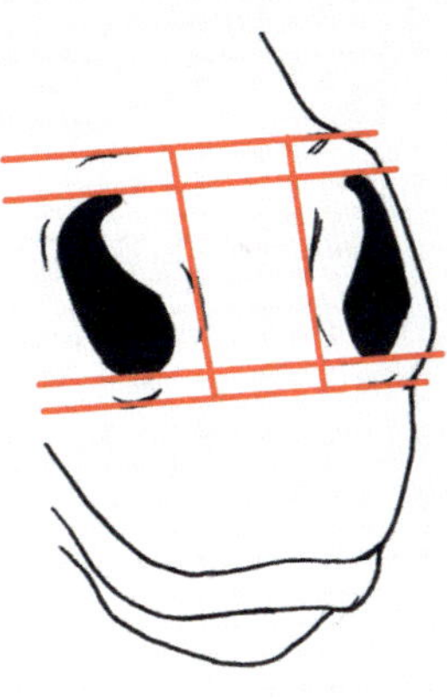

DEFINE CONTOURS AND NOSTRIL SHAPES

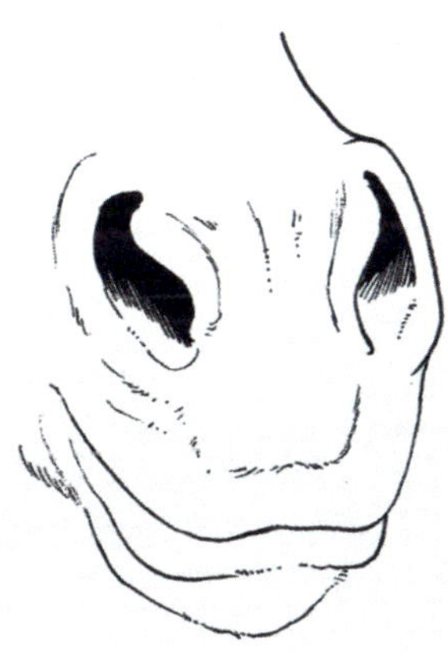

USE THE NOSTRILS AS AN ANCHOR POINT AS YOU ELABORATE ON THE DETAILS OF THE NOSE

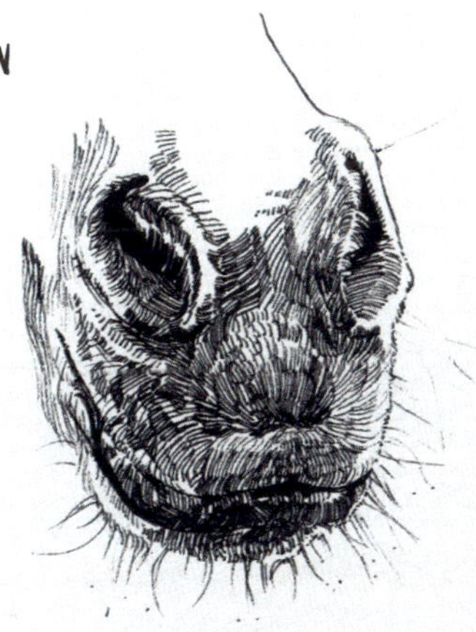

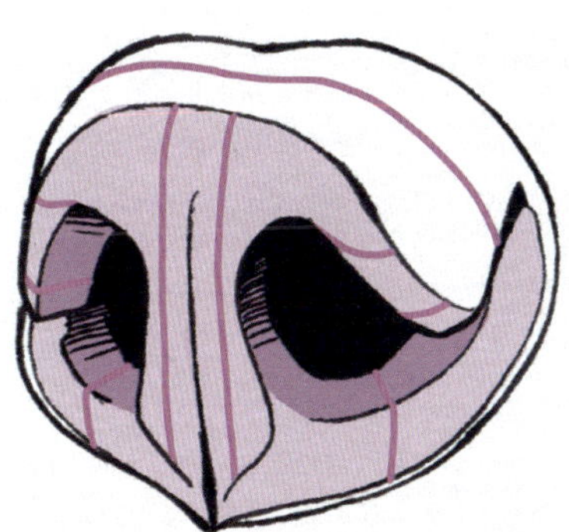

WHILE ITS STRUCTURE VARIES BETWEEN ANIMALS, YOU WILL OFTEN NOTICE CLEAR PLANES TO THE TOP, FRONT AND SIDES OF THE NOSE

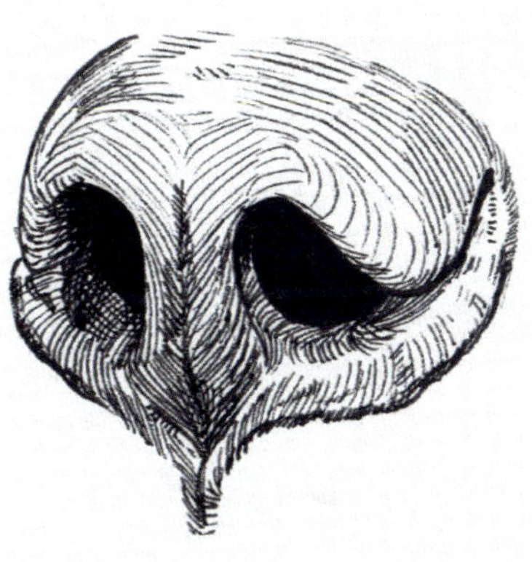

PART 02: STRUCTURES

MOUTHS

The expression of the mouth is defined by the shape of the opening – from the slim line of a closed mouth to the expansive shape of open jaws. Notice how the top of the mouth hinges away from the bottom, and to enrich your drawings, get to know the anatomy within the open mouth.

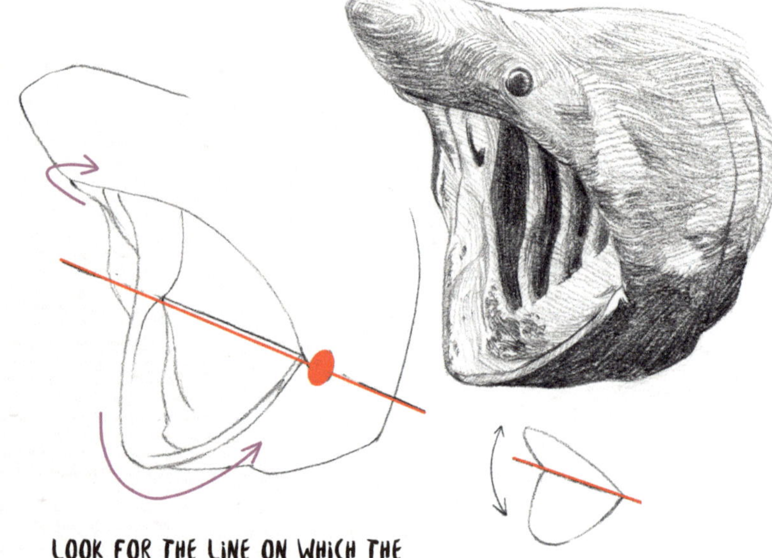

LOOK FOR THE LINE ON WHICH THE MOUTH HINGES. FROM HERE, THE JAWS SWEEP OUT IN A CURVE. MORE COMPLEX FORMS CAN BE BUILT UP ON TOP.

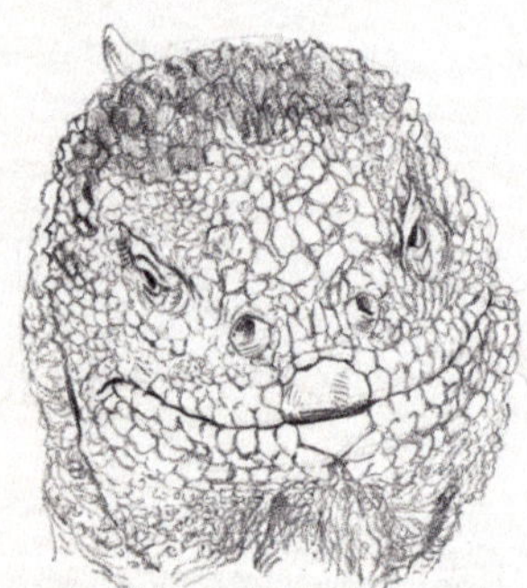

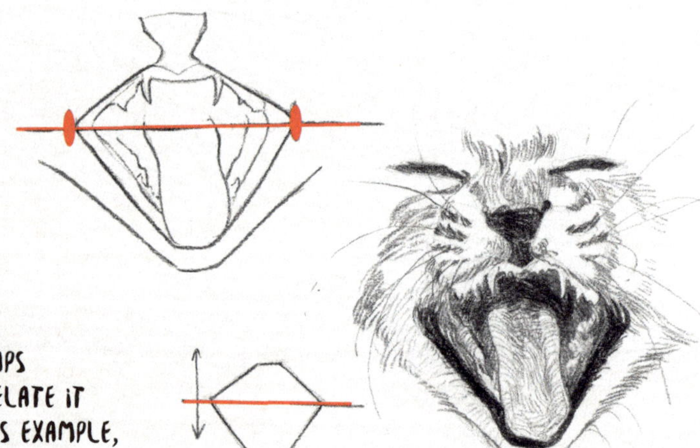

THE LINE OF THE MOUTH WRAPS AROUND THE FACE. TRY TO RELATE IT TO OTHER FEATURES – IN THIS EXAMPLE, THE CORNERS OF THE MOUTH LINE UP WITH THE BOTTOMS OF THE NOSTRILS.

LIPS AND OTHER SOFT TISSUES MAKE UP THE EXTERIOR FORMS OF THE MOUTH IN MANY ANIMALS, ADDING ROUNDED VOLUMES.

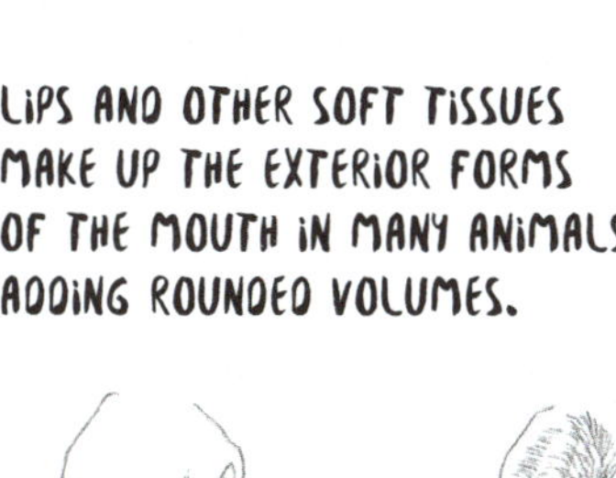

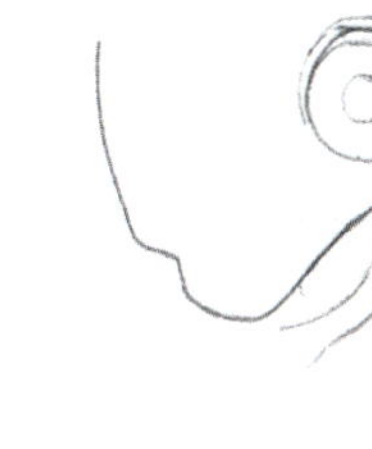

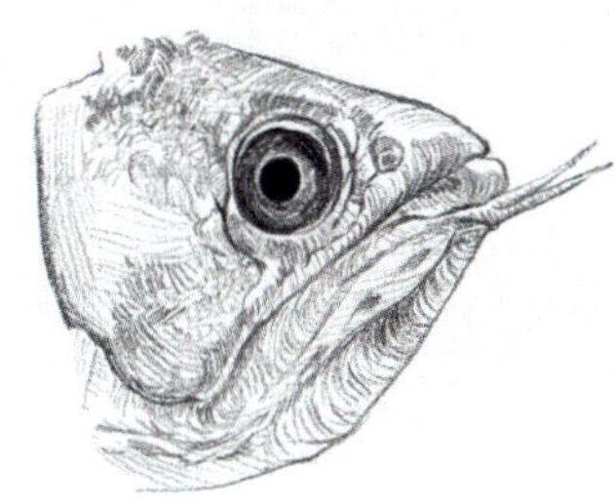

WITHIN THE MOUTH, THE JAWBONE HAS A THICK, CURVED, OFTEN HORSESHOE-SHAPED FORM ON WHICH THE TEETH ARE MOUNTED AND AROUND WHICH THE LIPS ARE WRAPPED.

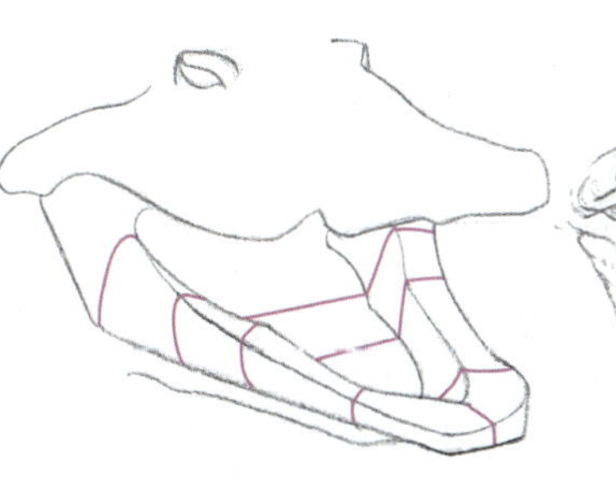

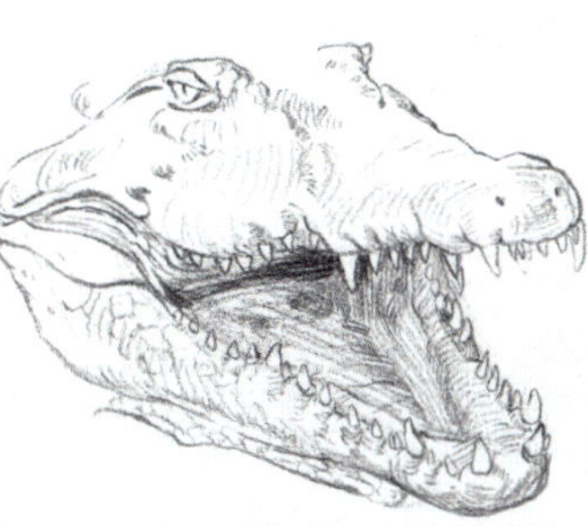

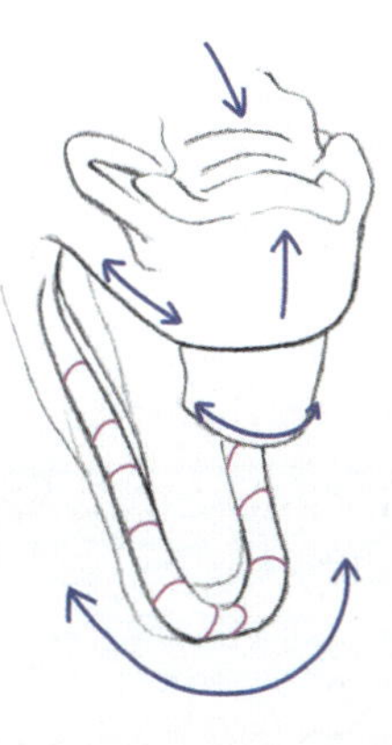

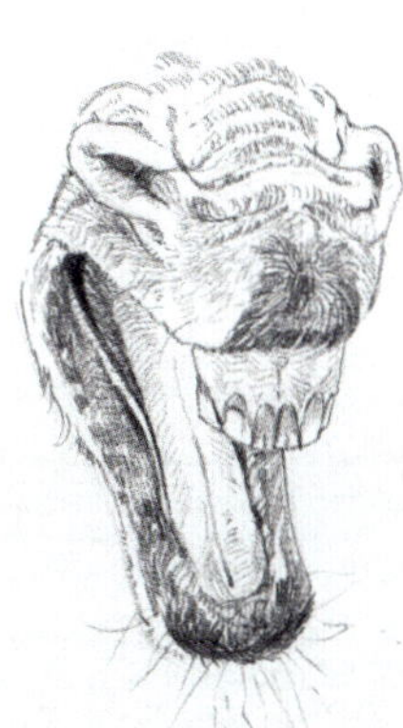

MORE FLEXIBLE ANIMAL LIPS CAN DISTORT INTO DIFFERENT SHAPES BUT ARE STILL MADE OF ROUNDED VOLUMES.

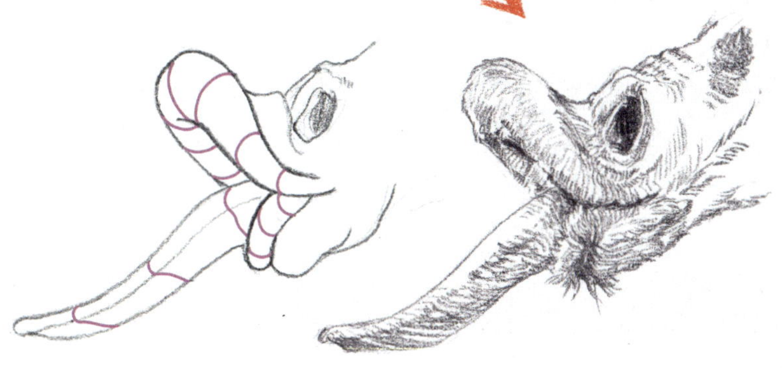

TEETH COME IN MANY SHAPES AND SIZES. TRY TO LOOK FOR THE CURVED RHYTHMS THEY CREATE WITH THE GUMS, AND WHERE THEY TAPER TO A POINT.

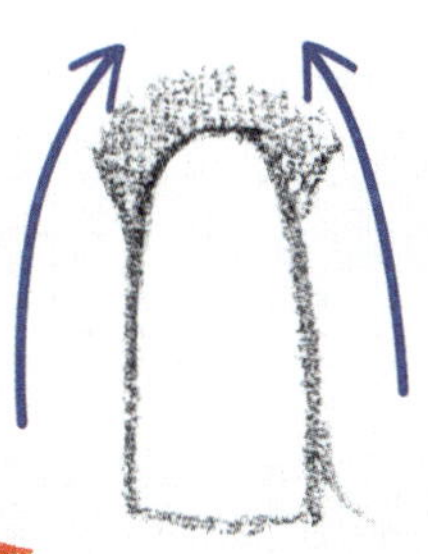

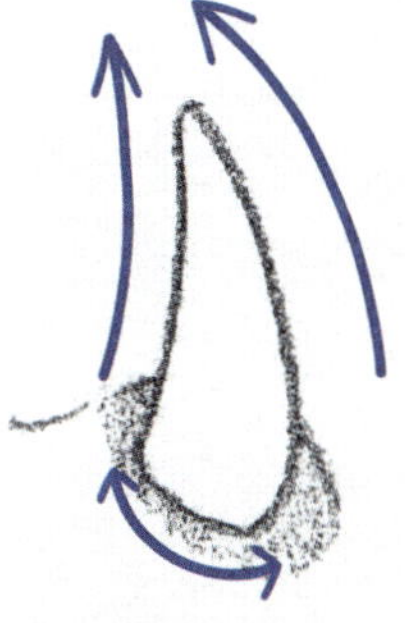

PART 02: STRUCTURES

BEAKS

Just like mouths, the shapes of beaks relate to the type of food their owner eats. Their hard forms give them a satisfyingly clear shape which you should practise drawing from a variety of different angles.

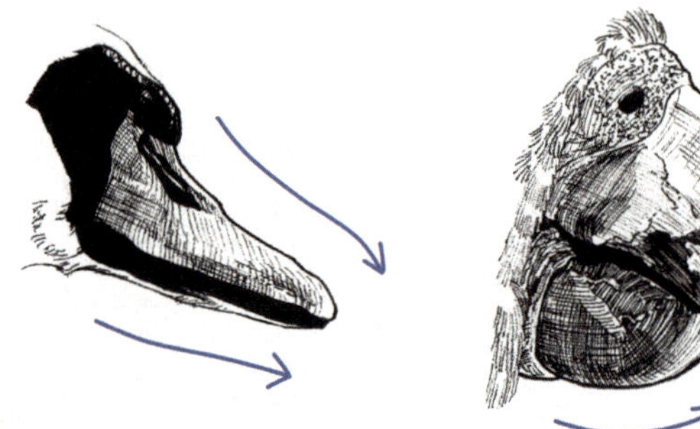

IDENTIFYING THE OVERALL RHYTHM TO THE CURVE OF A BEAK HELPS MAKE IT DISTINCT. THE NOSTRILS ARE ALSO PART OF THE BEAK AND TEND TO FIT ALONG A RHYTHM LINE WITH THE EYE.

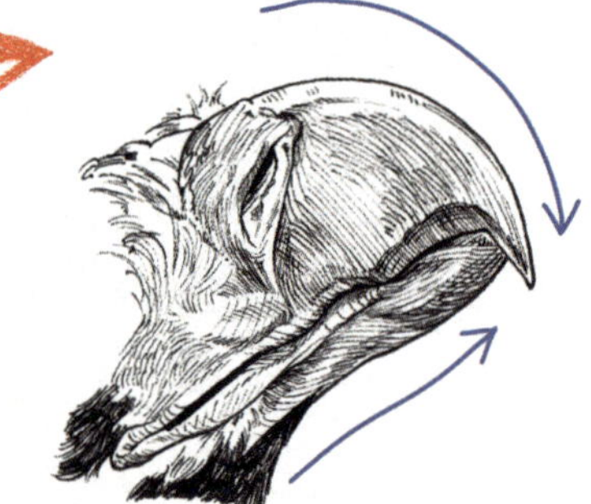

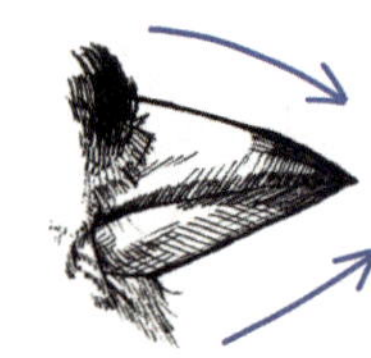

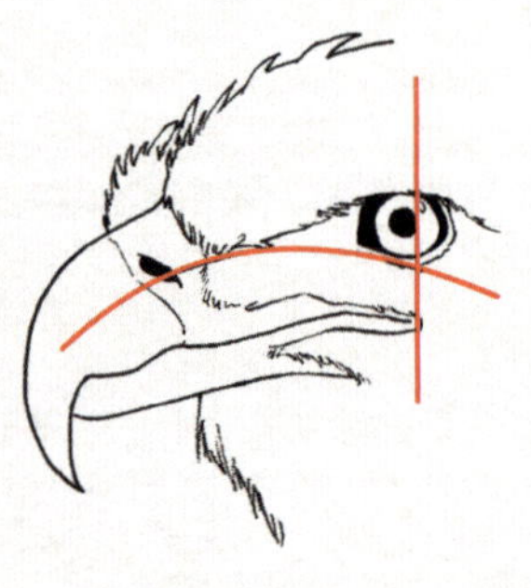

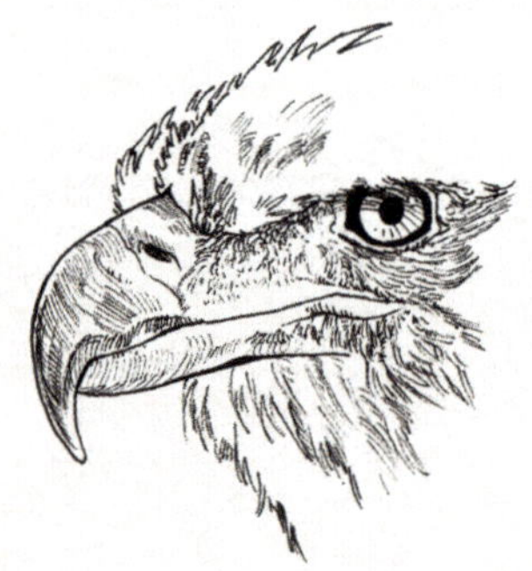

BEAKS HINGE MUCH LIKE JAWS. THIS IS OFTEN BELOW THE EYE, THOUGH THE JOINT MAY BE HIDDEN UNDER A FLAP OF SKIN.

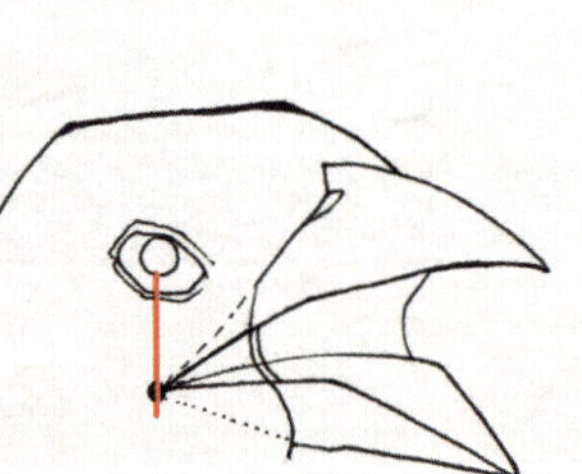

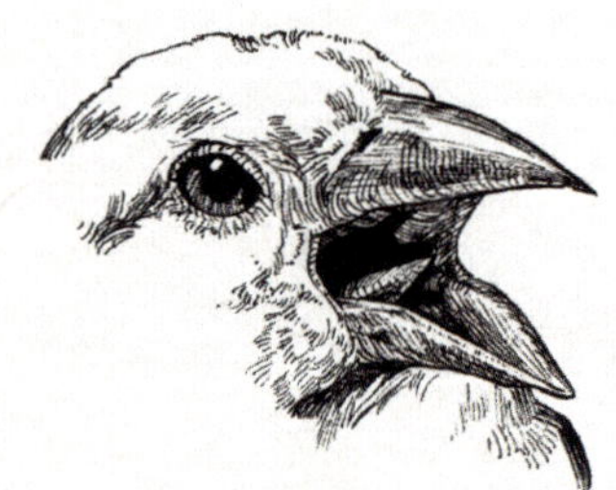

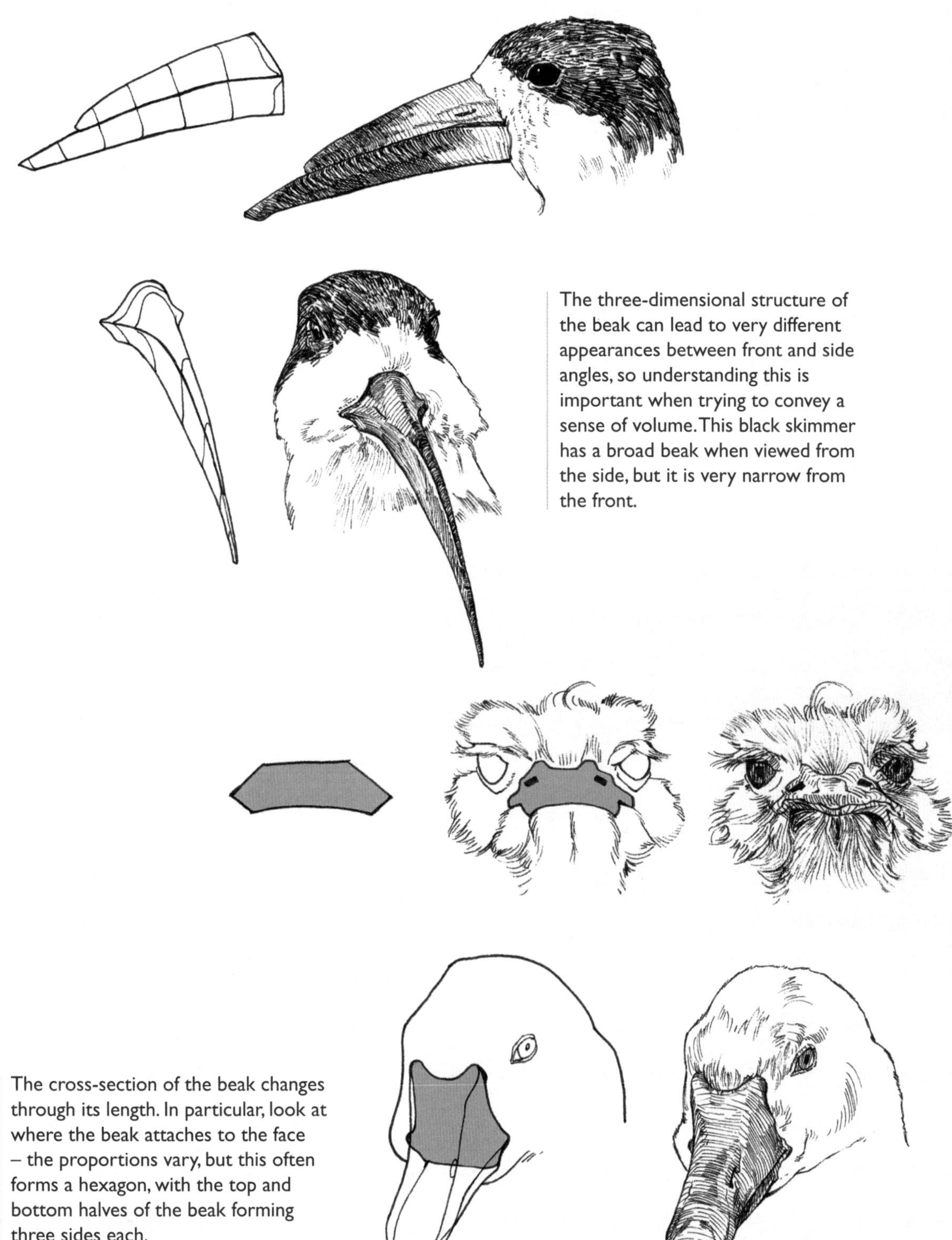

The three-dimensional structure of the beak can lead to very different appearances between front and side angles, so understanding this is important when trying to convey a sense of volume. This black skimmer has a broad beak when viewed from the side, but it is very narrow from the front.

The cross-section of the beak changes through its length. In particular, look at where the beak attaches to the face – the proportions vary, but this often forms a hexagon, with the top and bottom halves of the beak forming three sides each.

PART 02: STRUCTURES

EYES

The elements that frame the eye – eyelids, eyebrows, sockets or stalks – are important for how the eye itself looks. Our gaze is naturally drawn to the eyes of both people and animals, so they are often a focal point in a drawing.

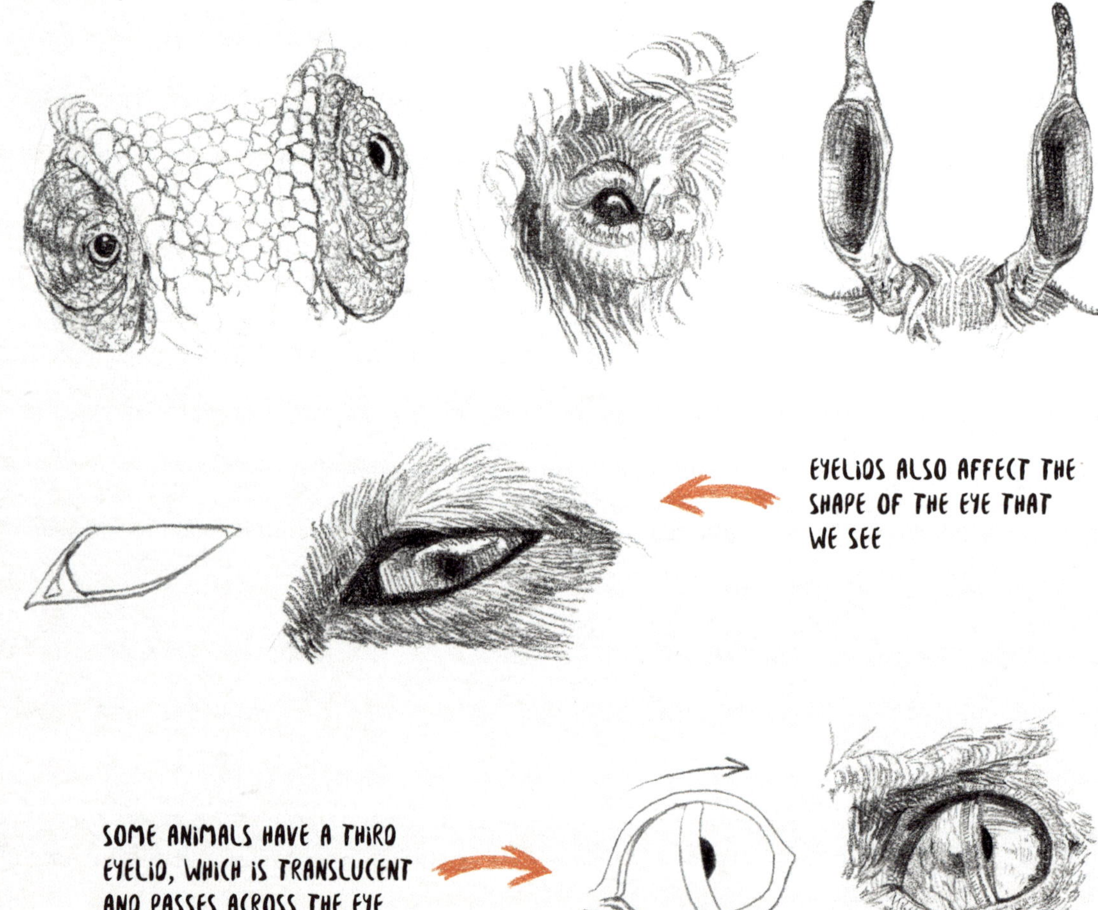

THE SHAPE OF THE PUPIL VARIES WIDELY IN DIFFERENT ANIMALS – FROM SIMPLE CIRCLES, THROUGH HORIZONTAL OR VERTICAL SLITS, TO LETTER-BOX SHAPES.

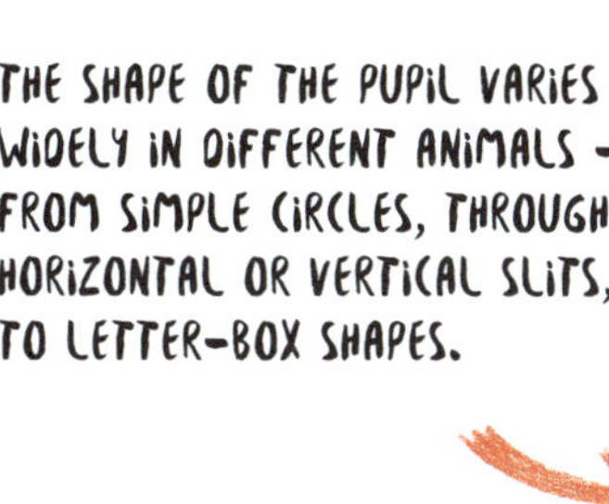

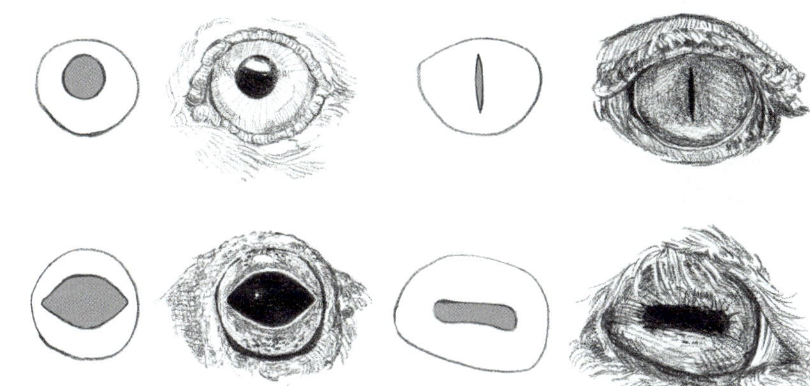

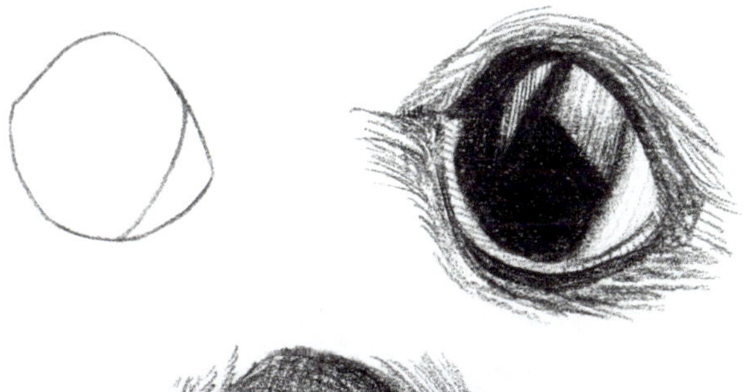

IN MANY ANIMALS, WE MIGHT NOT SEE MUCH OF THE SCLERA, OR WHITE OF THE EYE. WHEN VISIBLE, IT CREATES A SMALL, WHITE NEGATIVE SPACE. IN SOME CASES, THE SCLERA IS PIGMENTED BLACK IN ORDER TO CAMOUFLAGE THE FACE IN SHADY ENVIRONMENTS.

EYELIDS WRAP AROUND THE CURVE OF THE EYEBALL. THE EYELIDS ALSO HAVE THEIR OWN THICKNESS, WHICH WE CAN SEE AT CERTAIN ANGLES.

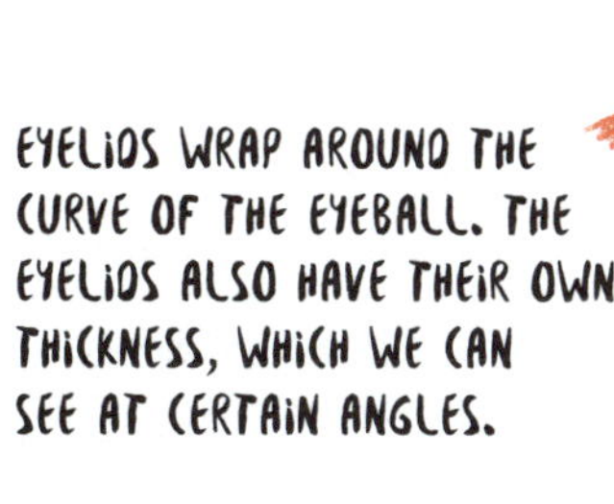

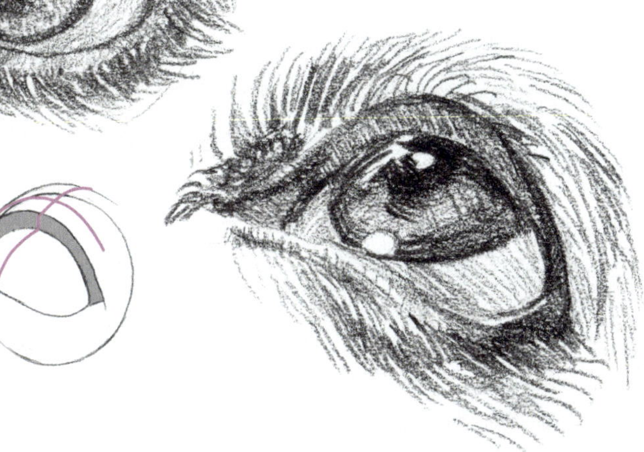

EARS

Just like noses, ears vary – they can range from simple holes in the side of an animal's head to large, complex external elements. While their primary function is to receive sounds, they are used for a range of other purposes in different species – from the communication of emotion in cats to cooling systems in elephants.

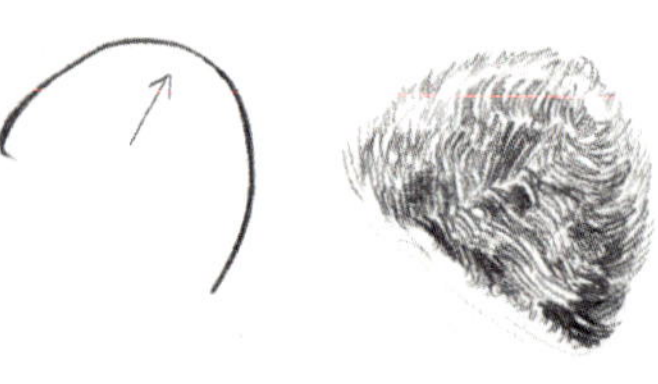

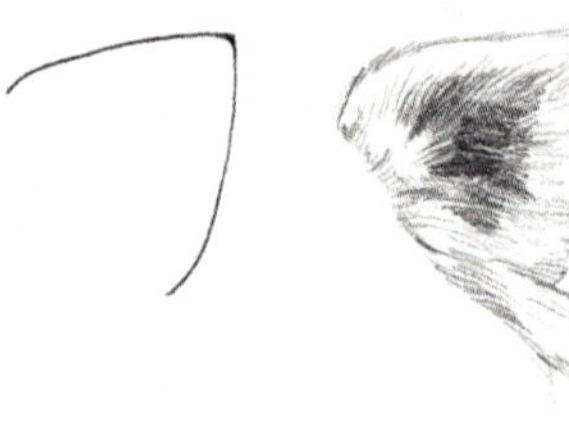

IDENTIFY THE OVERALL SHAPE OF THE EAR BEFORE BUILDING SURFACE TEXTURE OVER THE TO

WHEN THERE IS LESS FUR PRESENT, YOU WILL SEE MORE OF THE STRUCTURE OF THE EAR. TRY TO FOLLOW THE FLOW OF THOSE FORMS WITH YOUR MARK AND NOTICE HOW THEY CONNECT TOGETHER.

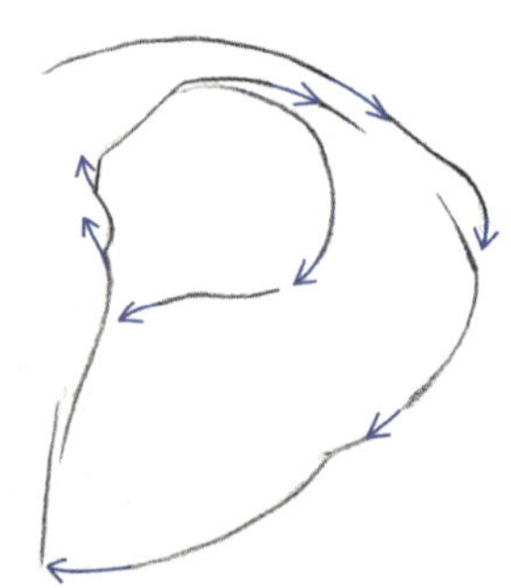

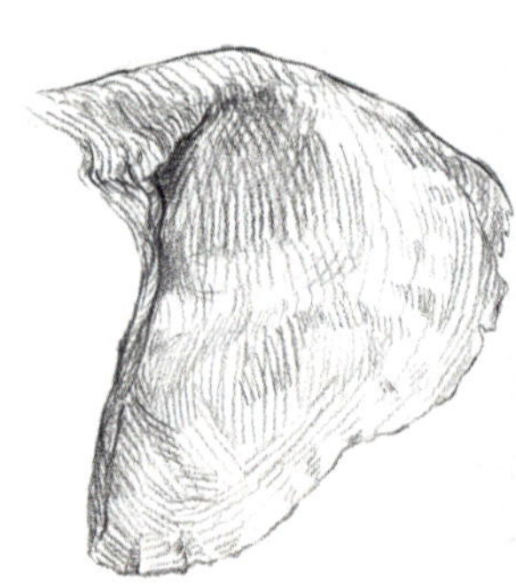

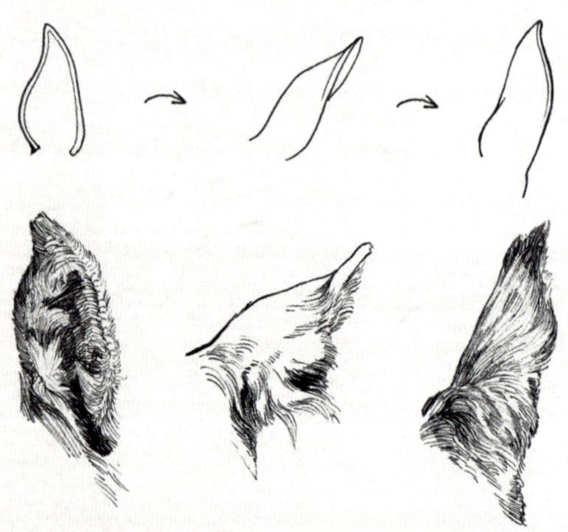

MANY ANIMALS CAN MOVE THEIR EARS TO EXPRESS EMOTION OR TO LISTEN FOR SOUNDS IN SPECIFIC DIRECTIONS. NOTICE HOW AN EAR MIGHT CHANGE ANGLE WHILE THE ANIMAL'S HEAD REMAINS STATIONARY.

For many animal ears, fur is a big part of what we see, and this can make drawing them challenging. Start by drawing the overall shape of the ear followed by the shape of the clump of hair that grows out from it before adding texture and tone to the hair.

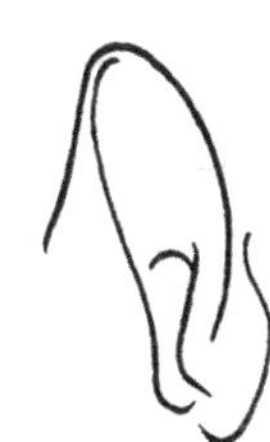

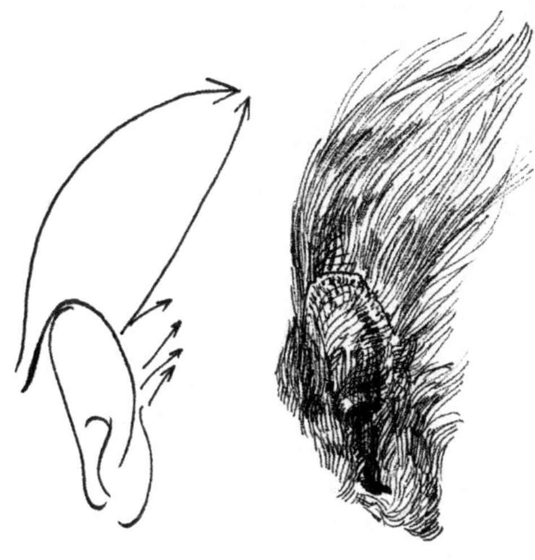

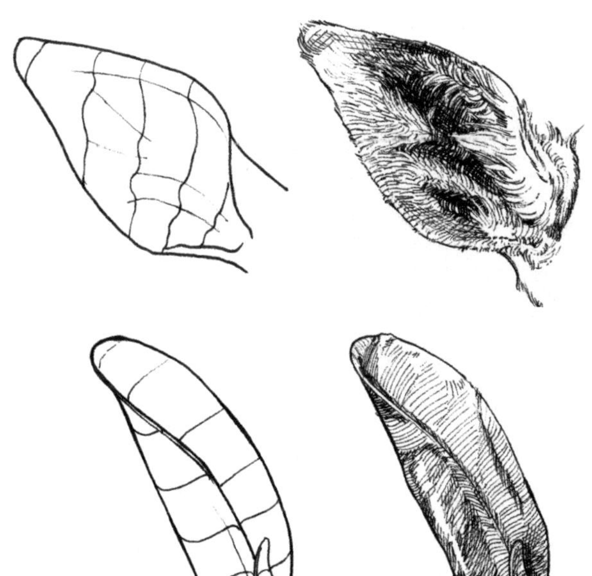

EARS HAVE THREE-DIMENSIONAL FORMS, AND MAY DEVELOP INTO CUPPED SHAPES, OR EVEN FOLD OVER ON THEMSELVES.

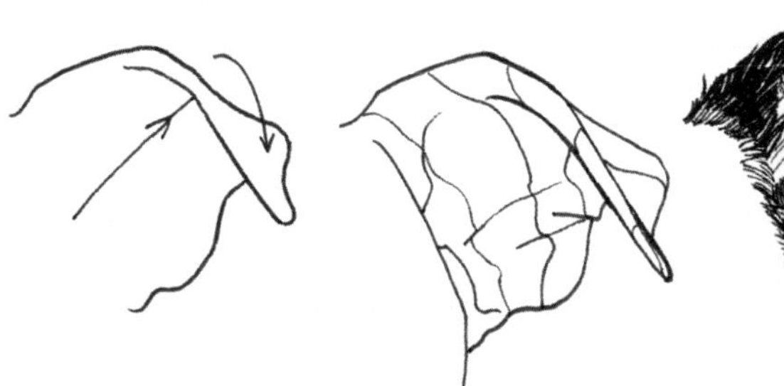

PRACTISE SOME FEATURE STUDIES HERE

PART 02: STRUCTURES

ANTLERS & HORNS

The horns and antlers that animals use as tools, decoration and weapons grow from very different materials in very different ways. They can appear on different parts of the head, and take a wide range of shapes, from simple to elaborate. However, they share the characteristic of being hard, consistent forms that are anchored to the skeleton of your subject.

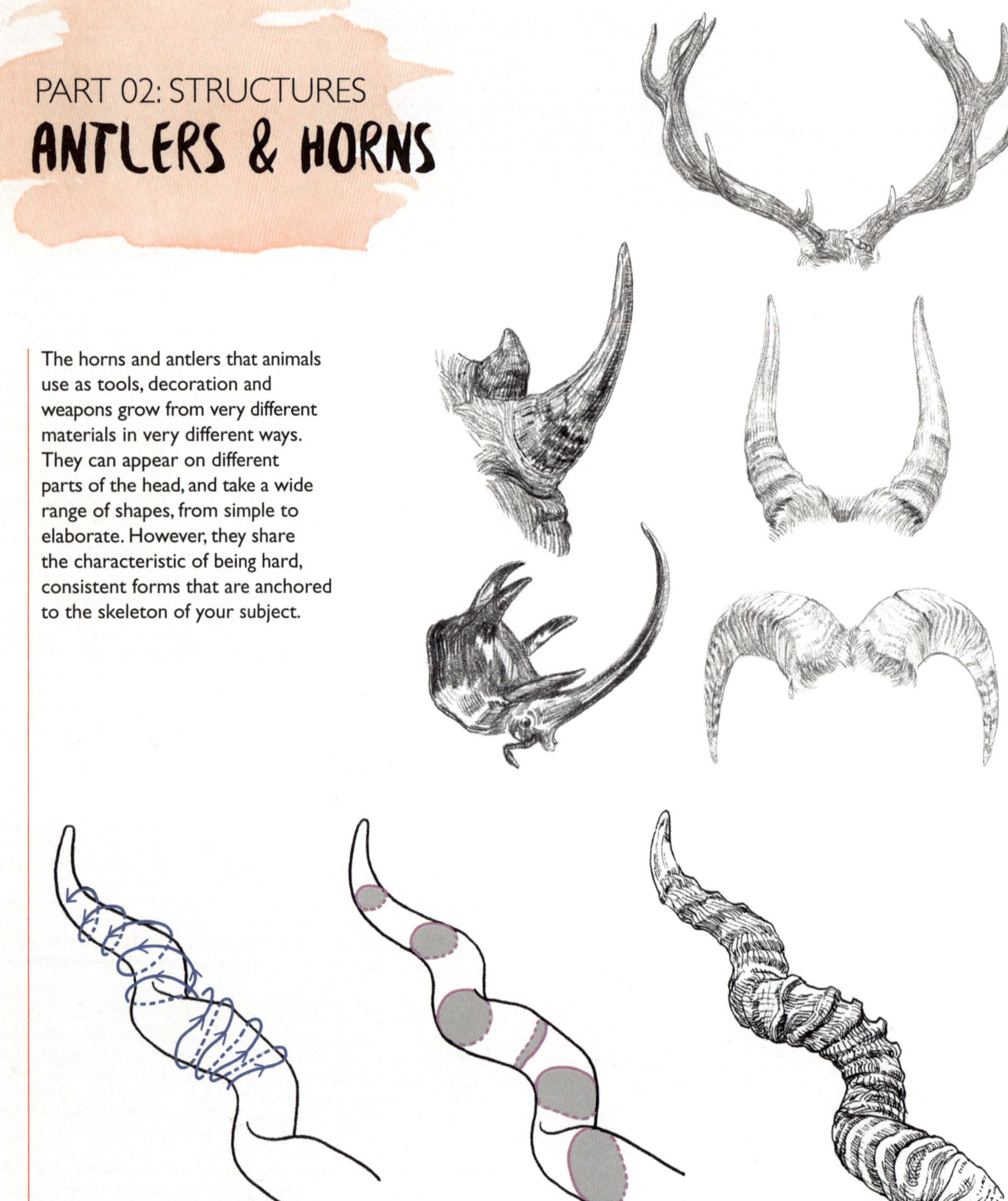

NOTICE HOW A HORN TAPERS AND HOW CROSS-CONTOURS DESCRIBE ITS FORM

TO HELP VISUALIZE CROSS-CONTOURS, IMAGINE THE CROSS-SECTIONS OF THE HORN

NOTICE HOW SURFACE TEXTURES FOLLOW CROSS-CONTOURS

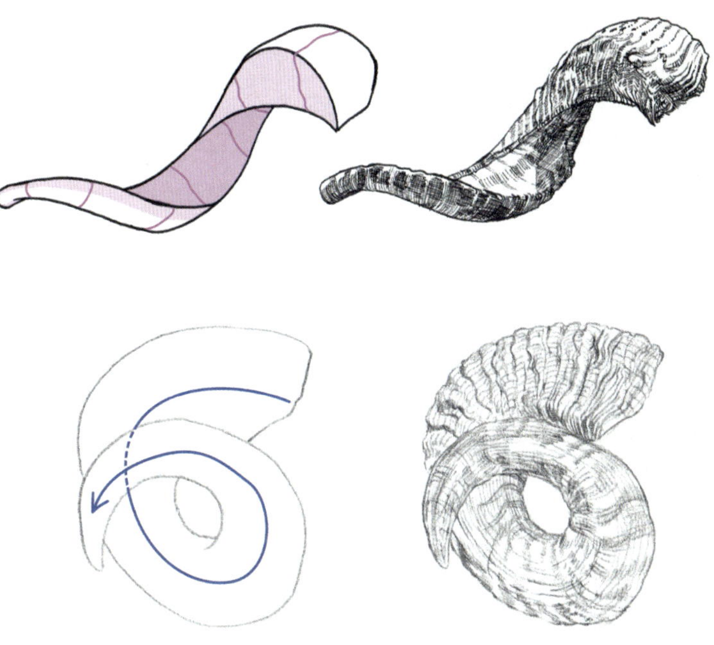

Horns can have more complex forms as they twist, or exhibit surface ridges. Try to follow any flattened sides you observe as they twist around. In this example, the ridge forms a spiral around the cylindrical form of the horn, so we need to combine the volume of the ridge with that of the horn. In curling horns and branching antlers, notice how one part of the form can overlap another.

The branching forms of antlers can seem overwhelming at first glance. Simplify the drawing process by focusing on the directions of the branches and negative spaces in between them before elaborating on the contour and surface textures.

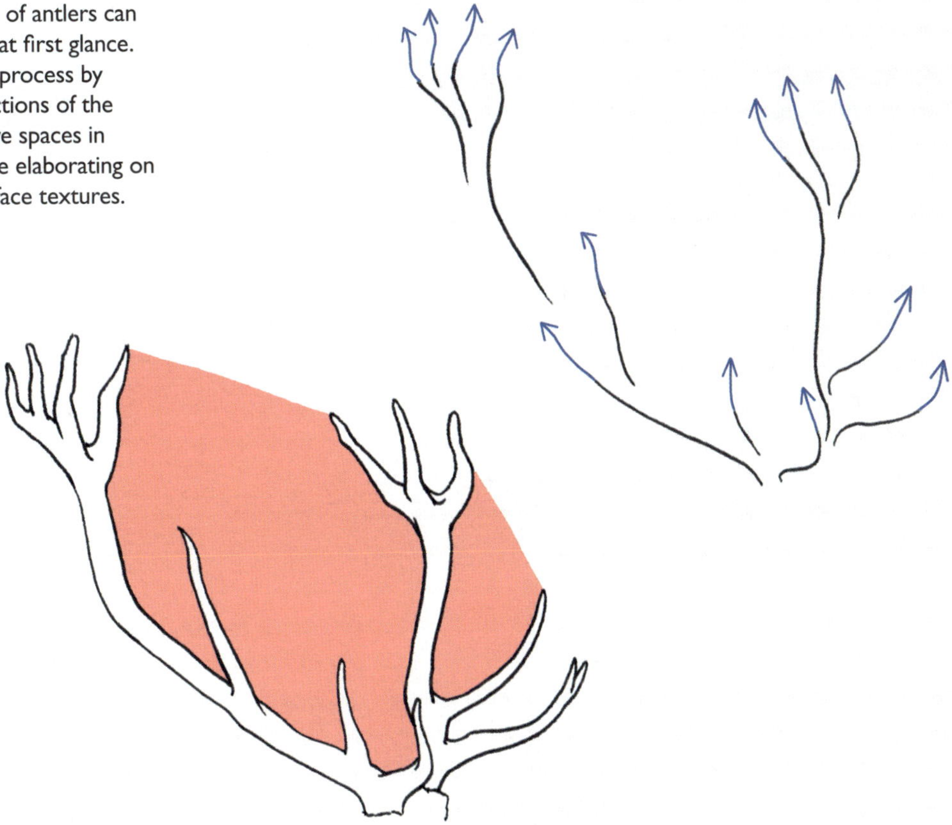

PART 02: STRUCTURES

HOOVES

Ungulate mammals typically walk on the toughened, horny tips of their toes. These hooves vary in expression between species, leaving recognizable tracks and presenting satisfyingly consistent shapes to draw. Ungulates can have one, two, three or four toes and are split into odd-toed and even-toed groups.

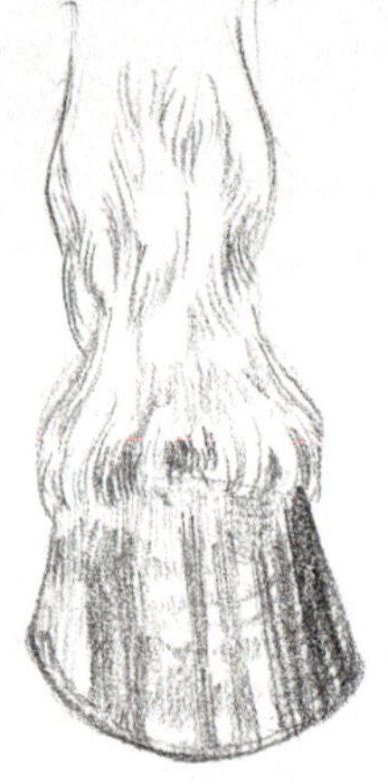

1-TOED (HORSE)

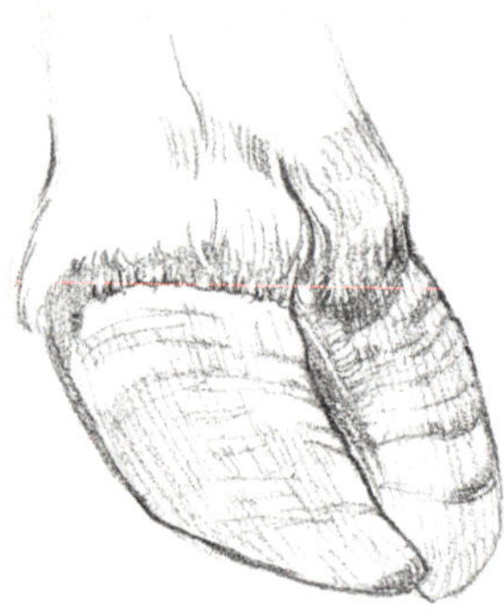

2-TOED (GOAT)

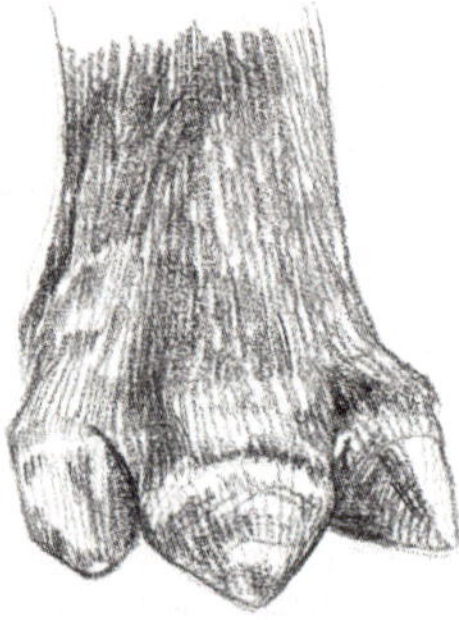

3-TOED (TAPIR)

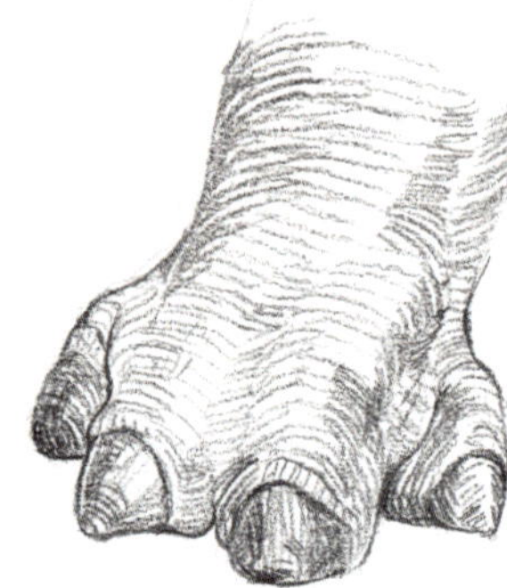

4-TOED (HIPPO)

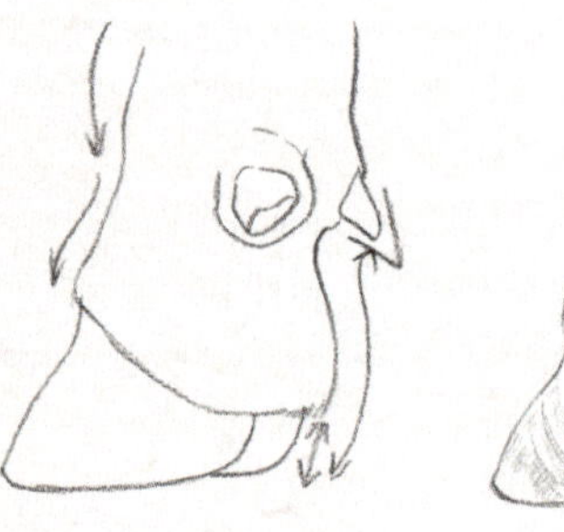

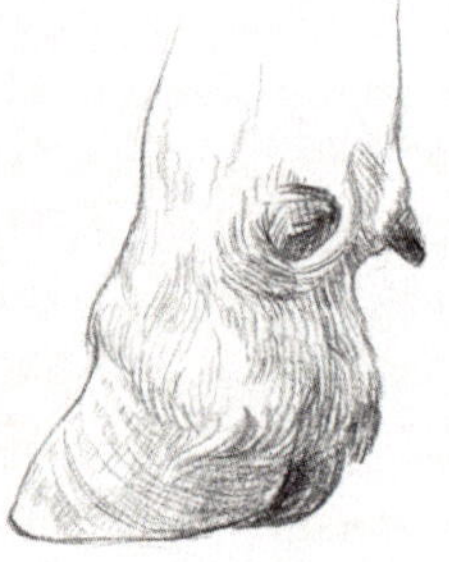

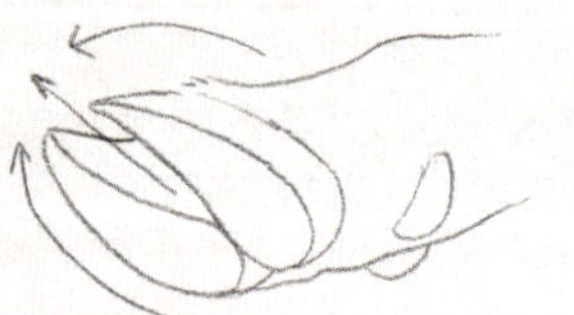

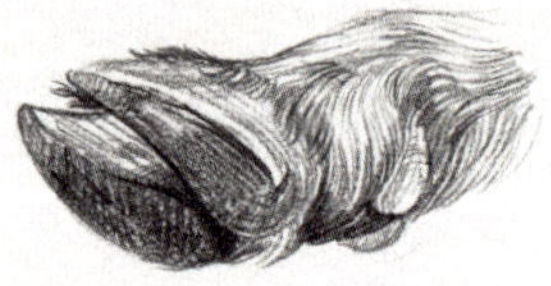

SOME EVEN-TOED UNGULATES HAVE TWO UNDEVELOPED EXTRA TOENAILS AT THE BACK OF THE FOOT

The individual toes of ungulates can take a roughly cylindrical form. The base of the foot might be a single solid toenail, as with horses, or split into multiple toenails. You'll often notice that the toes form a rounded arc, pointing towards a centre line.

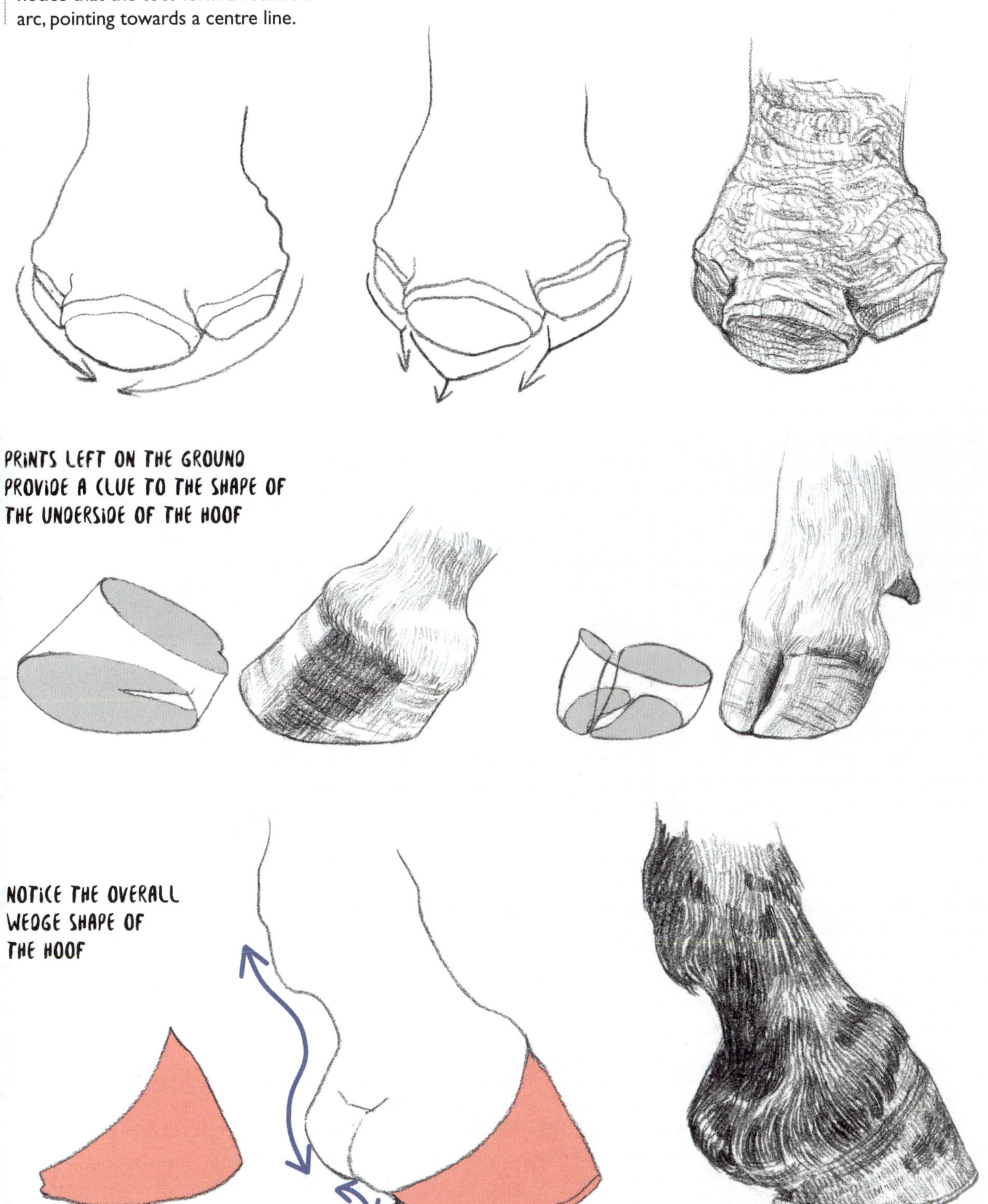

PART 02: STRUCTURES

PAWS, CLAWS & NAILS

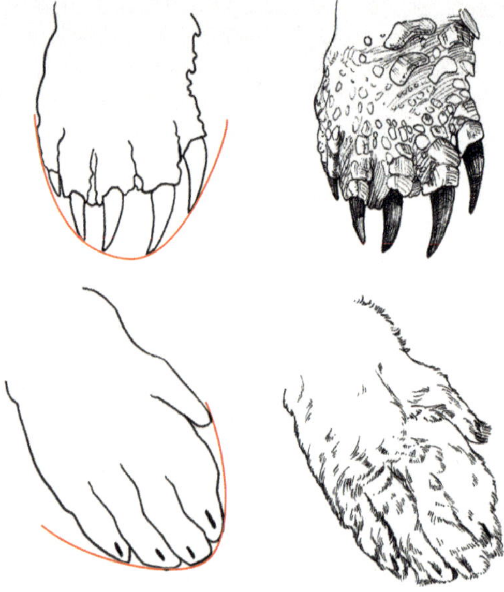

The paws, claws, hands and feet at the end of animals' limbs serve a multitude of purposes. Simplify the extremity into a series of 'landmarks' – the point at which the hand or foot pivots on a limb (the wrist and ankle of a human), the connected mass that follows it, the digits, and the claw or nail.

NOTICE THE ARC THAT JOINS THE TIPS OF THE TOES OR CLAWS OF YOUR SUBJECT

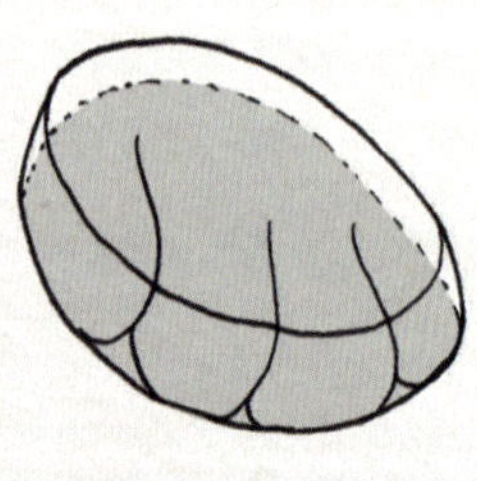

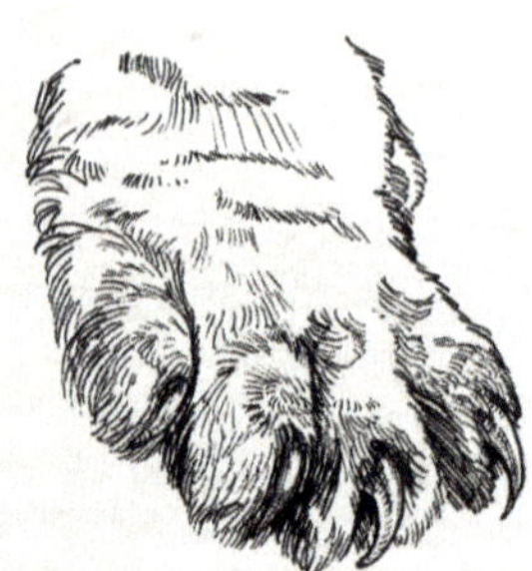

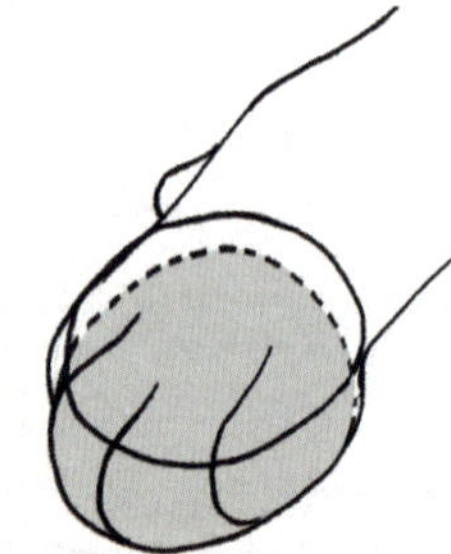

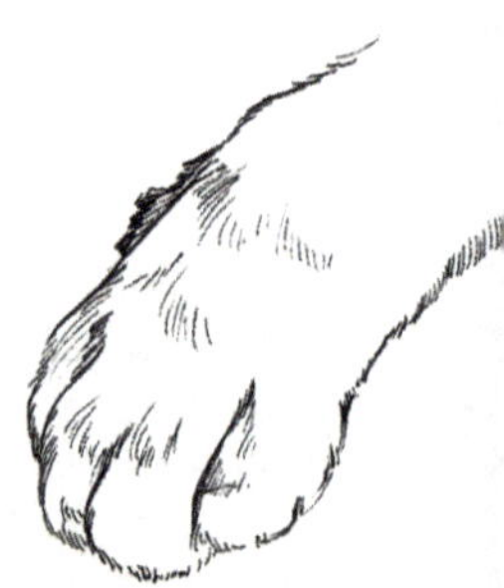

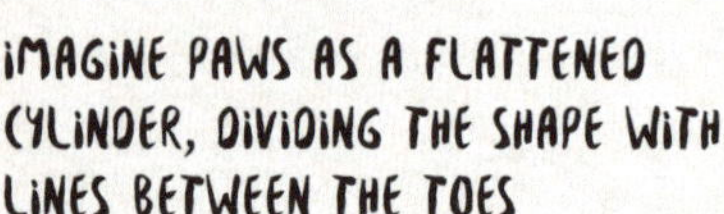

IMAGINE PAWS AS A FLATTENED CYLINDER, DIVIDING THE SHAPE WITH LINES BETWEEN THE TOES

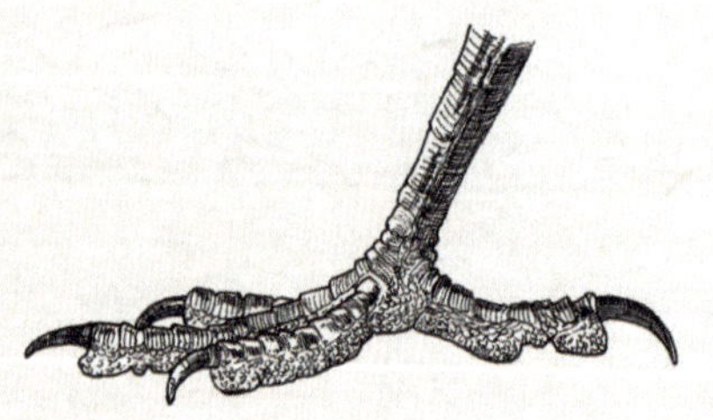

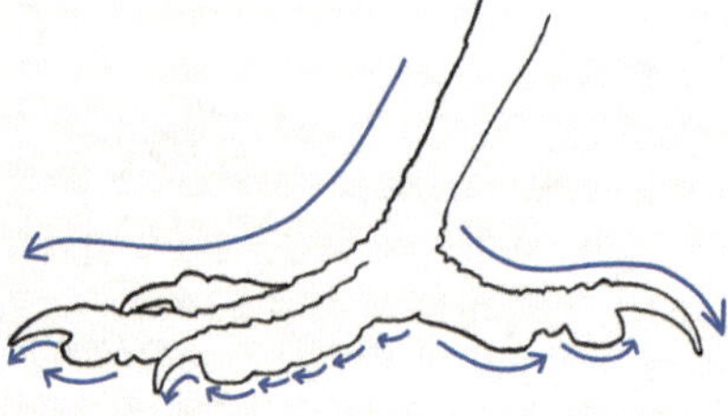

LOOK FOR THE RHYTHMS OF THE TOP AND BOTTOM OF TOES. THE JOINTS CREATE A STEP DOWN TO THE CLAW.

YELLOW – FOREARM
RED – PALM
BLUE – FINGERS

Amphibians, reptiles, mammals and birds have similar limbs, stretched out into different shapes. These forelimbs are (left to right) from a prairie dog, a horse and an iguana.

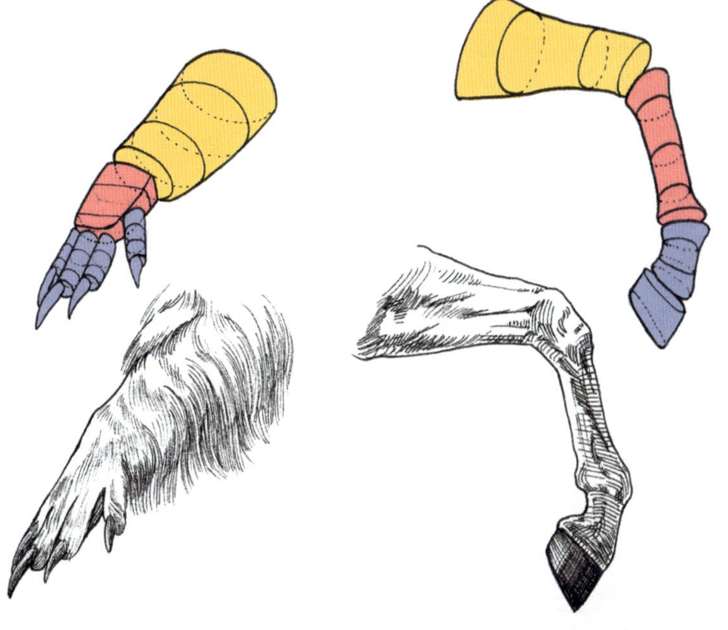

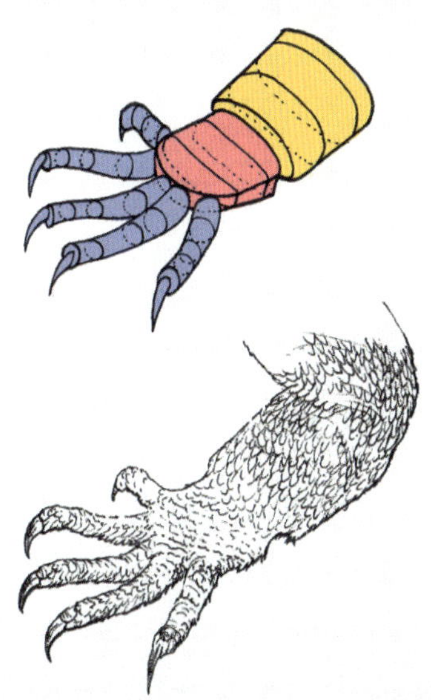

The foot starts at the ankle – the joint between the lower leg and the foot. In some animals, the bones of the foot are elongated – for example, in birds the ankle is halfway up the leg, while the knee and hip are hidden under feathers.

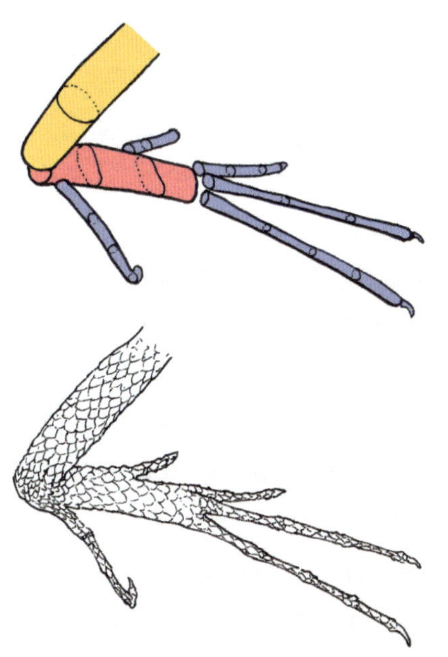

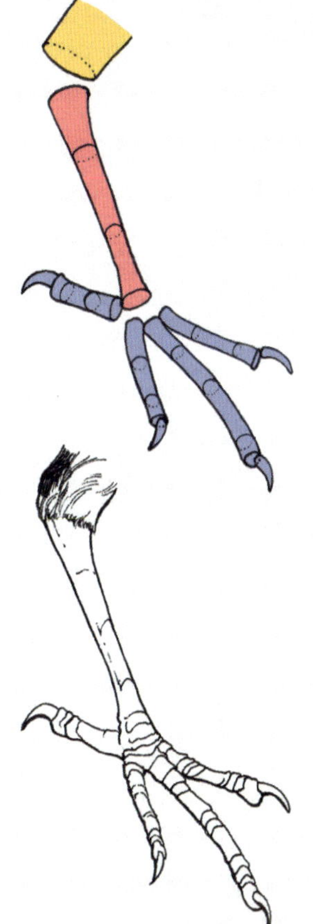

YELLOW – LOWER LEG
RED – FOOT
BLUE – TOES

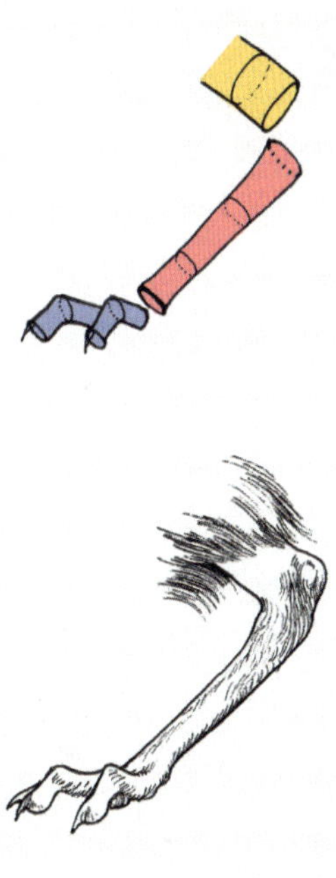

PART 02: STRUCTURES

SHELLS & CARAPACES

The hard shells of animals from snails to crabs to tortoises present clear, fixed forms. While they will still be subject to the visual distortions of foreshortening, they won't compact and bend in different poses. Interlocking armour plates on animals like armadillos or lobsters have a similar visual expression, sliding over one another as they move and change position.

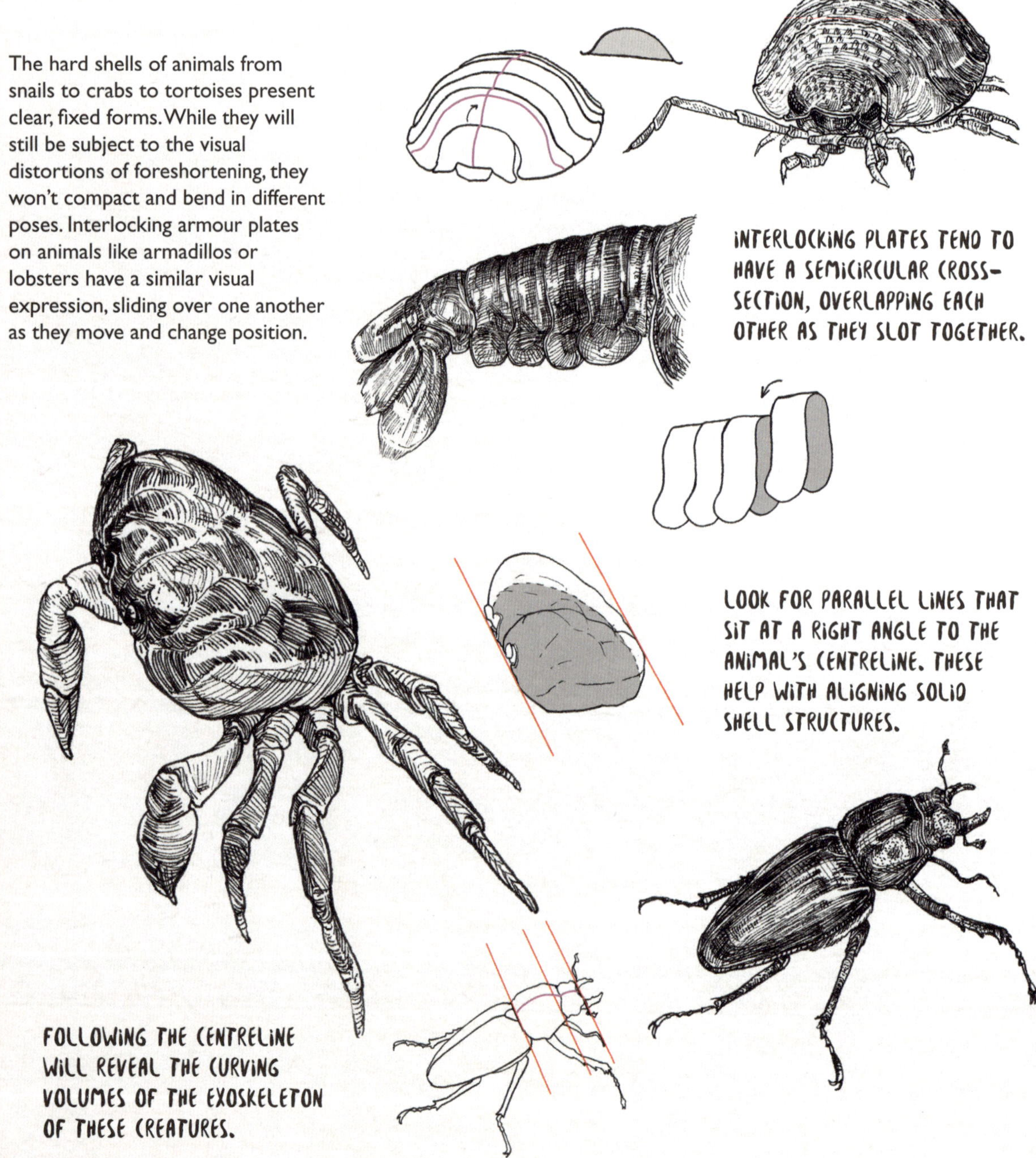

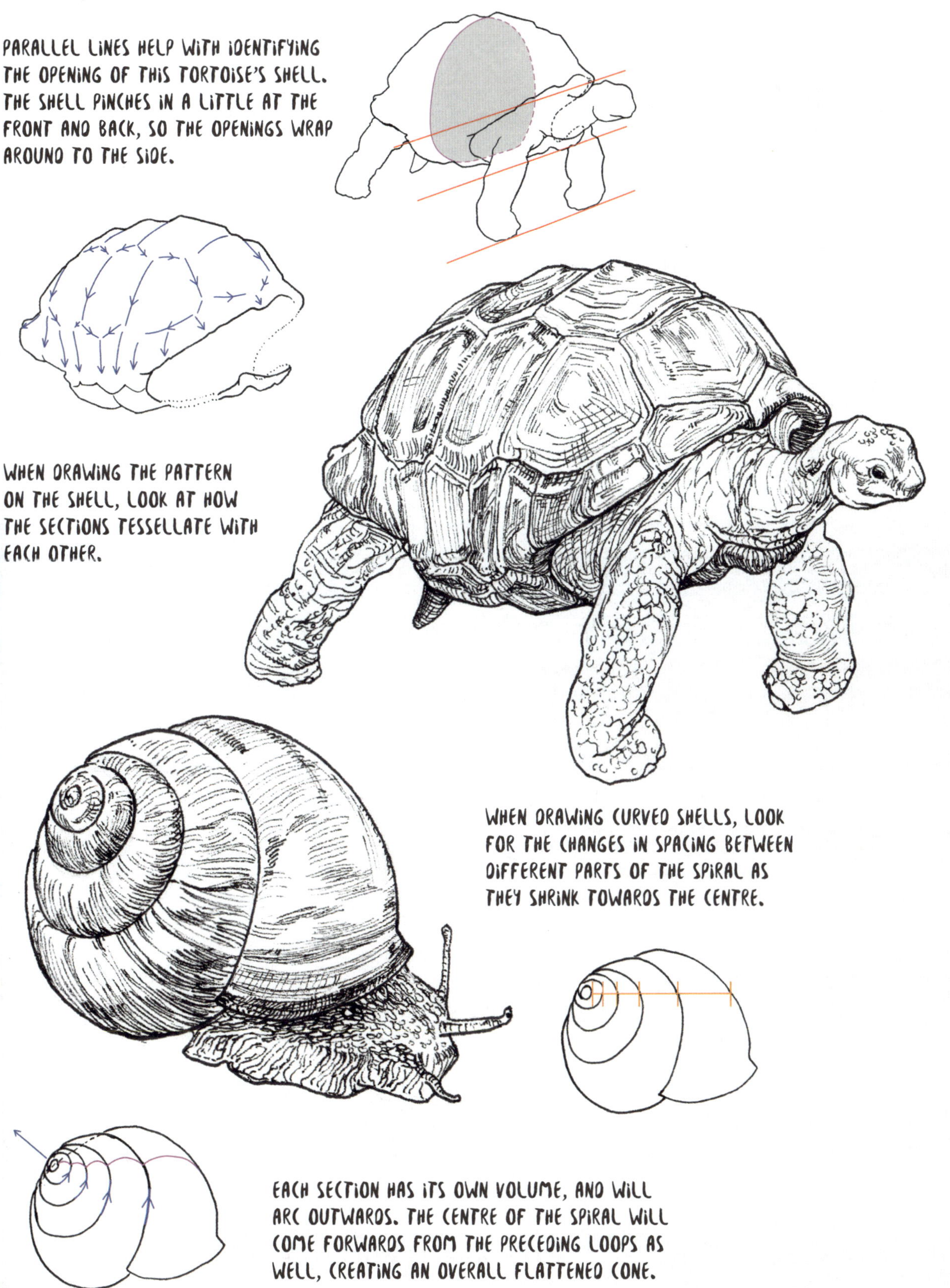
PARALLEL LINES HELP WITH IDENTIFYING THE OPENING OF THIS TORTOISE'S SHELL. THE SHELL PINCHES IN A LITTLE AT THE FRONT AND BACK, SO THE OPENINGS WRAP AROUND TO THE SIDE.
WHEN DRAWING THE PATTERN ON THE SHELL, LOOK AT HOW THE SECTIONS TESSELLATE WITH EACH OTHER.
WHEN DRAWING CURVED SHELLS, LOOK FOR THE CHANGES IN SPACING BETWEEN DIFFERENT PARTS OF THE SPIRAL AS THEY SHRINK TOWARDS THE CENTRE.
EACH SECTION HAS ITS OWN VOLUME, AND WILL ARC OUTWARDS. THE CENTRE OF THE SPIRAL WILL COME FORWARDS FROM THE PRECEDING LOOPS AS WELL, CREATING AN OVERALL FLATTENED CONE.

MAKE YOUR OWN NOTES ON
ANIMAL STRUCTURES HERE

PART 03

SURFACES

The luxurious tresses of a lion's mane and the characteristic pattern of a zebra's stripes illustrate how important textures and markings are in how we imagine animals. From fur to feathers and from scales to skin, the characteristics of those distinctive surfaces can be as important to your drawings as the structures that lie beneath them.

In this section, we'll explore some of the most prominent surfaces that you can encounter when you're drawing animals. Drawings don't need to be laboriously detailed to describe the surfaces of your subject, and a few well-placed, efficient marks can tell your eye enough about tone and texture for the viewer's brain to fill in the rest. Be inventive with your mark-making, borrow from the visual language of other artists (page 19), and experiment with your materials to create patterns that evoke the feel of different surfaces.

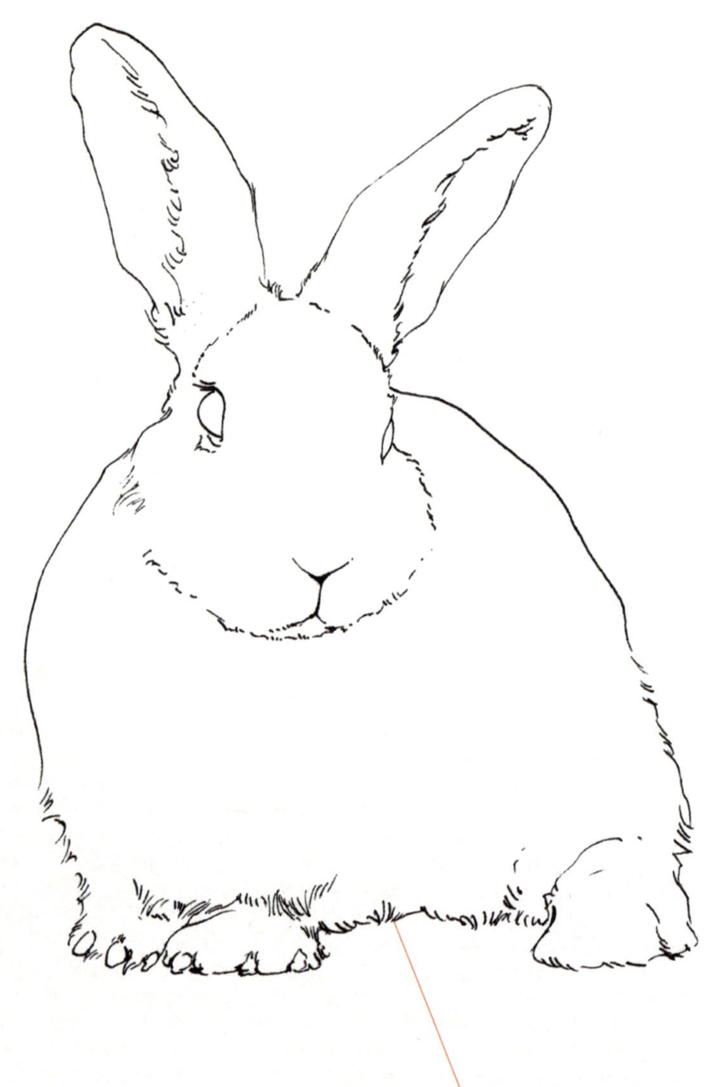

TEXTURAL CONTOUR DRAWINGS SUGGEST THE QUALITY OF THE SURFACE WITHIN THE CONTOUR WITHOUT NEEDING TO GO INTO FULL DETAIL

A SENSE OF TOUCH

Just as you brought your awareness of the physicality of an animal to weight and gesture, you must also bring your sense of touch to your studies of surface. Drawing is a tactile act, with the textures of your medium and surface feeding into the quality of marks that you make.

As you look at the surface of an animal's body, your own memories of touching similar surfaces will feed into the marks that you make, helping anybody who looks at your drawing to connect more directly with the subject you've drawn. It is this memory of physical connection that gives you an advantage over a camera or a computer program and allows you to make drawings that are more than just photographs.

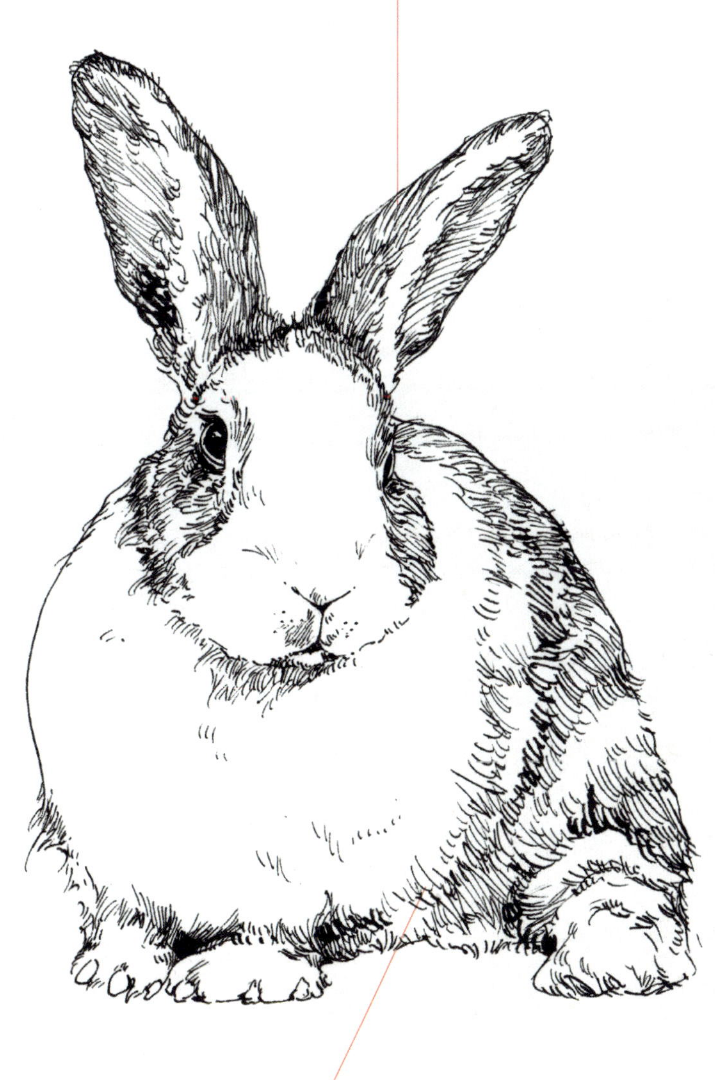

PART 03: SURFACES

HAPTIC DRAWING – EXERCISE

WHAT YOU NEED

- A pencil or pen
- A pet who likes being stroked

Our sense of touch contributes towards every drawing we make – both in the feedback we receive from the paper as our pencil makes contact with its surface, and the way in which our observation of fur, scales, skin and feathers elicits a memory of texture.

For this exercise you'll need a pet who likes to be stroked or held and a spot where you can comfortably balance a sketchbook, with one hand free to draw and the other to touch. Where you would usually use your eyes to perceive and your hand to draw, this exercise will require you to use one hand to gather information and the other to respond to it; you needn't look at your paper as you draw.

Start with whatever contact your pet most enjoys – a belly rub or a tickle behind the ears – and as you stoke them make abstract marks on the page which record the tactile experience of the textures that you feel. If their hair is short and smooth, you might explore short dashes on the paper. Dense curls might require whirling marks, while long wisps encourage a lighter touch on the page. The rough pads of paws or scaly skin might require dots or circles, while smooth claws call for sharp marks. Gently notice the resistance of bone and muscle beneath the surface of your pet's skin and find marks which communicate the feeling of those forms.

The drawing should end once your subject has had enough and chooses to leave. The drawing left behind will contain unexpected, abstracted marks which you can then use to inform the visual vocabulary of future observational drawings.

Variation

If you don't have an animal nearby to draw, be your own subject, making a self-portrait by touch alone.

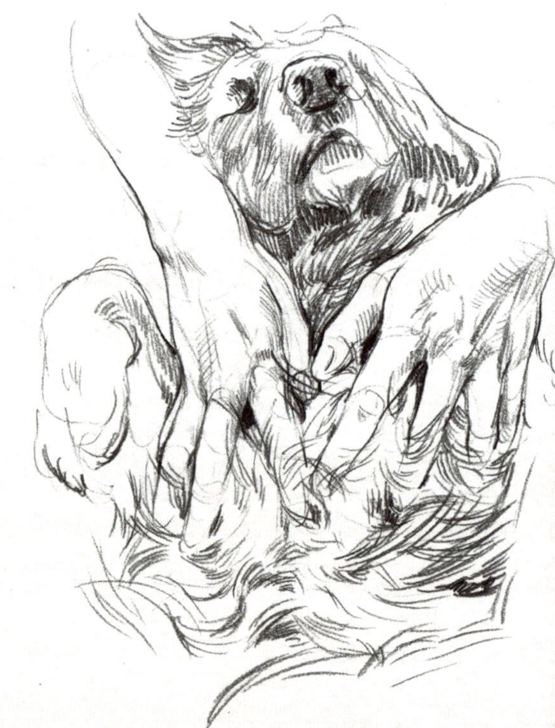

MARKS MADE BY TOUCH ALONE

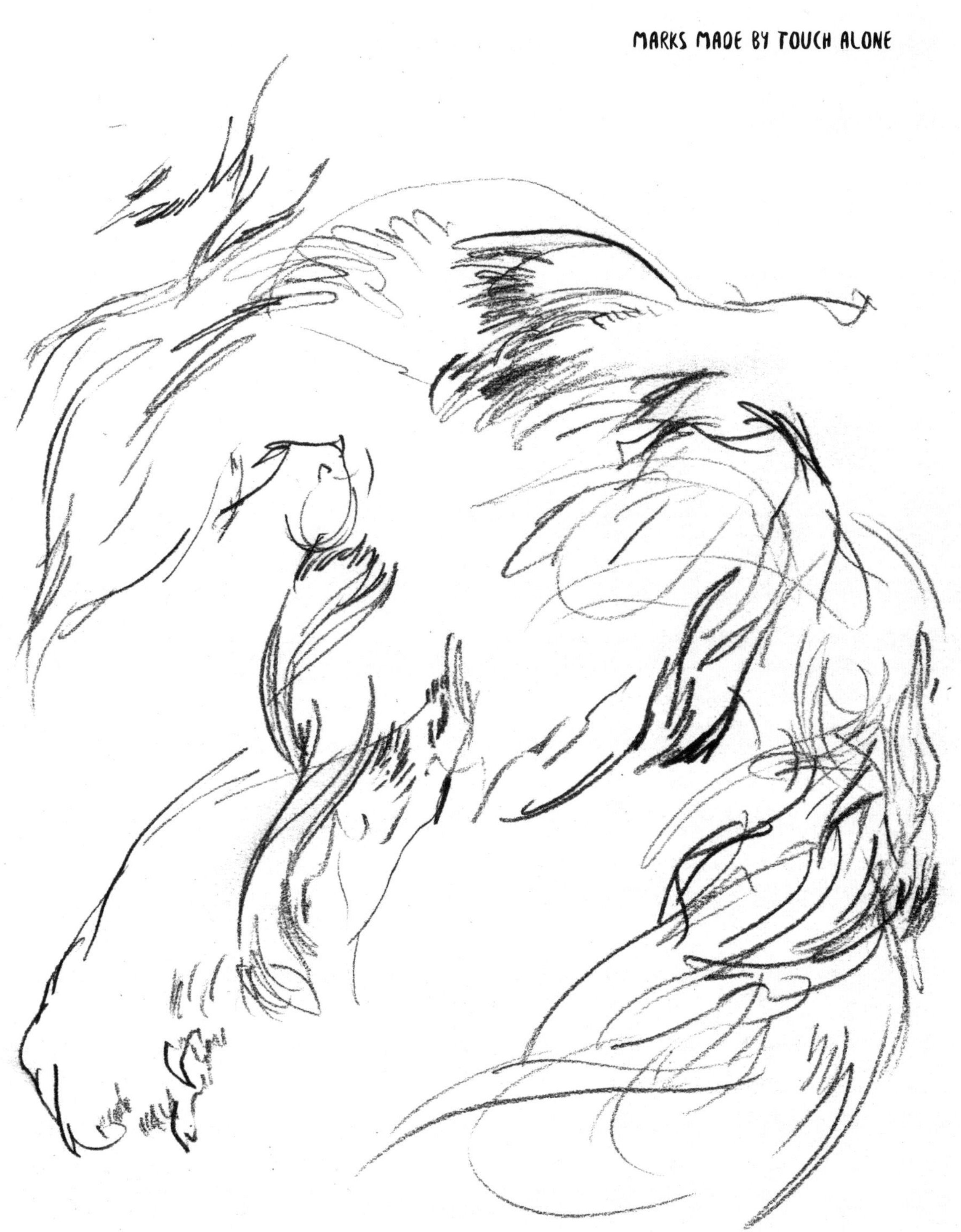

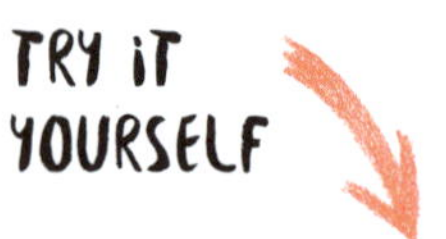
TRY IT
YOURSELF

PART 03: SURFACES

SKIN

The shadows and highlights on the surface of skin readily express the shape of underlying anatomy. The animal world presents us with a range of skin far beyond that of humans – from transparent to leathery, thin to thick, and smooth to heavily textured. To draw skin well you must become sensitive to the textures of its surface and how it creases, folds and hangs in different poses.

As the drawings on the right show, skin varies from animal to animal, with the elephant and babirusa having fine lines and wrinkles, while the frog skin is more bumpy. The babirusa shows an example of hanging skin folds. While these animals have different skin textures, these can be conveyed in your drawing using a similar process.

First, draw out the shape of the creases which define the major folds of the skin. Add some tone to help suggest volume. Next, add the secondary creases in the skin, before elaborating on the finest textures that you can see.

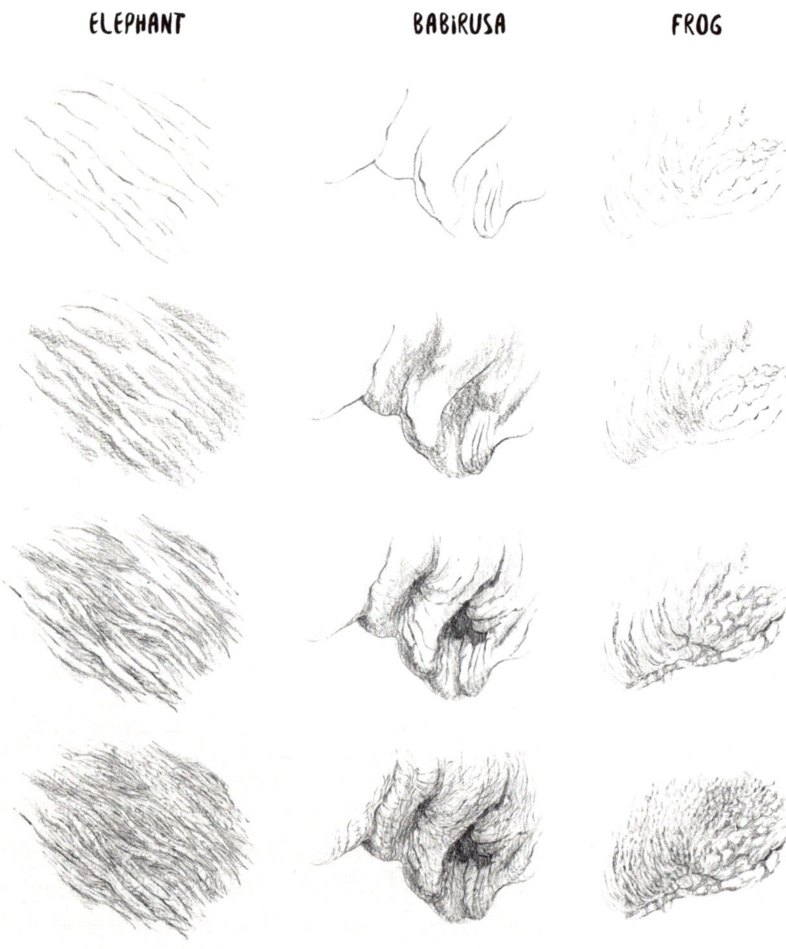

Think about the fabrics we wear as analogous to different animal skins. The thick skin of a rhino forms large, bunched folds around the neck and shoulders, like the stiff folds of a leather jacket.

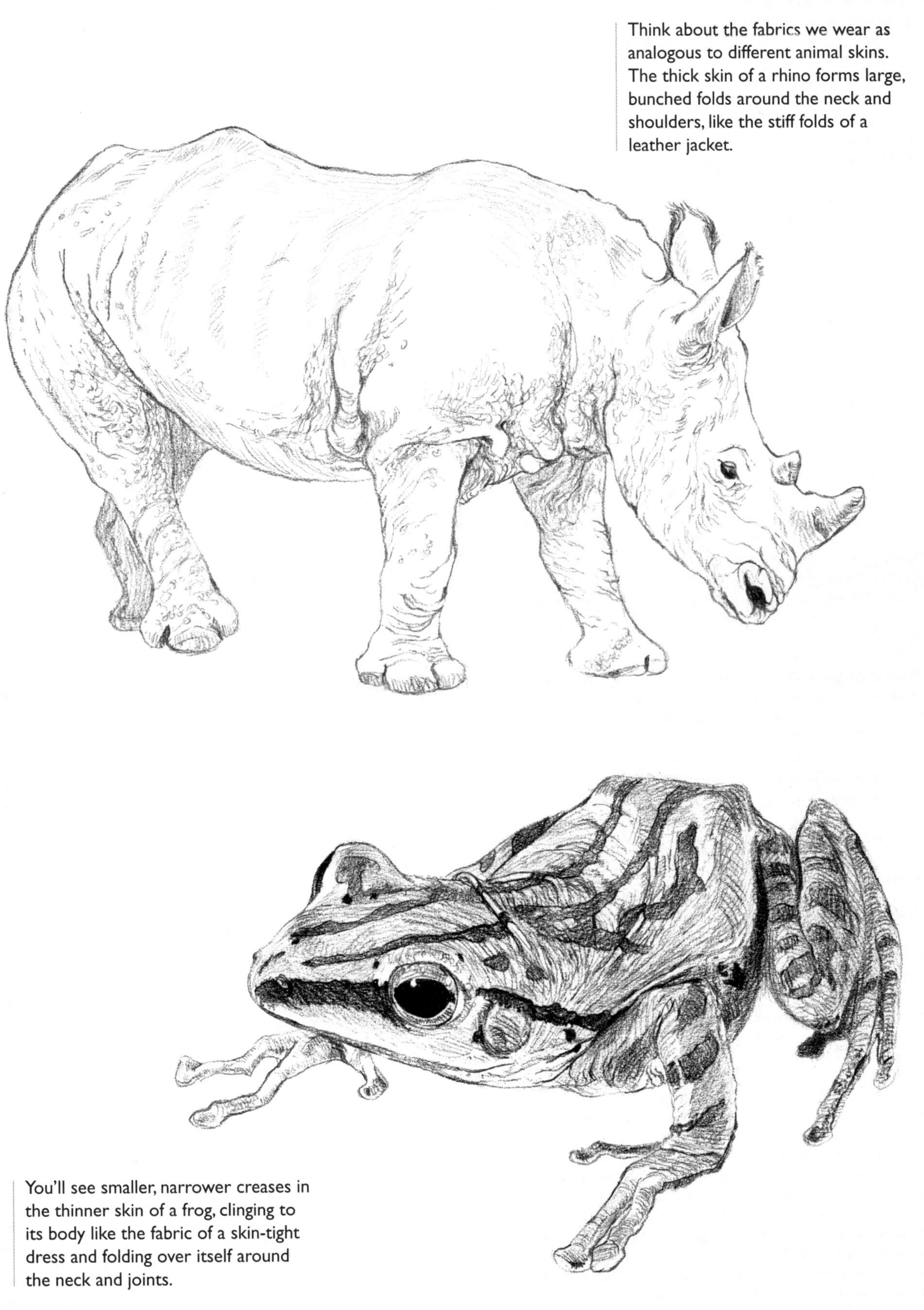

You'll see smaller, narrower creases in the thinner skin of a frog, clinging to its body like the fabric of a skin-tight dress and folding over itself around the neck and joints.

PART 03: SURFACES

SCALES

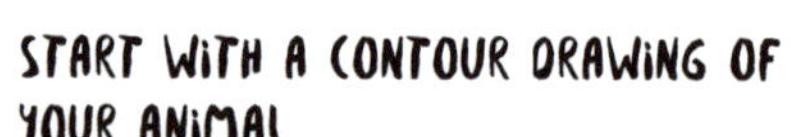

START WITH A CONTOUR DRAWING OF YOUR ANIMAL

Macroscopic scales create tessellating patterns on the surfaces of an animal's body, forming interlocking textures that can be represented in full, or implied with a few well-placed marks. Rows of scales that follow the cross-contours of the body can tell the viewer something about the form of the body, while markings are often expressed as a mosaic of scales in different colours and tones.

Each of the animals on the right has very different scales, but we can use a similar process to draw them. It is fine to simplify or skip some scales as long as the ones you do include follow the lines that wrap around your subject.

SKETCH OUT LIGHT LINES TO MAP THE DIRECTION OF GROUPS OF SCALES

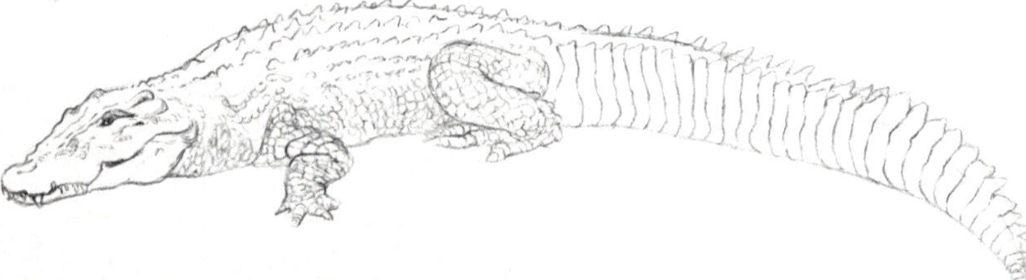

ADD SCALE SHAPES, FOLLOWING THE FLOW OF THOSE WRAPPING LINES

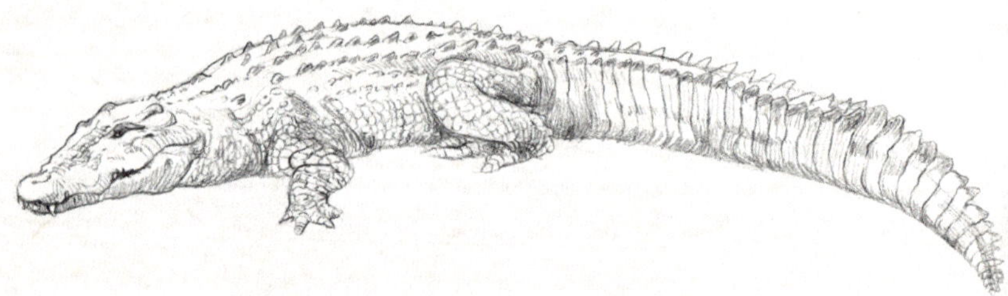

FINALLY, ADD TONE TO SUGGEST MARKINGS AND SHADOW PATTERNS

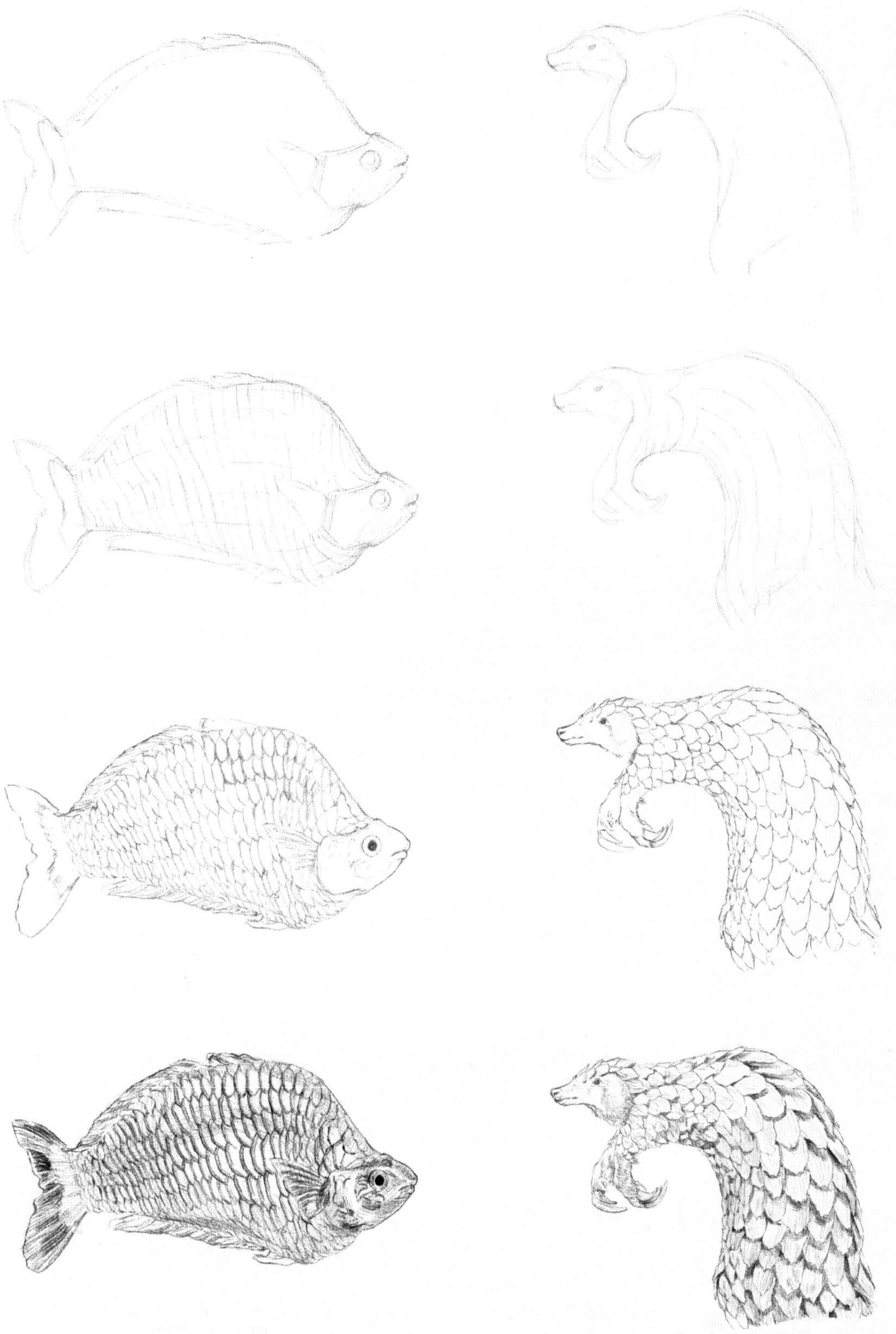

PART 03: SURFACES

FEATHERS

Individual feathers are beautiful objects in their own right, but it is their contribution to the whole that is most important to their expression on birds. Varying shapes of visually distinct wing feathers perform different roles in flight, while a build-up of smaller, softer feathers adds volume to the body.

The key to a successful drawing of a wing is to start with larger shapes, and break those shapes down into smaller groups of similar feathers. You'll find more examples of wing drawings on page 83.

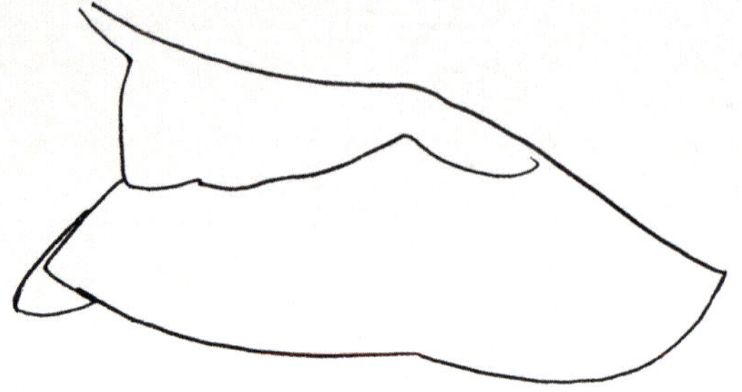

START WITH THE OVERALL SHAPE OF A WING

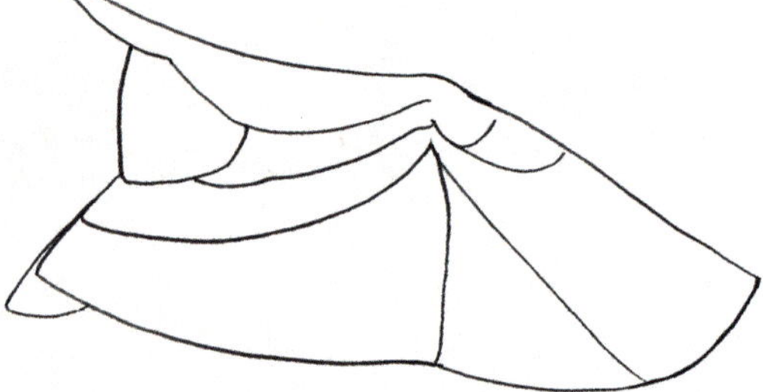

BREAK THE SHAPE DOWN INTO GROUPS OF SIMILAR FEATHERS

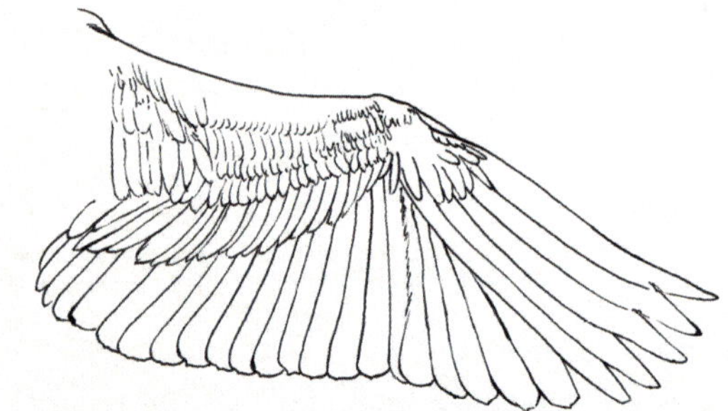

DRAW IN THE CONTOURS OF THE FEATHERS IN EACH GROUP

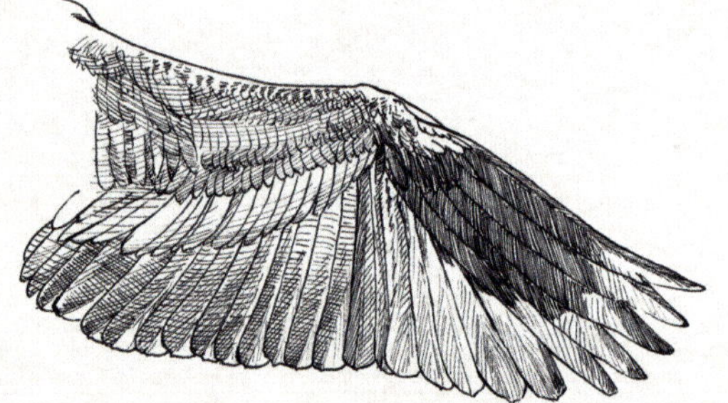

ADD FURTHER TONE AND TEXTURE TO THE FEATHERS

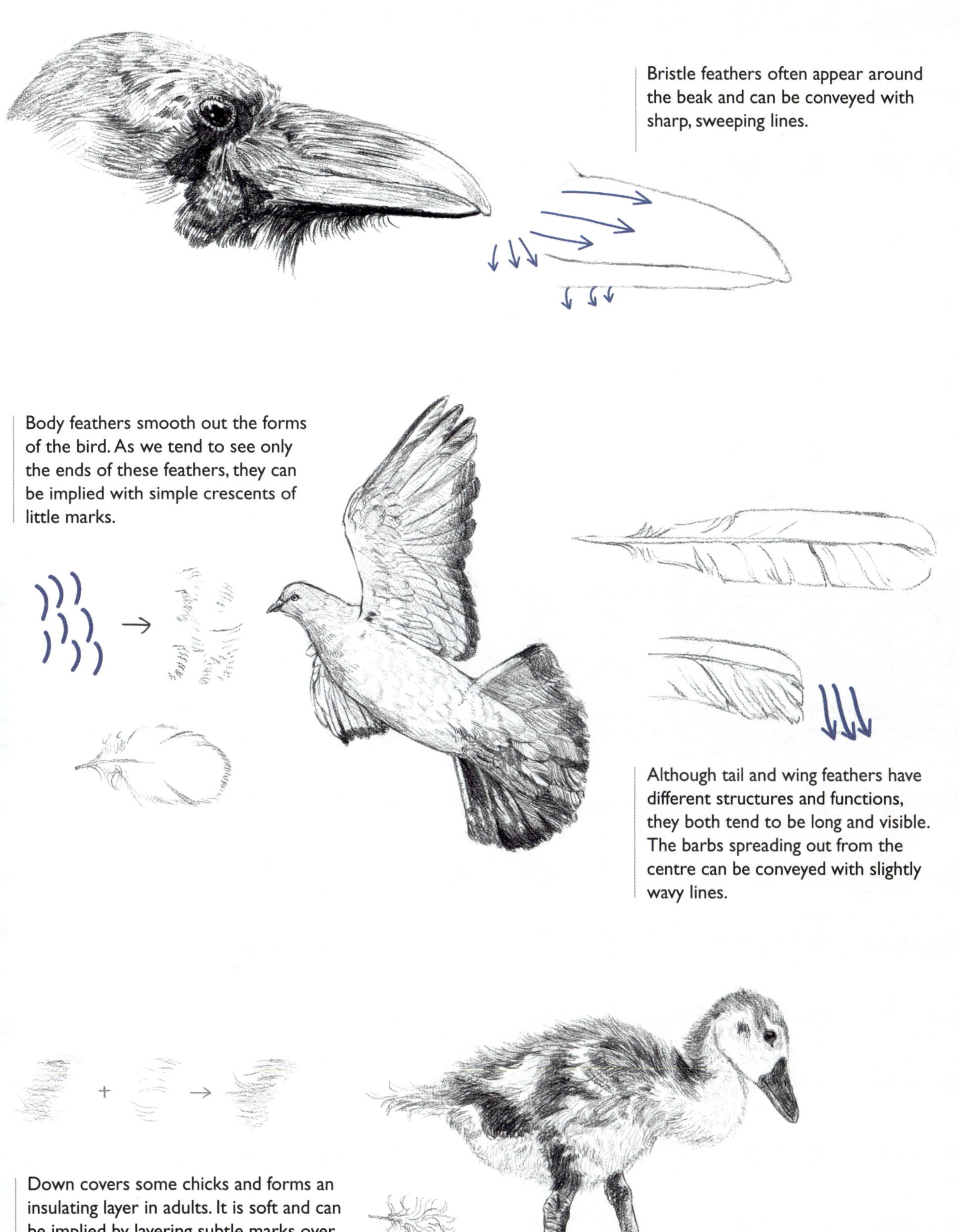

Bristle feathers often appear around the beak and can be conveyed with sharp, sweeping lines.

Body feathers smooth out the forms of the bird. As we tend to see only the ends of these feathers, they can be implied with simple crescents of little marks.

Although tail and wing feathers have different structures and functions, they both tend to be long and visible. The barbs spreading out from the centre can be conveyed with slightly wavy lines.

Down covers some chicks and forms an insulating layer in adults. It is soft and can be implied by layering subtle marks over tone. Pay special attention to how soft the outline is.

PART 03: SURFACES

FUR & WOOL

The way that hair expresses itself on an animal varies depending on how long it is, how coarse or soft it is, and whether it curls along its length. While it is tempting to try to draw every hair, it is the overall volume of the hair and the way it gathers in flows and clumps that is often most important at a distance.

Marks that mimic the length and direction of the hairs that make up the fur of your subject can be used to break up the contour of the animal you are drawing, or to efficiently show tone and texture at the same time. Make your marks in the direction you would stroke an animal's fur, and vary the length of your mark depending on whether your subject has short or long hair.

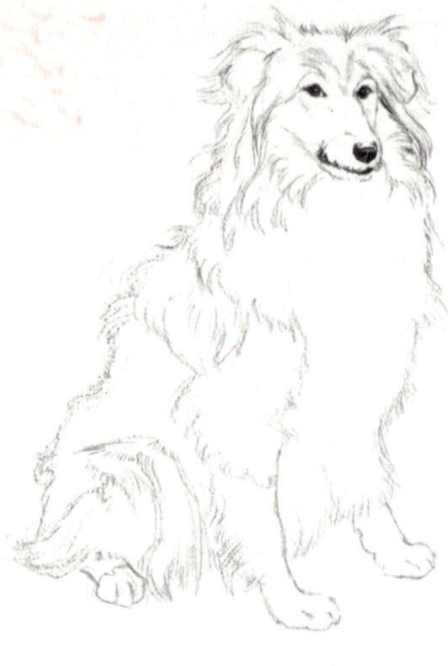

BROKEN CONTOURS SUGGEST FUR TEXTURE

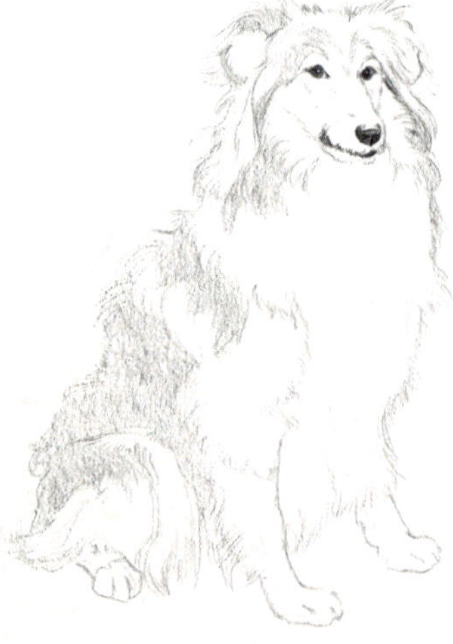

SIMPLE, TONAL SHAPES PROVIDE A FOUNDATION FOR MARKINGS

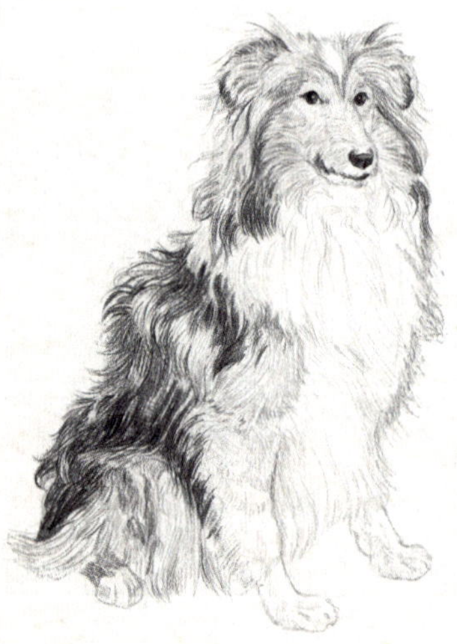

HEAVIER TEXTURAL MARKS CAN DESCRIBE TONE AND FUR TEXTURE AT ONCE

Wool readily clumps together and will often be defined by the shadow shapes between the clumps rather than the character of individual hairs. Viewed side on, it can often be seen as tufts that stand out from the boundary of the animal. As the form of the animal turns towards us, viewed end-on, the wool tends to have a more rounded, bobbled appearance.

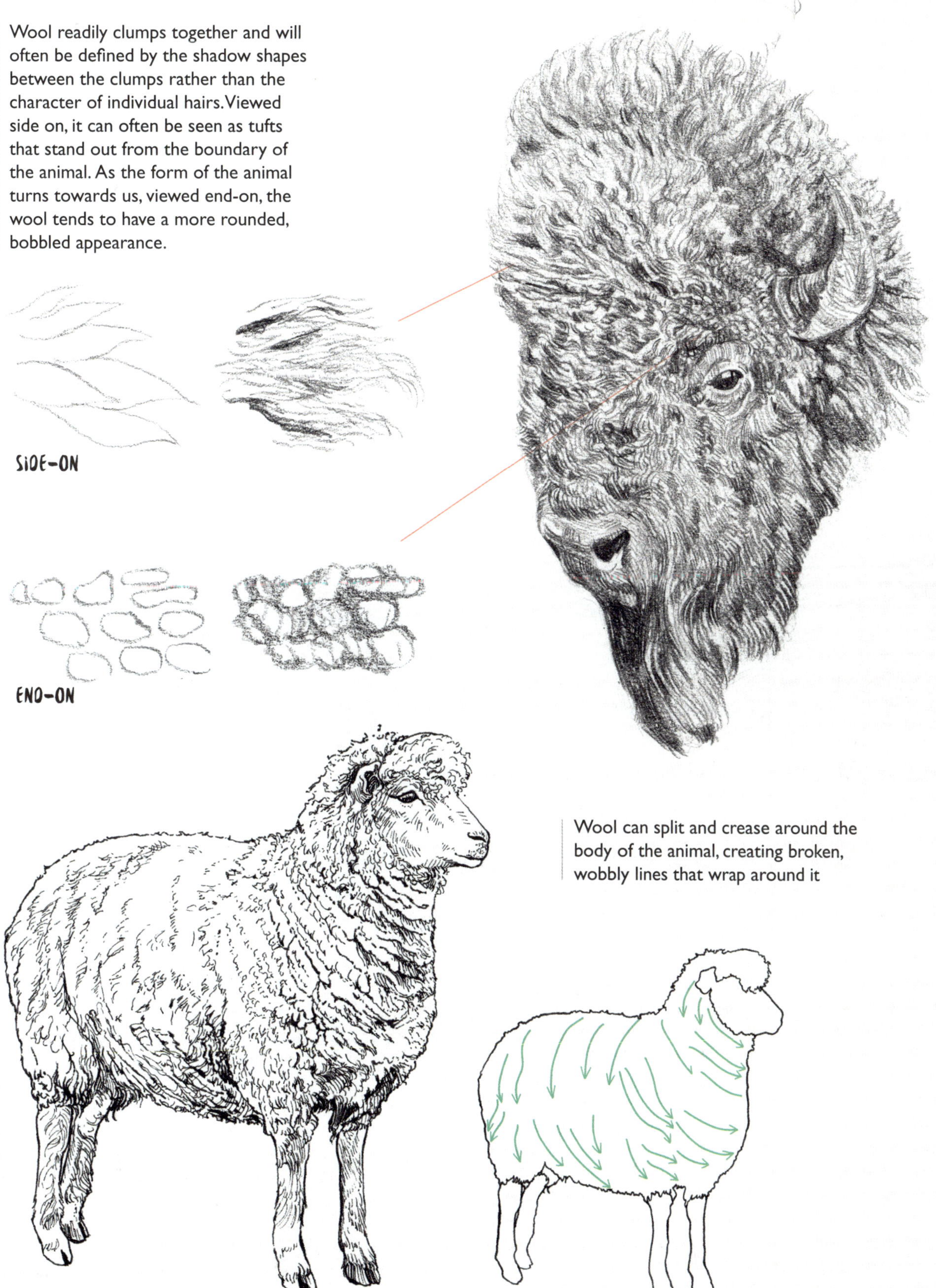

Wool can split and crease around the body of the animal, creating broken, wobbly lines that wrap around it

PART 03: SURFACES

SURFACE STUDIES – EXERCISE

WHAT YOU NEED

- A high-resolution image of an animal
- Your preferred drawing medium

Observational studies of isolated textures will help to inform the marks you make in a sustained study as well as informing the more minimal marks you might pick in brisker, more intuitive drawing exercises.

Take a high-resolution image and crop in to show an isolated square of surface. Make an observational study of that section within one of the boxes opposite, filling the boxes with other textures that you find elsewhere in the body of the same animal. Be playful with your mark-making and aim to find the most interesting and efficient ways of representing the surfaces you can see.

Variation
Copy an isolated section of another artist's work to borrow from their marks.

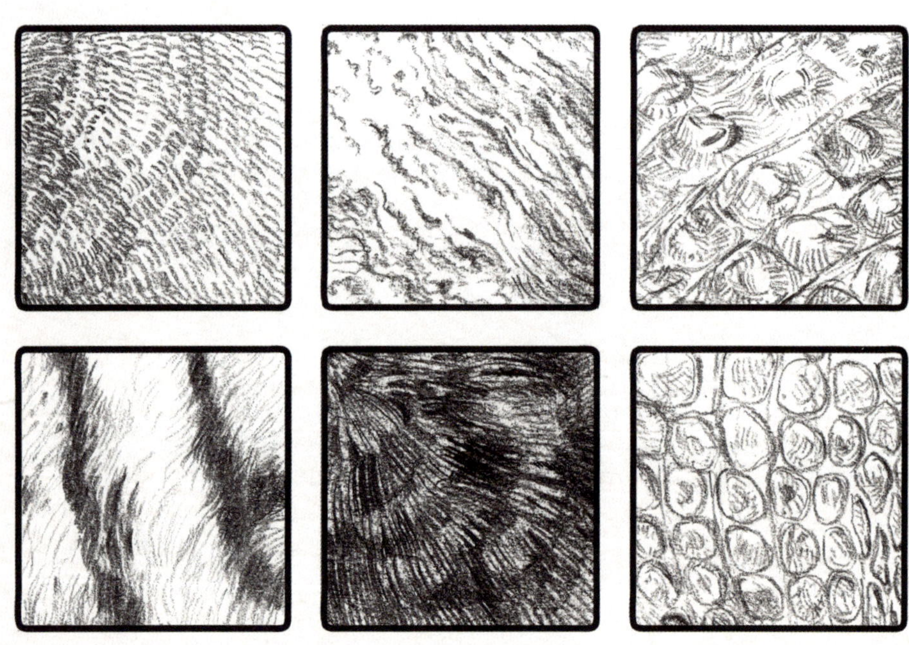

SPINES

While long hairs flow over and help to shape the surface of an animal's body, spines are more rigid, sticking out from its skin. Find marks which communicate a sense of sharpness when you're drawing a mass of spines, and steer clear of the exercise on page 118!

There's no need to draw every single spine on spiky subject. In this drawing of a puffer fish, spines stick out from the body to indicate the overall texture, while hatching follows the cross-contours of the body, indicating the form of the fish and preventing the texture taking on a 'scribbly' look.

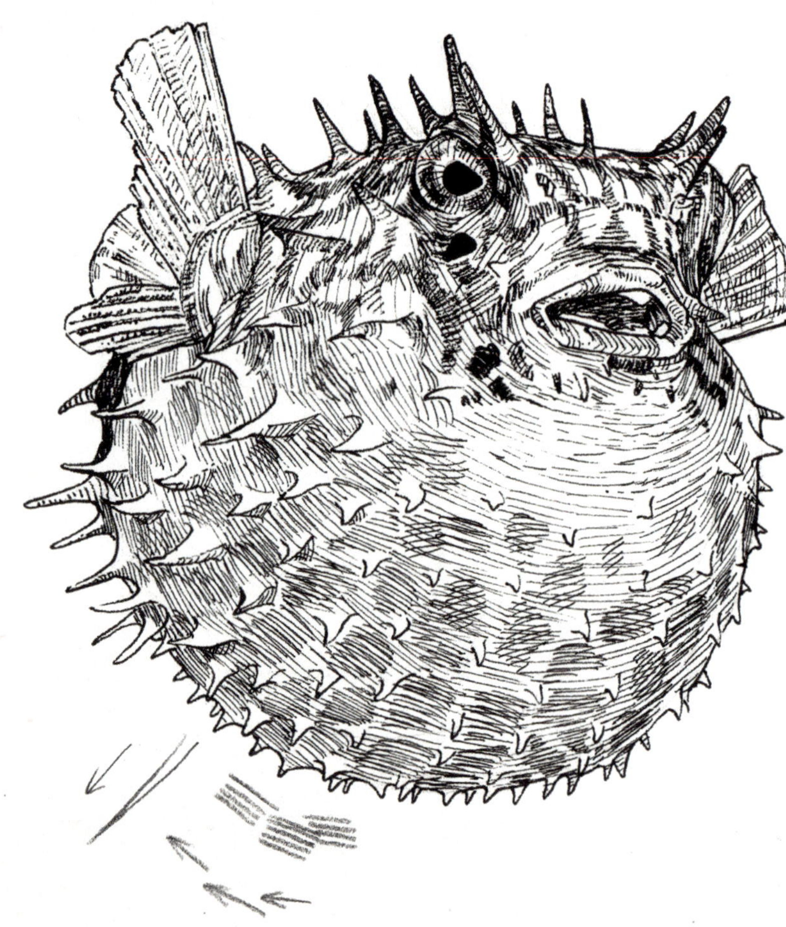

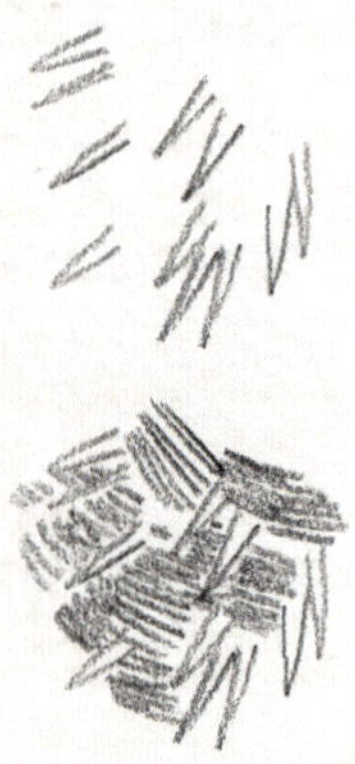

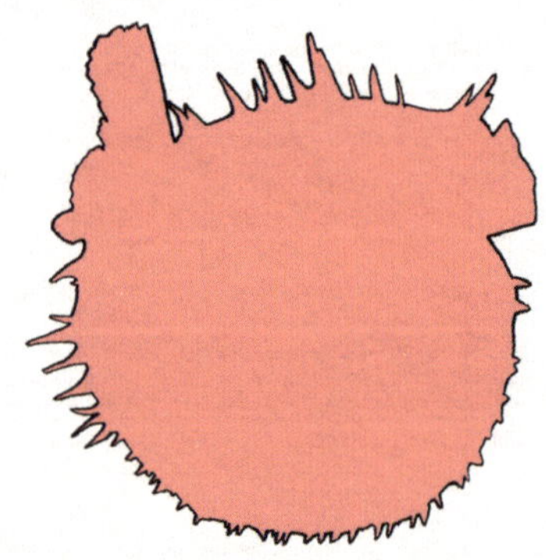

Be especially mindful of the silhouette, as this goes a long way in indicating a spiky texture.

Spines pointing directly at us appear end on, or as very tiny points, with more shadow between them. As the form of the animal turns away from us, we see them more side-on with less shadow.

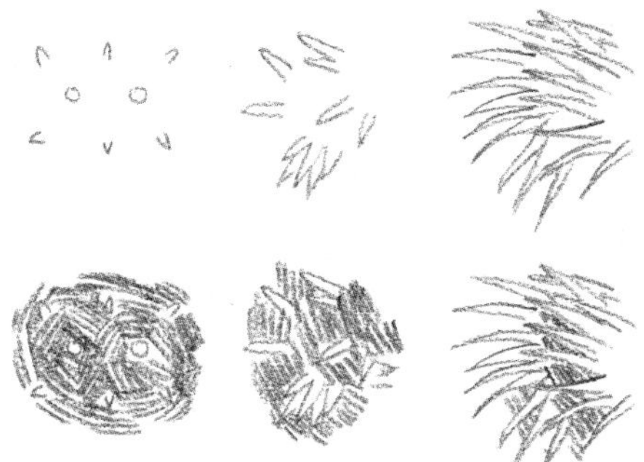

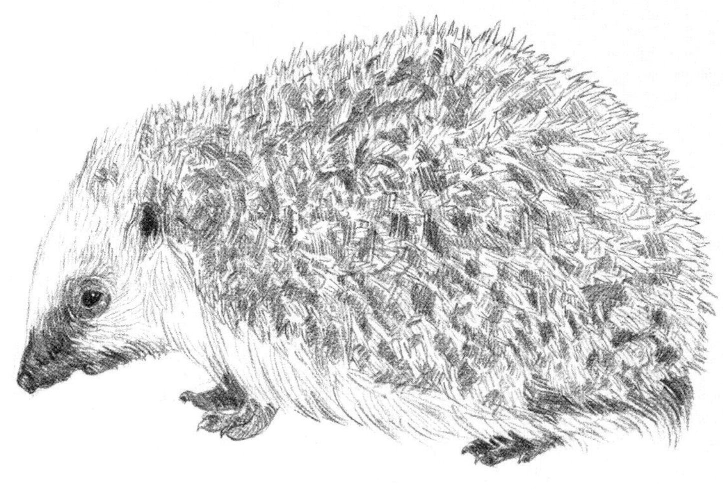

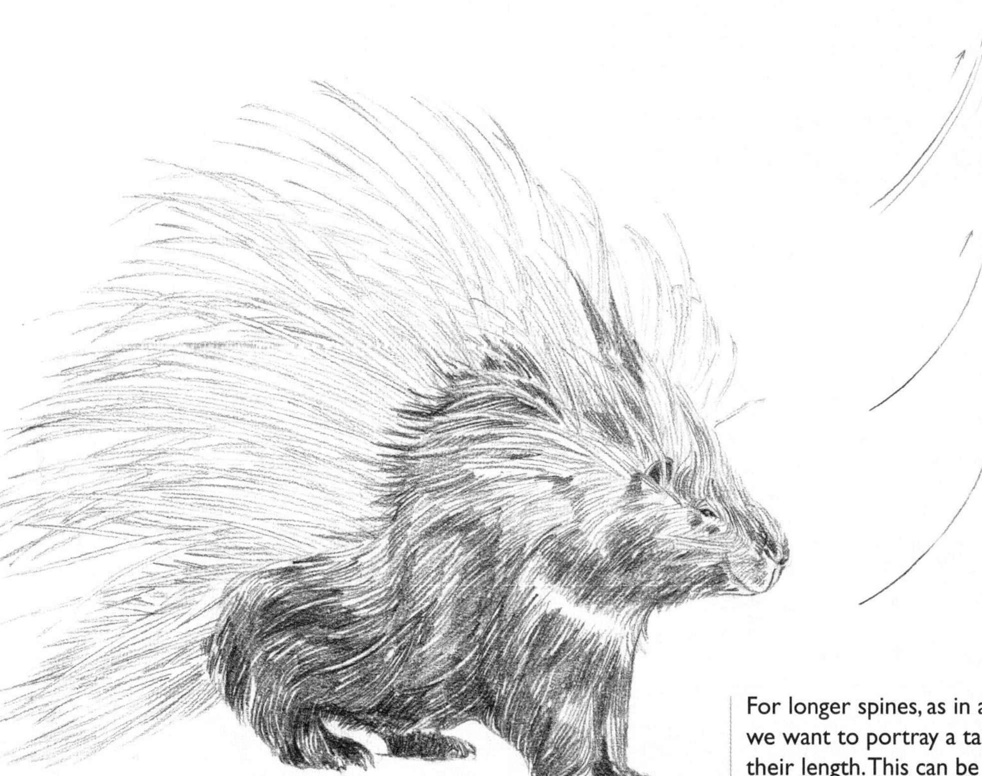

For longer spines, as in a porcupine, we want to portray a tapering down their length. This can be achieved by letting the shape of the spine taper, but also by controlling the line quality. The thickness of the line can narrow down its length. Very fine tips might also be indicated with broken lines.

PART 03: SURFACES

REFLECTIVE SURFACES

Whether you're looking at wet eyes or silvery scales, shiny surfaces reflect light. Reflected light must be communicated by contrast, so that the bright light of the reflection sits in a darker context. This might mean working on a darker paper with a light medium, leaving white paper behind as you draw around it, or erasing light back into charcoal or graphite.

The highlights on this fish were added in white gouache paint, which sits on top of the pencil. Try experimenting on scrap paper before adding highlights to a drawing.

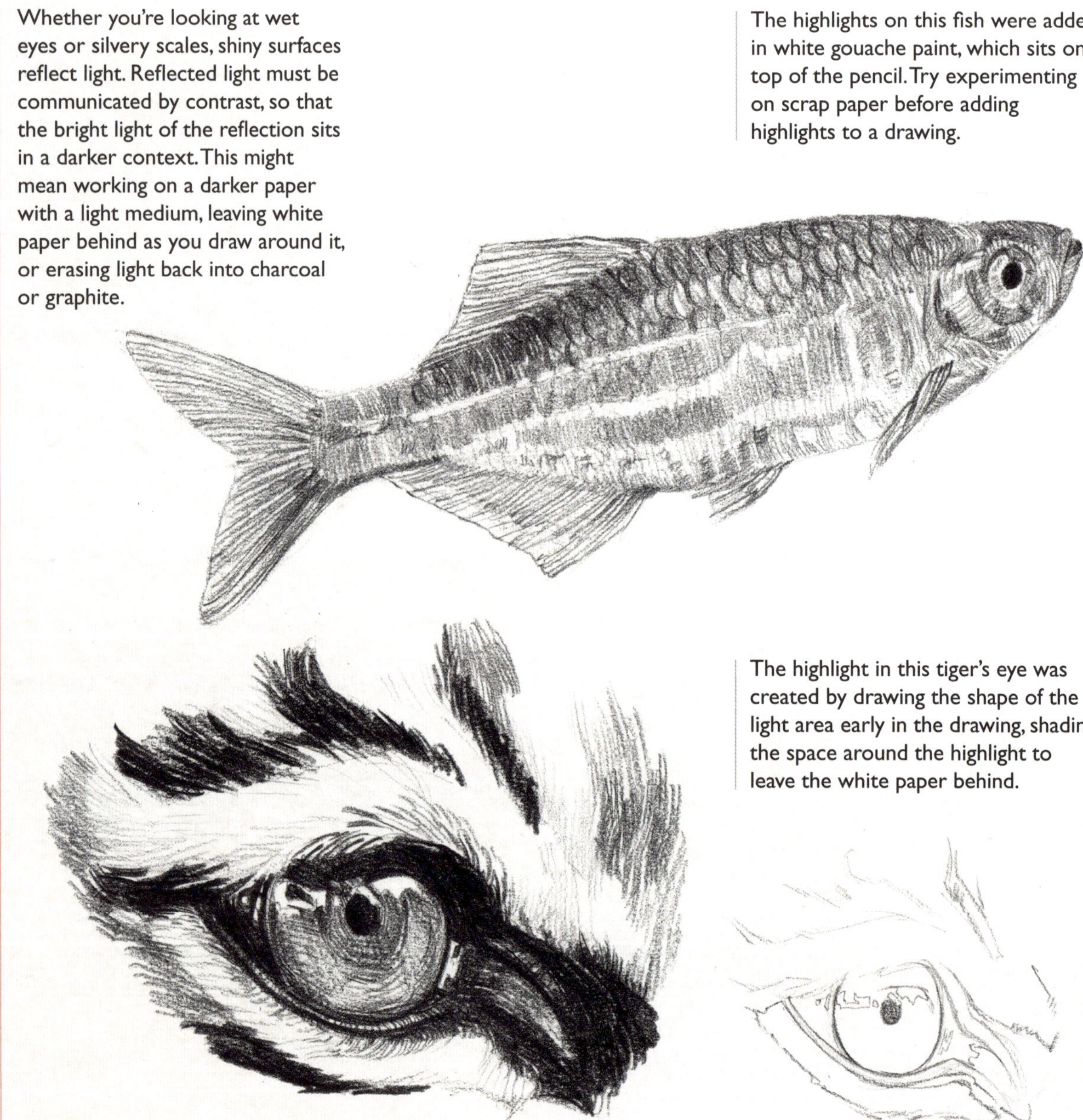

The highlight in this tiger's eye was created by drawing the shape of the light area early in the drawing, shading the space around the highlight to leave the white paper behind.

This dolphin has highlights added in by erasing away the charcoal. Putty erasers produce softer, broad marks, while an electric eraser can pick out the details.

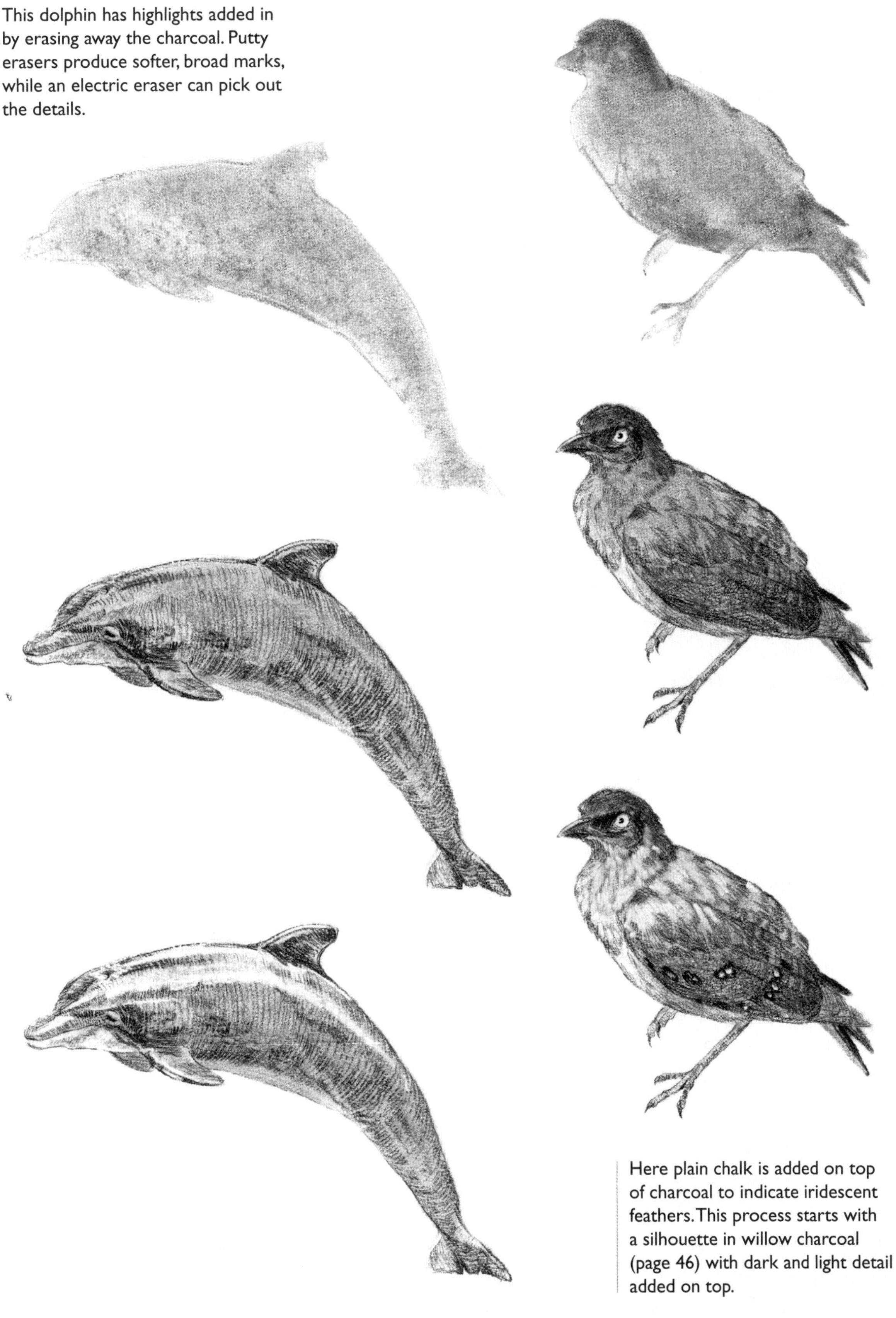

Here plain chalk is added on top of charcoal to indicate iridescent feathers. This process starts with a silhouette in willow charcoal (page 46) with dark and light detail added on top.

PART 03: SURFACES

PATTERNS & MARKINGS

The individual markings on an animal are key to achieving a likeness. If you are repeatedly returning to the same subject, you might want to map their markings onto a line drawing as a supporting study to remind you of their patterning when making further drawings.

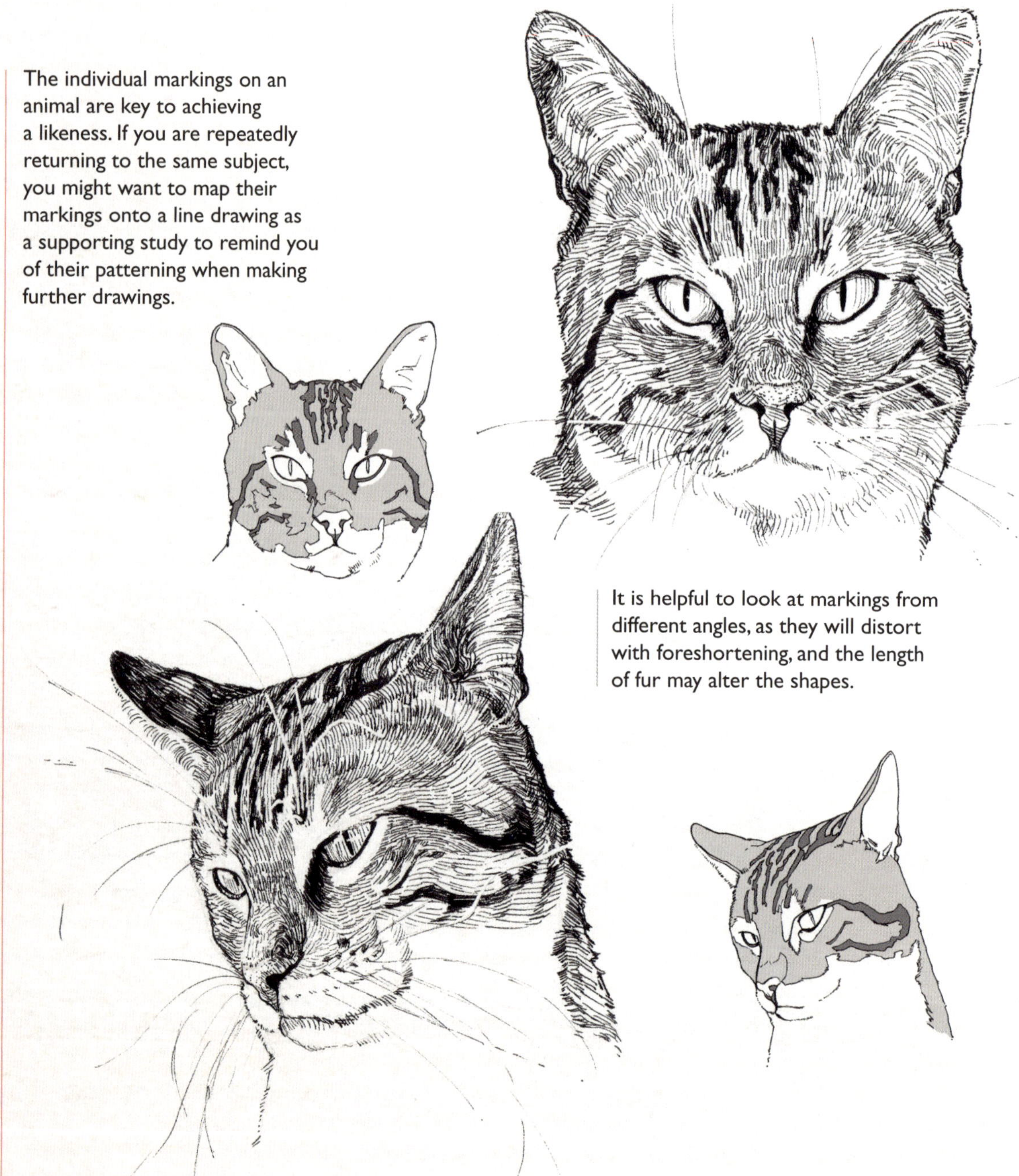

It is helpful to look at markings from different angles, as they will distort with foreshortening, and the length of fur may alter the shapes.

Observing the negative spaces (page 44) between the pattern shapes can help with positioning them.

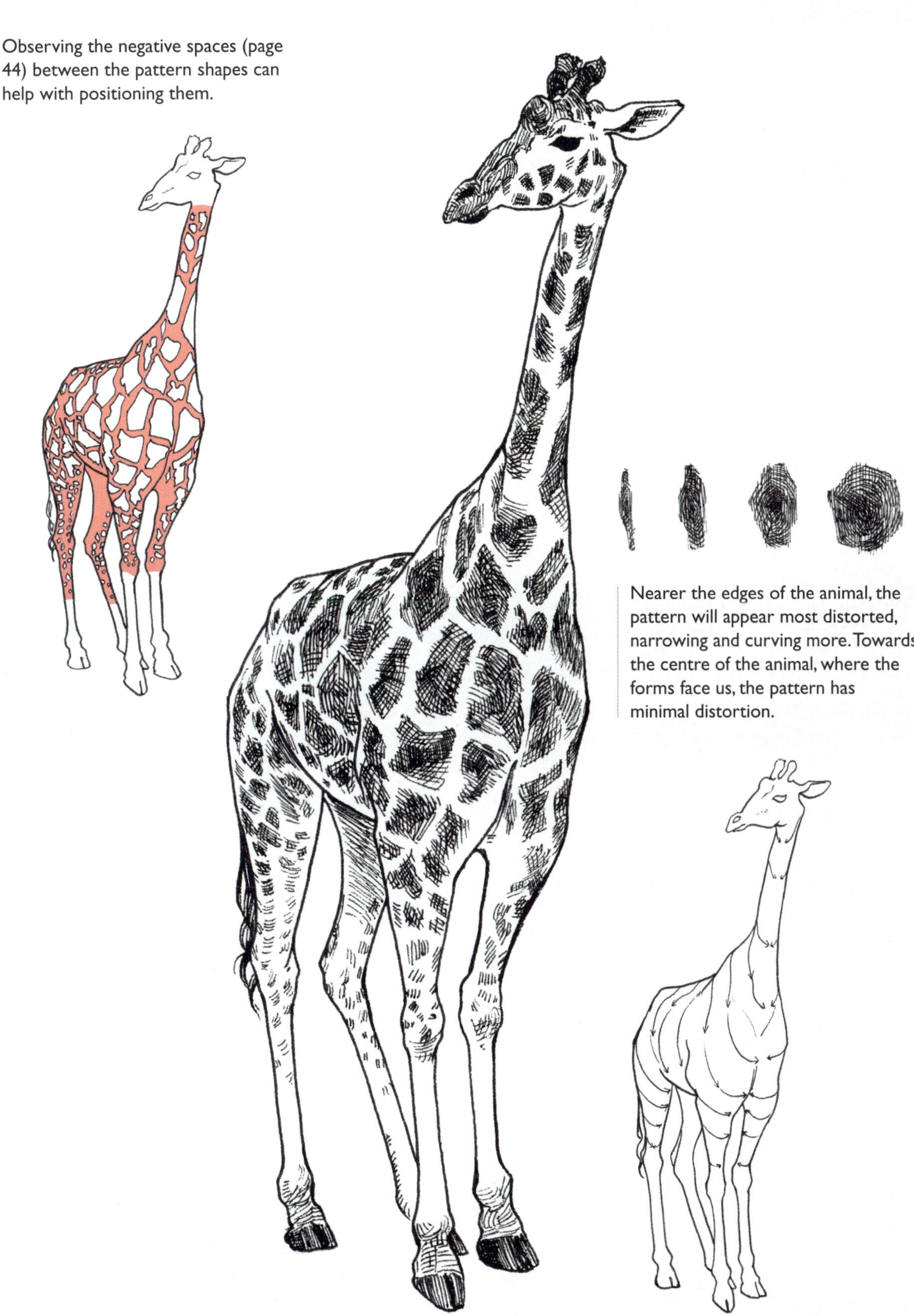

Nearer the edges of the animal, the pattern will appear most distorted, narrowing and curving more. Towards the centre of the animal, where the forms face us, the pattern has minimal distortion.

PART 03: SURFACES

A COMPLETE PROCESS (ii)

This page picks up from the process described on page 60, further elaborating on the surfaces of your subject and incorporating some of the ideas from Part 03 into a single, practical observational process.

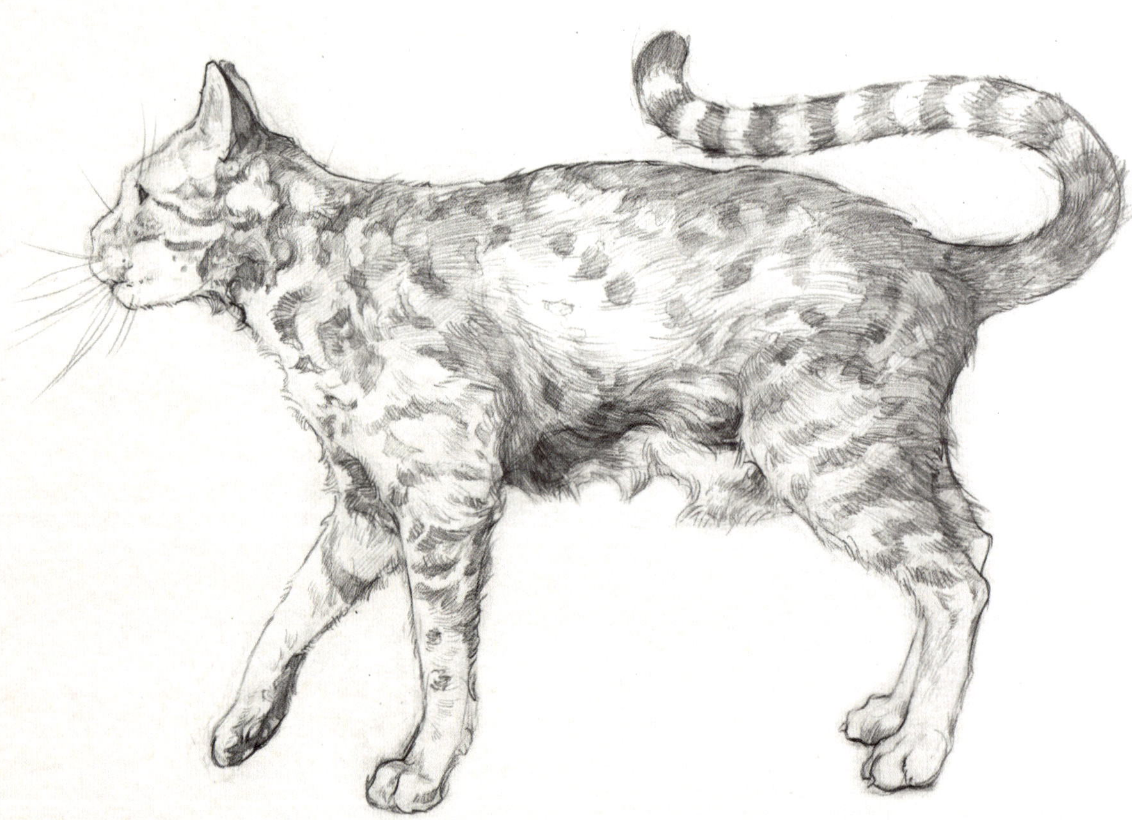

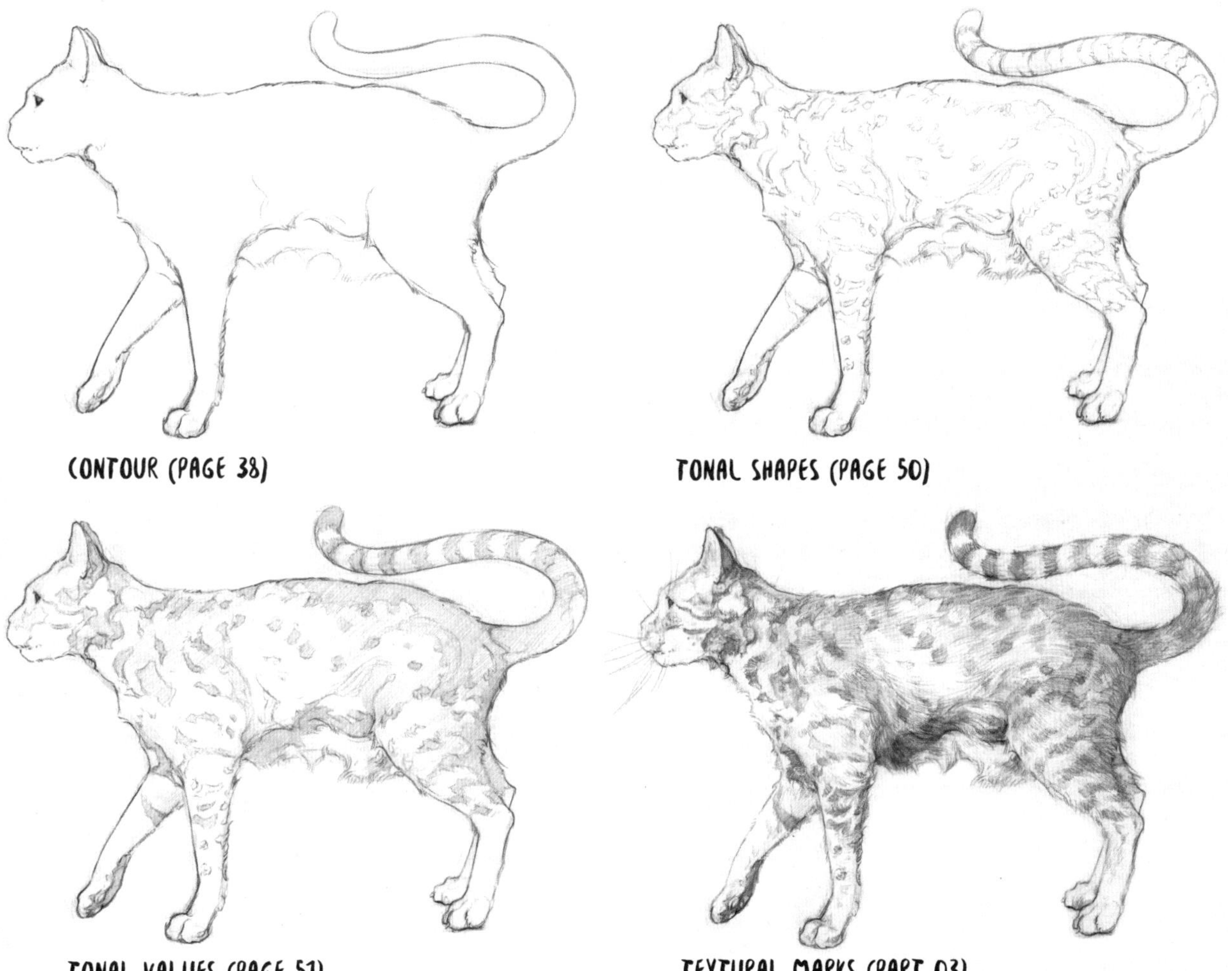

CONTOUR (PAGE 38)

TONAL SHAPES (PAGE 50)

TONAL VALUES (PAGE 51)

TEXTURAL MARKS (PART 03)

PART 04

APPLICATION

As you become more confident and competent in your drawing, you'll be able to put the skills you've developed into practice in your own personal projects. This part introduces exercises that can help you to take your drawing further, exploring animal portraiture, movement studies, and playful approaches to creating imaginary animals.

This part, like those that precede it, should be a springboard into a more regular and personal drawing practice. As you practise more, you'll discover more about yourself – which animals you like to draw, what mediums you like to use, and how you want to apply the skills you have learned. You might even find your tastes in other artists' work changing as you gain more insight into the processes that they use.

Return to the exercises in this book to keep yourself grounded in the observed world and add your own notes to the pages, adapting the exercises as you might adapt a recipe to your taste. In your first year of drawing, it is a good habit to keep all of your work – both the drawings that you like and the ones that you don't – so that you can look at the former to boost your confidence and at the latter to help you remember just how far you have come.

MAKING SUCCESSFUL DRAWINGS

A engaging drawing shows something new to a viewer – it is a story about the subject told in drawn marks rather than words. A good storyteller can reveal the beauty and interest of a mundane situation, whereas an inexperienced storyteller can flatten the most profound experience into a tedious ramble.

The more you draw, the better you will become at telling these visual stories. Through spending time watching and drawing from animals you will create the opportunities to notice more about them and become more articulate in describing what you have seen. You can only judge the success of your own drawings by measuring them against your intention. While any single drawing can succeed or fail, the more vigour and curiosity you put into the process, the better and more engaging your drawings will become.

ANTHROPOMORPHIC ANIMALS

Animation and character design often seeks to anthropomorphize animals, either by imposing human facial expressions and mannerisms, or by combining animal and human anatomy. We see so many anthropomorphic animals in popular culture that we often have to remind ourselves of the reality of animal expression and behaviour. As this book focuses on drawing animals as they are, to support your own imaginative interpretations, you'll need to seek out further tutorials on the conventions and methods of combining animal and human anatomy.

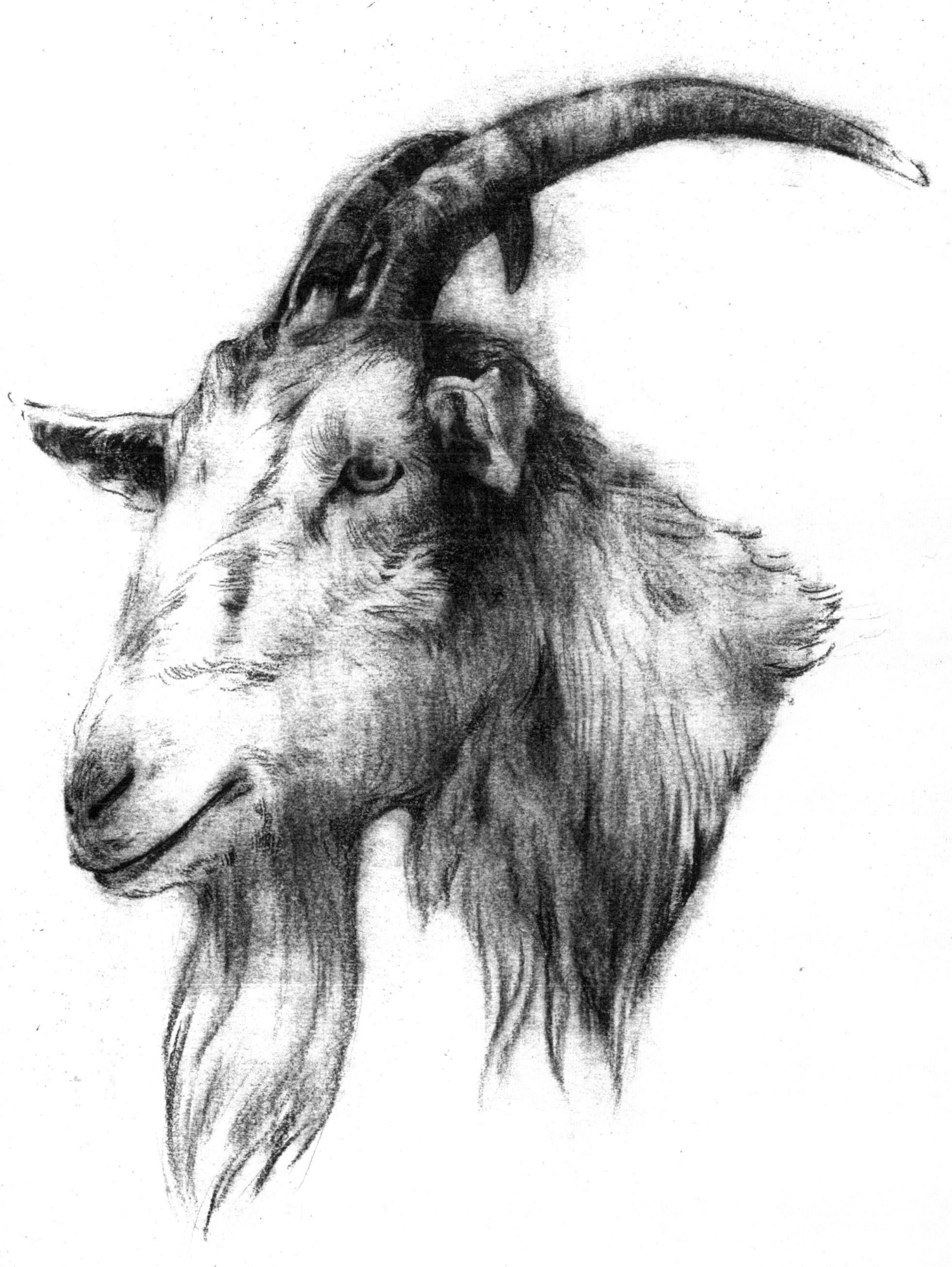

PART 04: APPLICATION

CONTEMPORARY ANIMAL PORTRAITURE – EXERCISE

WHAT YOU NEED

- An animal that you have met
- Your medium of choice

INSPIRATION

Zahra Akbari's drawings of Shane

A portrait drawing should respond to the character of its subject – it shouldn't just be a just a picture of a dog or a cat, but a portrait of Kiki the dog or Garry the cat. When you're developing a portrait, don't just settle for a single head-and-shoulders reference photograph but capture dozens of photos and videos of your subject over a day and make sketches that record their movements, mannerisms and repeated poses. Take your sketches, photos, recordings and memories away and draw from them, exploring different compositions and non-representational colour choices. Test all of your ideas in a series of playful sketches, looking for inventive and original ways to represent the character of your subject before developing a more considered drawing.

Variation

Include a person in your portrait – hands holding a gerbil, or a friend curled up on their sofa with their dog.

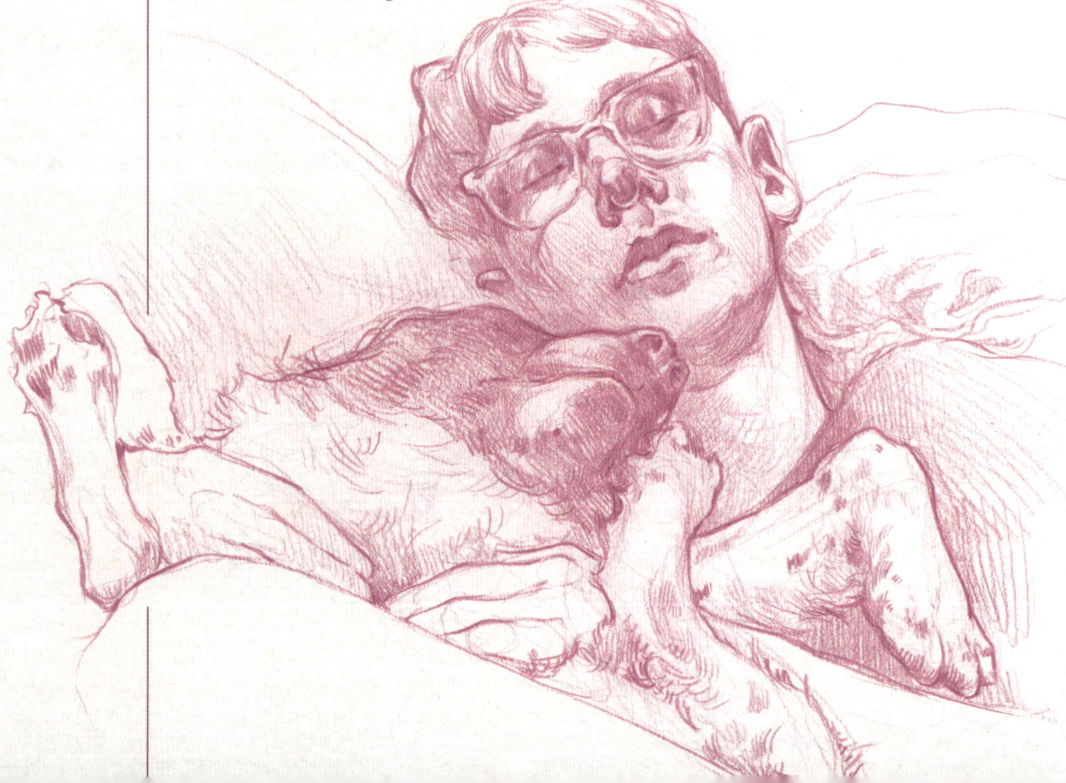

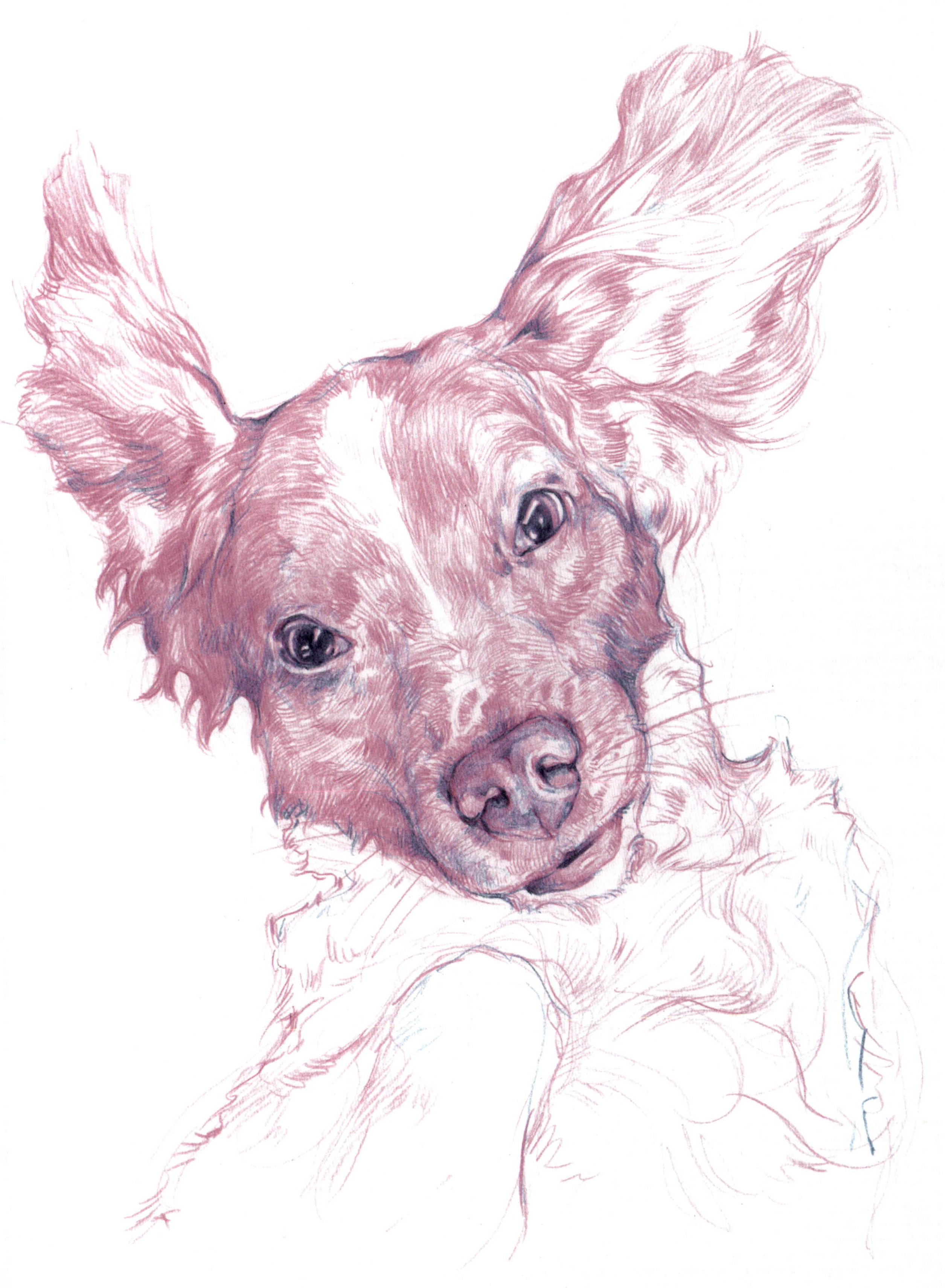

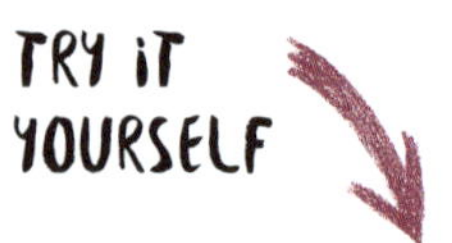
TRY IT
YOURSELF

PART 04: APPLICATION

RECORDING MOVEMENT – EXERCISE

WHAT YOU NEED

- Recorded footage of a moving subject
- A medium capable of fast, energetic marks.

Drawings made from photographs replicate the moment captured in the split second of the camera shutter's opening, but that fractional moment is one that is both preceded and followed by activity. In our drawings we can find different ways to respond to that activity. This exercise will introduce you to three ways to record movement – use each of the following approaches to make drawings from the same piece of recorded footage:

DRAWING 1: SEQUENTIAL POSES

Play your footage from the beginning and pause it every few moments, making a quick drawing from each paused frame. This will help you to chart a particular movement, either as an end in itself or as studies to support an animation.

DRAWING 2: REPEATED STUDY

Play the footage at a slower speed, focusing on one unit of the body – a leg or head perhaps. Make multiple quick studies of its changing shape and position. This will help you to notice the specific shapes that make up a movement and will exercise your visual memory.

DRAWING 3: CHARTING MOVEMENT

Place your pencil on the page and stare at the screen, playing the footage at natural speed and focusing on a single landmark in the body. Notice as it bumps, jerks and sweeps through space, following that journey with a dance-like mark that has the speed of a written signature.

Variation

Apply any one of the approaches to a live subject, remaining energetic and responsive.

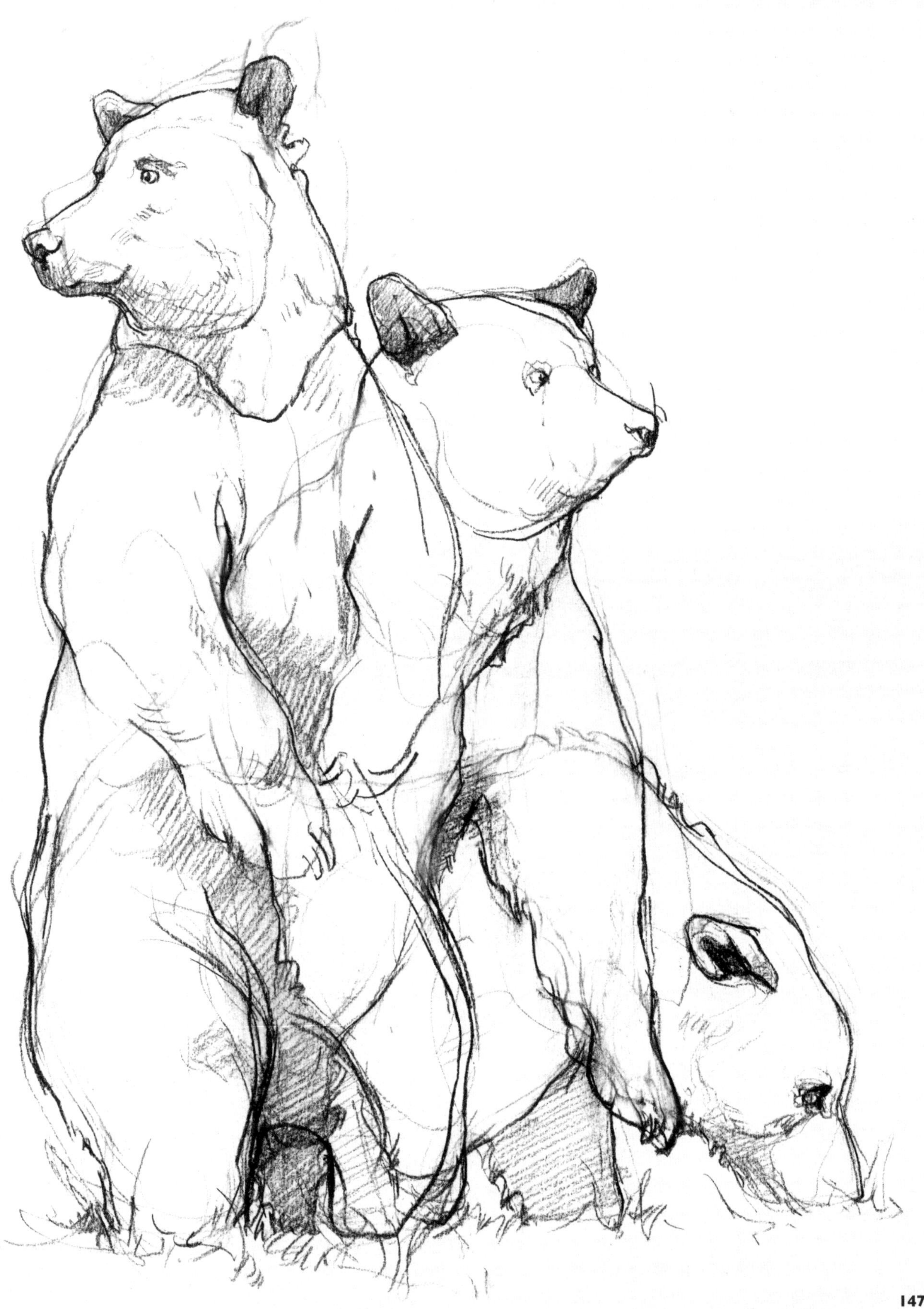

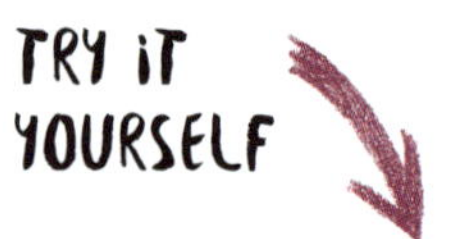
TRY IT
YOURSELF

PART 04: APPLICATION

ACTIONS

When you are drawing from a moving animal you need to find a balance between responding energetically within a limited time and making a visually coherent sketch of the subject. You can use focused studies from life and paused videos to get to know the stages of a particular action – in much the same way you made studies in Part 02 as a way of getting to know an animal.

The following pages examine a few common animal movements – use them as a starting point for your own explorations, making studies of an animal's behaviour, its physical expression of emotion, and its most prominent actions – hunting, eating, trotting, running, swinging, flying and swimming.

STANDING

As a starting point for understanding an animal in action, notice how it stands still – is its head near to the ground, or raised up high? How do its limbs, tails and wings contribute towards its balance? In a still pose, an animal's centre of gravity must sit between the limits of its stabilizing base – notice where it connects with the ground and visual cues like shadows that suggest that contact.

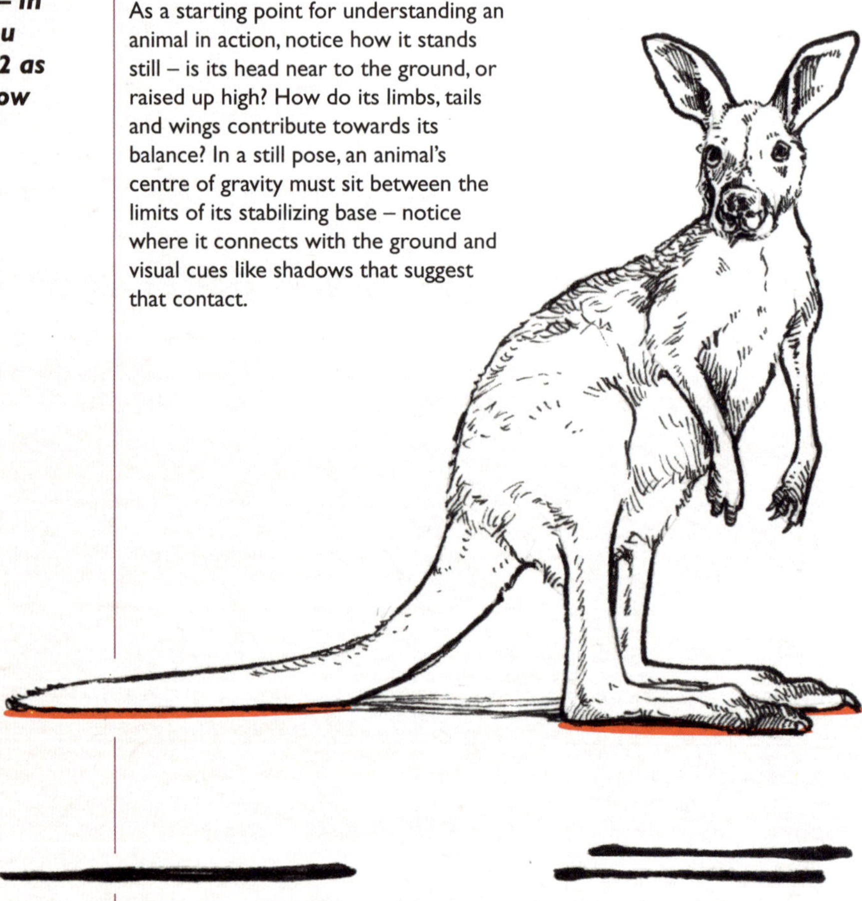

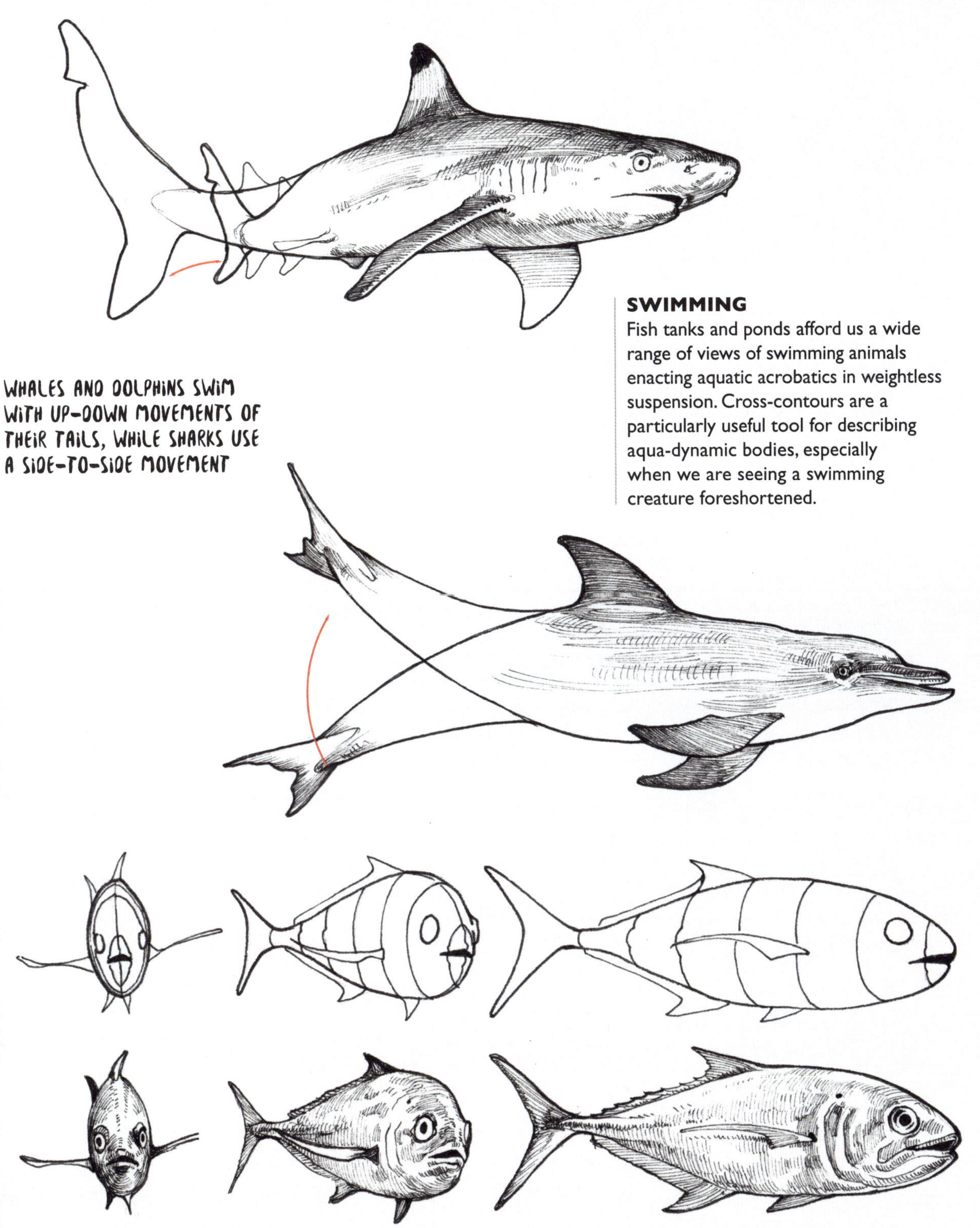

SWIMMING

Fish tanks and ponds afford us a wide range of views of swimming animals enacting aquatic acrobatics in weightless suspension. Cross-contours are a particularly useful tool for describing aqua-dynamic bodies, especially when we are seeing a swimming creature foreshortened.

THE SHAPE OF A FISH SWIMMING TOWARDS YOU CHANGES DRAMATICALLY AS THEY SWIM PAST. NOTICE HOW THEIR PROMINENT EYES APPEAR TO CHANGE FROM A SQUASHED ELLIPSE TO A CIRCLE.

RUNNING

The pioneering photographs of Eadweard Muybridge (1830–1904) showed the order in which a horse's hooves struck the ground, proving for the first time that all four hooves leave the ground at a gallop. You, too, can use sequential photos and paused video to analyze and draw from a running sequence.

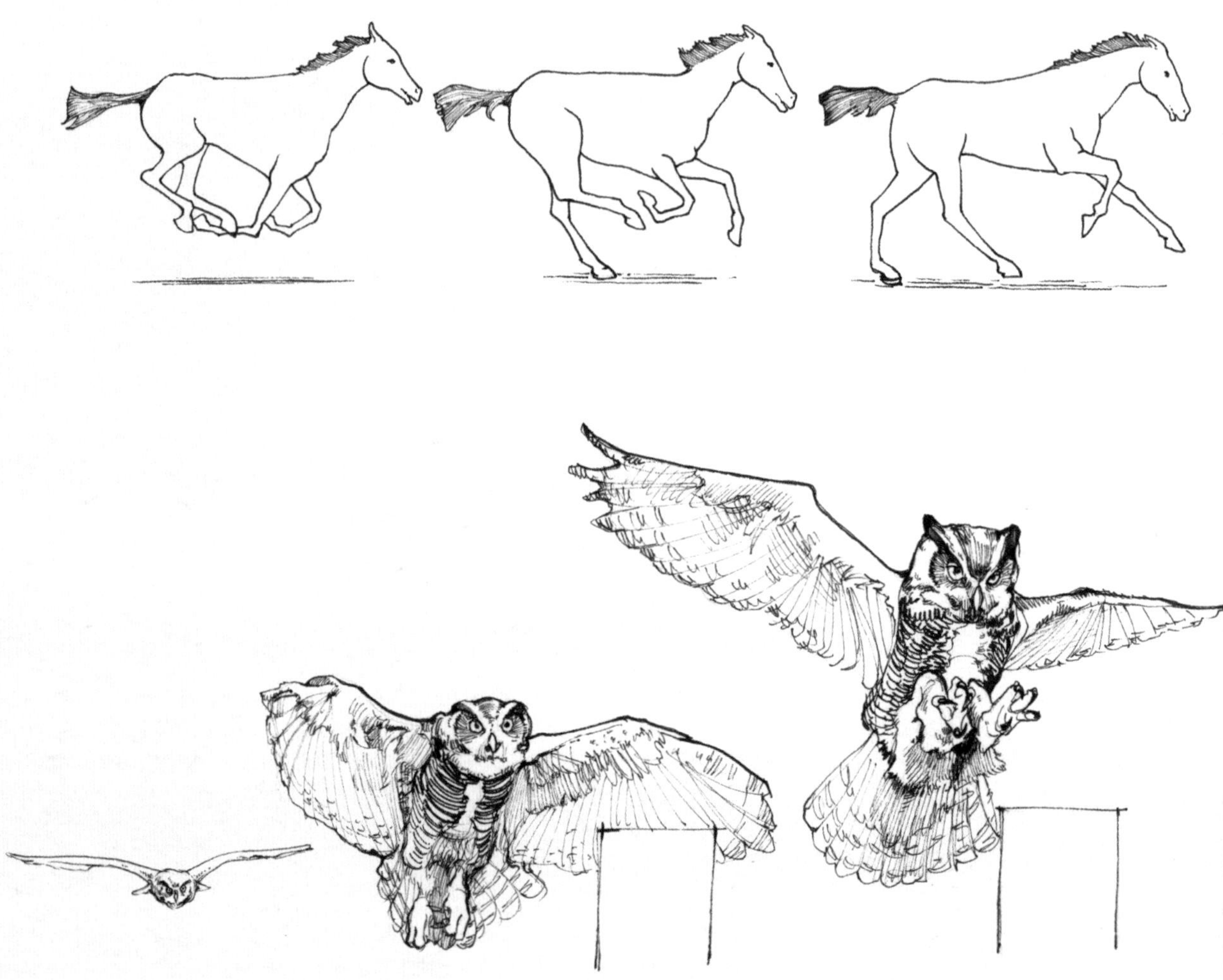

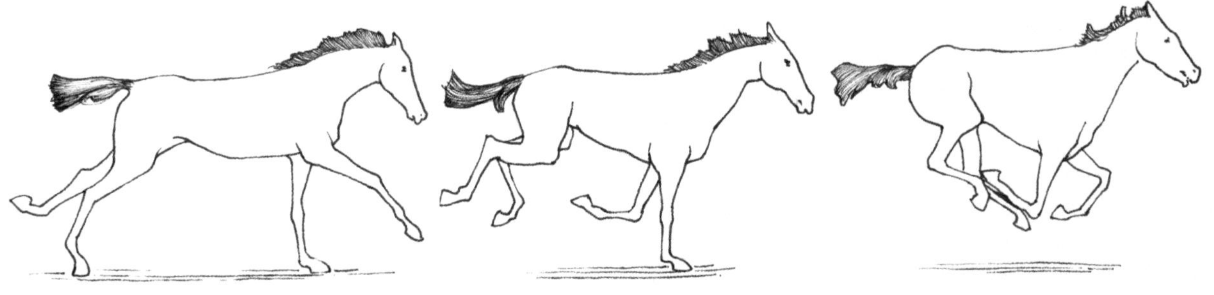

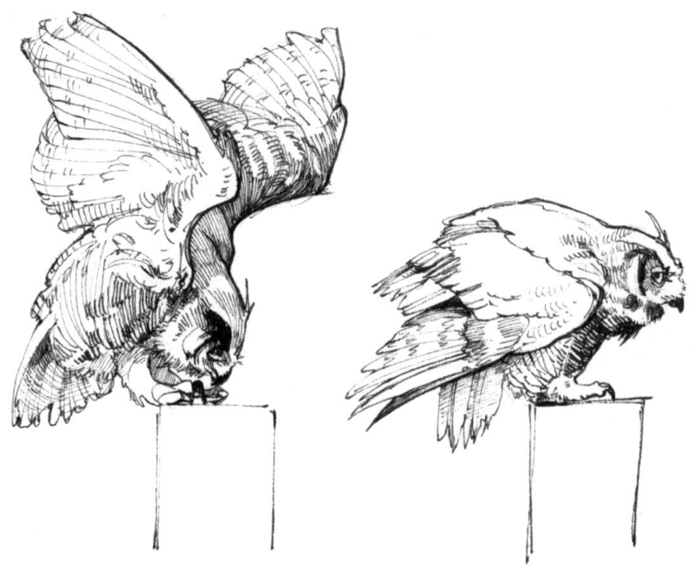

FLYING

From below, we identify soaring birds from the silhouette of their outstretched wings, recalling the exercise in Part 01 (page 46). Make drawings of paused video of birds taking off and landing to understand their movements.

INCLUDE YOUR OWN MOVEMENT STUDIES HERE

INVENTED ANIMALS – EXERCISE

WHAT YOU NEED

- Reference images of the animals you would like to combine, from a variety of different angles
- Your medium of choice

INSPIRATION

The invented creatures of Emily Hare

Part 02: Structure and Part 03: Surfaces in this book looked at the modular sections that make up an animal, rather than the morphology (overall form) of a particular species. You can take those textures, shapes and body parts and combine them to design your own invented creatures. Some animals already look made up – a duck-billed platypus looks as though it combines an otter's body shape and fur texture with a duck's beak and flippered paws; a flying squirrel looks like a weird hybrid of a rodent and a bat.

Whether you are drawing inspiration from mythological imagery to create dragons and chimeras, or inventing your own fabulous beasts, the most convincing fantasy creatures are rooted in the physical expressions of existing animals. Your imaginative process can combine a playful attitude to the purpose, shape and pose of your invented animals with supporting imagery drawn from real-world observational studies.

Variation

For a drawing game to play with friends, try a variation on the Surrealist technique known as Exquisite Corpse. Find an explanation online and play it on a horizontal axis with animal tail, hindquarters, forequarters and head.

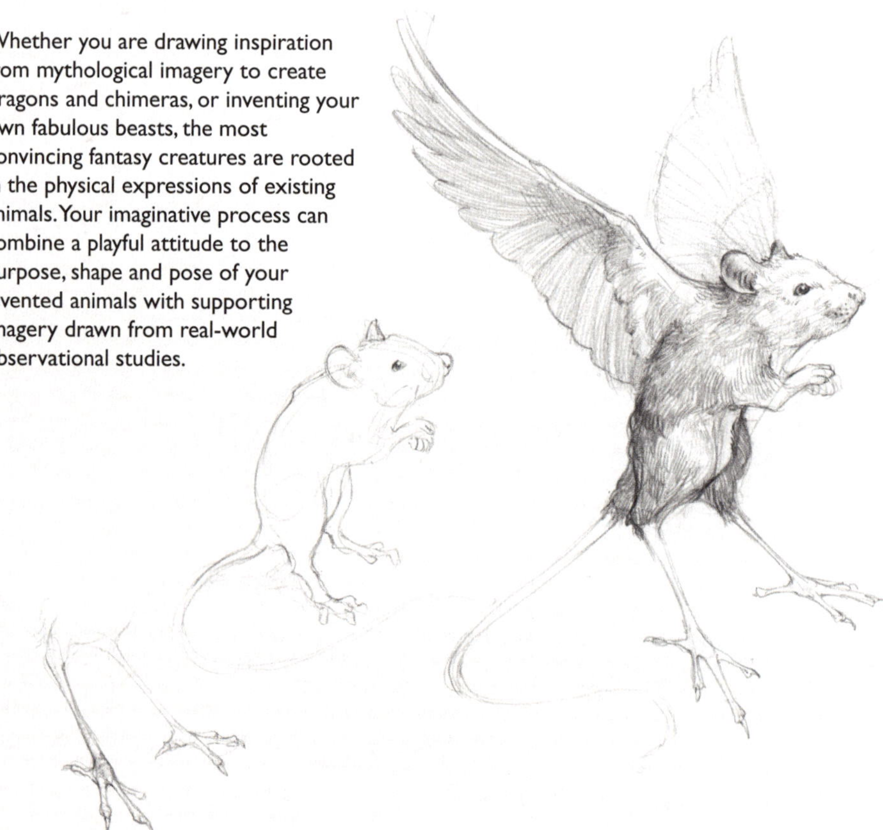

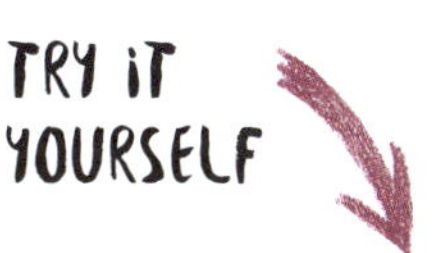
TRY IT
YOURSELF

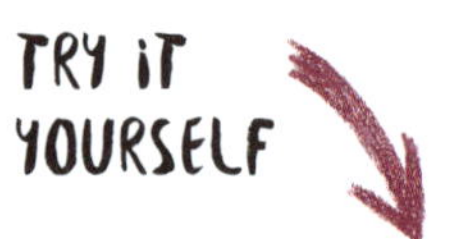
TRY IT
YOURSELF

REFERENCES & ACKNOWLEDGEMENTS

Thank you to everybody who made this book possible, especially Ellie Corbett, Rachel Silverlight and Ben Gardiner whose patience and tenacity have been deeply appreciated. Thank you to Ellie Lopez, Scarlett, Toby the cat and to the Draw Brighton community for their ongoing support, and to the menagerie of animals who lent their likenesses to this book. Thank you also to the champions of animal drawing: Jennie Webber of Wild Life Drawing, James Ort, Tom Shepherd and to the regional museums of natural history around the world, whose collections provide an invaluable resources to us all. Finally, special thanks to Lancelot Richardson for joining the project at a late stage to partner on the book and ensure that it was able to be completed.

OTHER BOOKS BY JAKE SPICER

Figure Drawing

How to Draw

You Will be Able to Draw by the End of this Book

You Will be Able to Draw Faces by the End of this Book

You Will be Able to Draw by the End of this Book: Coloured Pencils

You Will be Able to Draw by the End of this Book: Ink

ONLINE

Both Lancelot and Jake teach online and in person at Draw Brighton.

www.jakespicerart.co.uk
@jakespicerart

www.lancelotrichardson.com
@lancelotrichardson

www.draw-brighton.co.uk
@draw_brighton

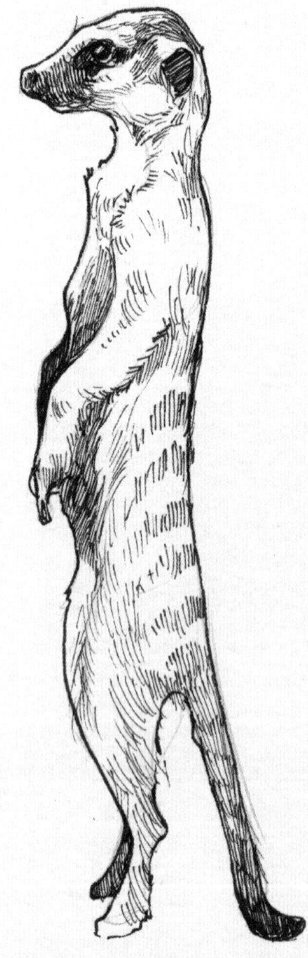